How to Do *Everything* with Your

GPS

Rick Broida

McGraw-Hill/Osborne

New York Chicago San Francisco Lisbon
London Madrid Mexico City Milan New Delhi
San Juan Seoul Singapore Sydney Toronto

The **McGraw·Hill** Companies

McGraw-Hill/Osborne
2100 Powell Street, 10th Floor
Emeryville, California 94608
U.S.A.

To arrange bulk purchase discounts for sales promotions, premiums, or fund-raisers, please contact **McGraw-Hill**/Osborne at the above address. For information on translations or book distributors outside the U.S.A., please see the International Contact Information page immediately following the index of this book.

How to Do Everything with Your GPS

1234567890 CUS CUS 019876543

ISBN 0-07-223171-8

Publisher:	Brandon A. Nordin
Vice President &	
Associate Publisher	Scott Rogers
Executive Editor	Jane K. Brownlow
Senior Project Editor	LeeAnn Pickrell
Acquisitions Coordinator	Athena Honore
Technical Editor	Dave Johnson
Copy Editor	Judy Ziajka
Proofreader	Susie Elkind
Indexer	Valerie Perry
Composition	Apollo Publishing Services
Series Design	Mickey Galicia
Cover Series Design	Dodie Shoemaker

This book was composed with Corel VENTURA™ Publisher.

For Dave, obviously.

About the Author

Rick Broida has written about computers and technology for over 15 years. A regular contributor to *Cnet* and *Computer Shopper*, he specializes in mobile technology. In 1997, recognizing the Palm PDA's unparalleled popularity and the need for a printed resource covering the platform, Rick founded *Handheld Computing* (formerly *Tap Magazine*). He currently serves as editor of that magazine, which now covers all handheld platforms and devices. Rick has conducted Palm training seminars across the Midwest and authors the Tech Savvy column for Michigan's *Observer & Eccentric* newspapers. He lives in Michigan with his wife and two children.

About the Technical Editor

Dave Johnson is the editor of *Handheld Computing Mobility* magazine and senior editor of *Handheld Computing Magazine*. He writes about digital photography for *PC World* magazine and is the author of the best-selling book, *How to Do Everything with Your Digital Camera*. He's the author of about three dozen books that include *Robot Invasion: 7 Cool and Easy Robot Projects*, *How to Do Everything with MP3 and Digital Music* (written with Rick Broida), and *How to Use Digital Video*. His short story for early readers, *The Wild Cookie*, has been transformed into an interactive storybook on CD-ROM. In his spare time, Dave is a scuba instructor and wildlife photographer.

Contents

Acknowledgments   xi
Introduction   xiii

CHAPTER 1   **Introduction to GPS** **1**
What Is GPS?   2
 What Is Real-Time Data?   3
History of GPS   4
How GPS Is Used Today   7
 How Consumers Use GPS   7
 How Businesses Use GPS   13
The Future of GPS   14
An Overview of GPS Hardware and Software   15
 The Important Role Software Plays in GPS   19
GPS Terminology Explained (and Made Simple)   22

CHAPTER 2   **Choosing a GPS Receiver** **25**
Identifying Your GPS Goals   26
 To Map or Not to Map?   29
GPS Receivers for PDAs   34
 The Upsides to PDAs   36
 The Downsides to PDAs   37
 What to Buy If You Don't Own a PDA Yet   39
 What to Buy If You Already Own a PDA   39
 Just the Software   41
Specialty GPS Receivers   43
 Two-Way Radio Meets GPS   43
 GPS for Golf   43
 GPS for Runners   44
 Child Safety Devices   46
Understanding GPS Features and Tech Specs   47
 Antenna Type   49
 Acquisition Time   49
 Battery Life   50

	NMEA Compatibility	50
	Number of Channels	50
	Number of Routes	51
	Tracking Points	51
	WAAS	51
	Waterproofing	51
	Where to Shop for GPS Gear	52
	Where to Find It	52
CHAPTER 3	**Driver's Ed: GPS Navigation for Cars**	**53**
	GPS Safety (Important!)	55
	Enter Directions Safely	56
	Rely on Voice Navigation	57
	Mount Wisely	58
	What You Need Before Hitting the Road	60
	Have a Backup Plan	60
	Loading Maps into Your GPS Receiver	61
	Entering Destinations in Your GPS Receiver	65
	Choosing a Destination from Your Contact List	67
	Routing Options	68
	Navigating with Your GPS Receiver	70
	What's on the Display	70
	Setting Zoom Level	72
	Dealing with GPS Flakiness	75
	Understanding Rerouting	76
	Where to Find It	79
CHAPTER 4	**Go Take a Hike: GPS in the Great Outdoors**	**81**
	The Ultimate Outdoor GPS?	83
	Understanding Waypoints	84
	Effective Waypoint Naming	85
	Understanding Tracking	87
	Downloading, Sharing, and Storing Routes and Waypoints	88
	Using GPS for Fishing	91
	The Right GPS Gear for Fishing	93
	How to Use GPS for Fishing	96
	Using GPS for Hiking, Hunting, Camping, and More	98
	The Right GPS Gear for Hiking, Hunting, Camping, and the Rest	98
	How to Use Your GPS for Hiking, Hunting, Camping, and the Rest	102
	Topographic Maps on Your GPS	102
	Where to Find It	107

CHAPTER 5   **Geocaching and Other GPS Games** **109**

What Is Geocaching? 110

    What's in the Box? 111

    Is Geocaching Really for You? 112

    How to Get Started 112

    Working with Geocaching.com 122

    Entering Coordinates into Your GPS 126

    Fair and Responsible Geocaching 130

My Dinner with Geocaching 130

Other GPS Games 134

    Where to Find It 135

CHAPTER 6   **Fore! GPS Goes Golfing** **137**

GPS on the Golf Course 138

GPS Gear for Golfers 139

    Dedicated GPS Receivers 140

    PDAs on the Golf Course 143

    Which Is Better: A Dedicated Receiver or a PDA? 145

    Where to Find It 147

CHAPTER 7   **GPS for Pilots and Sea Captains** **149**

GPS in Aviation 150

    How GPS Promises to Transform Aviation 152

    What Does GPS Offer a Pilot? 153

    GPS Receivers for Aviation 155

Marine GPS 162

    What Does GPS Offer a Mariner? 162

    Marine GPS Receivers 166

    Where to Find It 167

CHAPTER 8   **GPS in Business** **169**

Fleet Management and Dispatching 172

Dispatching 174

    Cell-Phone GPS or Vehicle Tracking? 174

Navigation 177

Team Building 178

    Where to Find It 182

CHAPTER 9   **How to Do Everything with Your Garmin iQue 3600** **183**

Introduction to the iQue 185

    The iQue's Key Features 188

    A Guided Tour of the Hardware 189

Getting to Know the Operating System   197
    The Icons   198
    The Menus   199
Entering Data into Your iQue   200
    Using Graffiti   202
    Using the Onscreen Keyboard   204
Introducing Palm Desktop   206
    A Word About Synchronization   207
    Map Selection in Palm Desktop   208
From Here to There: Routing with Your iQue   214
    Routing to a Street Address   216
    Routing to a Contact's Address   218
    Routing to Points of Interest   220
    Making Changes or Additions to a Route   223
    Using the iQue in the Great Outdoors   226
Improving iQue Battery Life   227
    Charging on the Road   227
Beaming Data and Programs   229
    How to Beam   230
    Selecting Items for Beaming   231
Working with Memory Cards   235
    What Price Memory?   237
    Memory 101   237
Beyond the Box: Doing More with Your iQue   240
    Where to Find It   241

CHAPTER 10   **Doing More with Your iQue 3600** **243**
How to Install Software   244
Playing Games   247
Listening to Music   251
    Watching Movies   254
    Getting Video into Your iQue   254
Reading Books   257
    Finding Free Stuff   258
    Finding Commercial Stuff   258
    Other Sources for Contemporary E-Books   260
Creating a Mobile Office   261
    Presentations in Your Pocket   263
    PDFs in Your Pocket   264
Keeping the Kids Happy   266
    Book Smarts   266
    Photo Op   267
    Paint and Scribble   268

Music Soothes the Savage Rugrat 269
That's Edutainment! 270
Games to Go 271
iQue Accessories 272
Troubleshooting Your iQue 276
Cure Most Problems with a Reset 276
Beaming Problems 278
Other Sources for Help 279
Where to Find It 279

Index. **281**

Acknowledgments

Hard? Nah, this book wasn't hard. Working 24/7 for three straight months is like being licked by kittens—especially when you're working on a second book at the same time. Fortunately, many, many people came to my rescue, and I'm deeply in their debt. Those people include:

Jane Brownlow, who believed in the idea from the beginning, championed it to the powers that be, and didn't freak out when the page count was low.

Editors Athena Honore, LeeAnn Pickrell, and Judy Ziajka, for keeping me sane with their good cheer and for catching all the embarrassing mistakes.

Doug Luzader, for plunging into thorny, bug-infested woods in search of a box full of junk, and for contributing an excellent treatise on piloting with GPS.

Craig Zurcher, for plunging into the same thorny, bug-infested woods in search of the same box of junk and finding it.

James Stewart, who had the good sense not to plunge into the woods and whose generosity made the whole thing possible.

Pat Valade, for giving me invaluable insight into marine GPS.

Stephen Davis, who provided a terrific example of how GPS can be used in a non-traditional way and then wrote about it.

Pete Brumbaugh, for providing a wide range of Garmin GPS equipment for testing and review.

The folks at ALK, DeLorme, Fugawi, Magellan, and Socket, for providing their own equipment for testing and review.

Navigation Technologies, for contributing a wonderful article on how maps are made.

Ashu Pande, Craig Schmidt, and Kevin Wolf.

Very special thanks to Garmin's Ted Gartner, a font of GPS information who not only helped me on countless occasions, but had the class to do so without hawking his company's products.

Finally, the biggest thanks of all goes to my wife, who effectively became a single parent while I was closeted away at my desk, and who did it all without complaint. I absolutely could not have managed this insane schedule without you, and I am eternally grateful to have you.

Introduction

Quick: What's invisible to the naked eye, moves very fast, and knows where you are? The Invisible Flash Santa-Claus Man, of course! Also, the satellites that comprise the Global Positioning System, or GPS. Actually, the satellites don't really know where you are (unlike certain covert government agencies, hint-hint), but they do make it possible for *you* to know where you are.

All you need is a GPS receiver—a device that locks on to the satellites' continuously broadcast timing signals and uses them to triangulate your position. This can be helpful information, to be sure, whether you're trying to find your way back to your campsite after a day hike or you're trying to find an alternate route around an Atlanta traffic jam (lots of luck).

This book gives you GPS from A to Z, starting with the history of the technology and ending with one of the most advanced and amazing devices ever to utilize it: the Garmin iQue 3600. In between you'll find information on using GPS to find your way to any street address, return to your favorite fishing spots, play the very cool sport of Geocaching, and lots more.

In most chapters you'll also find real-world case studies, written by consumers and industry professionals alike, that illustrate some of GPS's most amazing, unusual, and practical applications. You'll especially want to read the one in Chapter 7 about the guy who fell off a boat. GPS saved his life—true story.

Each chapter contains special elements to help you get the most from the book:

- ■ **How to...** These special boxes explain, in a nutshell, how to accomplish key tasks. Read them to discover key points covered in each chapter.

- ■ **Did You Know?** These are interesting facts and/or background information related to the subject at hand.

- ■ **Notes** These provide extra information that's often very important to gain an understanding of a particular topic.

■ **Tips**   These tell you how to do something smarter or faster.

■ **Sidebars**   These contain additional information about certain subjects that warrant special coverage.

I hope you find this book enjoyable, entertaining, and, most of all, helpful. If you have questions or comments, please feel free to steer them my way at **rickbroida1@excite.com**. Be sure to include "GPS" in the subject line so I don't accidentally overlook it. Thanks, and enjoy the book!

Chapter 1

Introduction to GPS

I t sounds a little spooky when you think about it: an orbiting system of satellites, built for the military and controlled by the government, that covers the globe and knows *exactly where you are*. Fortunately, the Global Positioning System, or GPS, has less to do with an *X-Files* plot than with simple, harmless, extraordinarily effective navigation. It is a remarkable technology with an increasing diversity of applications, and it may not be long before it becomes a part of everyday life.

Okay, but just what is GPS? What does it do? Where did it come from? How does it work? And why should you care? These are good questions—well done. I can see you're my kind of reader: inquisitive, intelligent, and a fan of questions both practical and esoteric. We'll get along just fine. Let's have lunch.

What Is GPS?

The Global Positioning System consists of 24 satellites in semi-synchronous orbit above our little blue-green marble. Semi-synchronous means that the satellite orbits are coordinated, but not identical; each satellite completes an orbit in 12 hours and does so at an altitude of about 11,000 miles. (Airplanes usually fly no higher than six miles, and the space shuttle orbits at 230 miles, so that gives you an idea of just how amazingly high up those satellites are.)

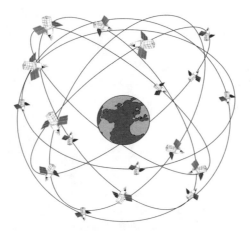

Each satellite performs a relatively simple primary task: it transmits a timing signal using its built-in atomic clock. When a device on the ground receives that signal, it can determine its distance from the satellite. That single measurement alone doesn't accomplish much, but when three satellites get in on the act—that is, when a ground receiver collects timing signals from three different satellites—the receiver can determine three precise coordinates: latitude, longitude, and altitude.

(Actually, a GPS receiver can determine even more than that—things like speed and heading—but for now let's stay focused on the three biggies.)

Armed with this information, you can now easily get from point A to point B. Okay, maybe "easily" is a relative term in this case, but you get the idea. The entire planet has been broken down into latitudinal and longitudinal points, and GPS feeds you that important data in real time.

What Is Real-Time Data?

Remember back in the old days when you'd call a number to get the exact local time? "At the tone, the time will be, one…thirty-seven…and 10 seconds. Beep!" After a few seconds, the recording would repeat. "At the tone, the time will be, one…thirty-seven…and 20 seconds. Beep!" This information was being fed to you in "real time," meaning it was both continuous and accurate. (The fact that it was real-time information about the *time* is confusing, I admit, but it seemed like a good example at the, uh, time.)

When you receive GPS data from the satellites, it's not just a one-time shot. And you don't have to manually request new data every time you want an update. The positioning information is "out there" all the time, and the devices that receive it do so in real time. That means that while a GPS receiver is on and active, it's constantly pulling in data from the satellites. Thus, as you move about, be it on foot, in a car, on a boat, or wherever, you're continually receiving updated and accurate latitudinal, longitudinal, and altitudinal data.

NOTE   *Nope, I didn't think altitudinal was a word either, but there you go.*

Did you know?

Three GPS Satellites Are Spares

Although the Global Positioning System consists of 24 satellites, the actual constellation—the system that makes GPS possible—consists of just 21. Why the extras? Spares, in case problems arise with one or more of the primary satellites. Oh, and in case you were wondering, there are also five ground stations scattered across the globe that monitor the satellites and send them updates as needed.

It is precisely because GPS data is received in real time that it's so incredibly valuable. In the pages to come, you're going to learn why. Before we delve into the real-world (not to be confused with real-time) marvels of GPS, however, let's take a quick peek at its history. It's pretty interesting.

History of GPS

It all started with the U.S. Department of Defense. In the early 1960s, the Department of Defense (or "DoD" to those of us who watch a lot of army movies) wanted to develop a global positioning and navigation system that would provide continuous, highly accurate data and that wasn't adversely affected by weather. The primary goal: to help weapons hit their targets with greater precision. Having dismissed the idea of putting guys with megaphones on top of towers planted every 30 feet or so, the DoD created and deployed experimental satellite systems.

The Navy got into the game first with a system called Transit, which consisted of seven low-altitude satellites and various ground stations and was made available to civilian users in 1967. Though fairly rudimentary, offering only two-dimensional positioning, it paved the way for GPS by proving that a space-based system was reliable enough for military use.

Flash-forward to 1973 (ooh, time travel—this book has everything!). Borrowing the best elements from systems created by both the Navy and the Air Force, the DoD approved development of what would ultimately become the Global Positioning System we know and love today.

> **TIP** *There's a dry-sounding but actually very interesting history of GPS's development (through 1995, anyway) available from the nonprofit institution RAND. It's Appendix B of "The Global Positioning System: Assessing National Policies," and you can find it here: **www.rand.org/publications/ MR/MR614/MR614.appb.pdf.***

Throughout the years-long development and deployment of GPS, nonmilitary enterprises began to take interest in the technology. Surveying became the first major profession to employ GPS. It enabled surveyors to save significant amounts of time and, as a result, oodles of money. According to estimates from the U.S. GPS Industry Council, GPS enables surveyors to work at one-fifth to one-tenth the cost of conventional surveying.

NOTE

Interestingly, the GPS constellation wasn't completed—that is, not all the satellites were in place—until the early 1990s, and it didn't reach full operational capacity until 1995, but it proved successful in military and commercial operations well before that. In other words, even operating at less-than-peak efficiency, GPS was a hit.

Next came aviation, one of GPS's original "niche markets." (That's in quotes because now it's a rather sizeable market, and it's going to get even bigger because the FAA recently approved GPS use for the nation's entire air-traffic system. More on that later.) Unfortunately, it took a tragedy to make it happen. In 1983, the Soviet military shot down a civilian Korean airliner that had drifted into Soviet airspace. As a result, President Reagan offered to make GPS available to civilian aircraft once the system became fully operational. Better still, airlines wouldn't have to pay a single penny to make use of the system.

In 1990, GPS faced its first major military test. Navigation played a pivotal role in Operation Desert Storm, and GPS made possible (or enhanced) activities like precision bombing, troop positioning, artillery fire support, and even search-and-rescue missions. When the fighting was all over, a military official cited two pieces of equipment that helped win the war: night-vision devices and GPS.

Interestingly, the Persian Gulf War marked the first time selective availability, or SA, was intentionally deactivated. SA, which had been implemented just months earlier, purposefully degrades the accuracy of the GPS signal, the idea being to hinder private and commercial use of the technology (though obviously even "hindered" GPS was beneficial to many). In July 1991, SA was reactivated—but in less than ten years, it would be shut off for good.

On May 1, 2000, President Clinton ordered exactly that. The decision was actually made back in 1998, with the plan being to terminate SA sometime between 2000 and 2006, but something happened in the late '90s that made it pointless to wait: various groups began deploying Differential GPS (DGPS), a collection of stationary GPS receivers designed to correct for SA's range errors. Put simply, DGPS enabled users to enjoy military accuracy, which kind of put the kibosh on SA. Here's a statement from one of the scientists involved with SA's termination:

In plain English, we are unscrambling the GPS signal. It's rare that someone can press a button and make something you own instantly more valuable, but that's exactly what's going to happen today. All the people who bought a GPS receiver for a boat or a car, or their riding lawn mower or whatever, to use in business and in recreation, are going to find that they're suddenly 10 times more accurate as of midnight tonight.

—Dr. Neal Lane, Director of the Office of Science and Technology

That's no exaggeration: with SA active, GPS could accurately pinpoint your location to within 300 feet. Today, with SA a thing of the past and the development of new technologies like DGPS and WAAS—see "GPS Terminology Explained (and Made Simple)" at the end of the chapter—GPS is accurate to within 10 to 30 feet. That's a huge difference, and it's one major reason the technology has become so popular seemingly overnight. (That, and the availability of small, affordable GPS receivers, which I'll discuss in detail in Chapter 2.)

Okay, so now you know how it all began. But what's the payoff? What can GPS do for you and yours? Find the answers to these and other compelling questions in the very next section.

NOTE   *By now you may be wondering, "If GPS stands for Global Positioning System, why don't you say 'the GPS' instead of just 'GPS'—as in, 'Everybody likes the GPS.'" If you're going to be asking oddball grammar questions like that, you'd better be prepared to explain "weird," which blatantly violates the "I before E except after C" rule. Or maybe a better example is* Star Trek: Voyager, *my all-time favorite* Trek *show. In the original series, they always referred to "the Enterprise," but on Voyager they just called the ship "Voyager." Where GPS is concerned, it's kinda like that. Sorta. Kinda.*

Free Lunches, No. Free GPS—Yes!

Perhaps the most impressive thing about the Global Positioning System—especially given that the government spent roughly six bajillion dollars on it—is that it costs nothing to use. Sure, you need to buy some sort of receiver to access and make use of the data (see "An Overview of GPS Hardware and Software" later in this chapter), but there are no subscription or airtime fees. The GPS receiver is your sole out-of-pocket expense. Okay, well, maybe a few bucks' worth of your taxes go toward GPS, so it's not *totally* free. Either way, you might as well take advantage of it, right?

How GPS Is Used Today

I'm willing to bet a book-author's ransom (put your $5 on the table) that until very recently, you'd never heard of GPS. Or you'd heard of it, but didn't really know what it was. But now you do know, so let's talk about how it's used. GPS has become the navigation tool of choice for boaters, fishermen, private pilots, hikers, a wide variety of businesses, and everyday drivers. GPS has emerged as a key component in safety-oriented location systems. And GPS has even become something of a recreational tool, offering game-improving assistance to golfers and a unique kind of treasure-hunting fun to thrill seekers. Let's take a closer look at these and other GPS applications.

How Consumers Use GPS

I'm not saying GPS will be the next DVD, but there's no question that its stock is on the rise. I know this because I'm the editor of *Handheld Computing* magazine (blechh—what a gratuitous and shameless plug; I feel just awful), and the last year or so has witnessed a huge increase in PDA-compatible GPS receivers and specialized GPS products, to say nothing of a dramatic improvement in the software that goes with them. Meanwhile, enterprising companies continue to come up with new uses for GPS, like wristwatches that help track lost children and gadgets that help golfers improve their games. Most of all, GPS is quickly becoming an indispensable in-car navigation tool.

In-Car Navigation (How Not to Get Lost)

This is the big one, the *cause célèbre* that has attracted so much of the recent attention to GPS. Basically, in-car navigation combines GPS data with a map that's displayed on a screen. (This can be the screen on a laptop computer, a PDA, a special system built into your car, or even a cell phone. More on this stuff later in the chapter.) As you know, GPS provides real-time positional updates. But the big deal here is that the map gets updated as well, meaning it moves as you move. (That's probably why they call it a "moving map.") As you drive down the highway or up the street, the map scrolls right along with you, displaying your relative position. (It's kind of like tracing your finger along a paper map, only the map is electronic and the GPS data takes the place of your finger.)

But wait, there's more. With most GPS-mapping systems, you can specify a destination—a street address, an intersection, or whatever—and the software will generate a route based on your current location. Now the system is actually guiding you from point A to point B. It may even *speak* to you, telling you when to make the next turn and which direction to go.

This is such a huge deal, there's a whole chapter devoted to it. Suffice it to say, if you've ever gotten lost behind the wheel of a car, or you just frequently find yourself traveling to unknown destinations, you'll want to hurry to Chapter 3. Right after you finish this chapter and the next one. Chop-chop!

Hiking, Fishing, and Other Outdoor Activities

Whether you're hiking in the mountains or trying to revisit a favorite fishing spot, nothing beats GPS for navigation. There are GPS receivers designed specifically for these kinds of outdoor diversions, very often with PC interfaces so you can download maps, waypoints, and other useful data.

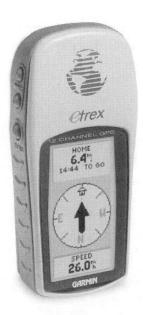

For instance, suppose you're camping in Rocky Mountain National Park. You've set off from your campsite for a daylong hike, but an unexpected storm sets in. You could wander blindly and risk getting lost, or just use your GPS to navigate back to the campsite.

NOTE *This would probably be a good time to point out that GPS signals aren't affected by weather. Although you do need a clear line of sight from the receiver to the satellites, the nature of the technology is such that even a blinding snowstorm won't interrupt the signal.*

In Chapter 4, you'll learn all about the cool ways to use GPS in the outdoors. You'll also learn that while weather doesn't affect GPS signals, dense foliage can.

Private Aviation

Pilots of small, private aircraft have flocked to GPS like seagulls to parking lots. That's because the technology affords the kind of crucial information that was previously unavailable, or at least prohibitively expensive. Products like the Garmin GPSMAP 196 provide real-time visual maps (also known as moving maps), flight management (such as automatic logging of flight time and departure and arrival locations), a ground-speed indicator, and plenty of other helpful features.

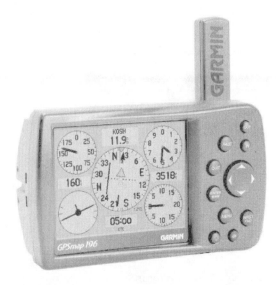

Of course, simple positioning is perhaps the most valuable data afforded by aircraft GPS receivers. That's because of the nation's newfound sensitivity to the location of every aircraft. You fly a bit too close to Washington, D.C., and you can wind up with a pair of F-16s on your six. So says my pilot buddy Doug, who lives in D.C. Thus, GPS is not only practical for pilots, it's important as well.

See Chapter 7 for information on using GPS in aviation.

GPS on the Links

I'm not much of a golfer (I know which end of the club to hold, and that's about it), but if I were, you can bet I'd be taking a keen interest in these newfangled GPS helpers. Some are stand-alone devices, others are designed to work with PDAs, but all have the same goal: to help you shave strokes off your game by telling you the exact distance from you to the pin. That way, you know exactly which club to select.

If you're interested in knowing more about GPS tools for golfers, skip ahead to Chapter 6. As long as you can live with missing all the witty and insightful stuff between here and there, that is.

Geocaching: The Sport of Geeks

Yes, Geocaching is a little geeky, but only because it's the first sport to rely on sophisticated technology. Actually, now that I think of it, radar guns that measure the speed of a fastball are pretty high-tech, so maybe baseball is the sport of geeks. Geocaching, then, must be the sport of hip, cool, smart people.

Though it's not really a sport—more a pleasant way to spend an afternoon. Geocaching is a kind of high-tech treasure hunt, a game in which you use a GPS receiver to navigate to a hidden something—a cache—that's usually located in some out-of-the-way place.

Sounds a bit unusual, I know, but trust me when I say it's a lot of fun. It's also the subject of Chapter 5—and I wouldn't devote a whole chapter to it unless it was really worth it.

The Spy in the Sky: Personal and Child Safety

Although GPS is a one-way technology—the satellites broadcast data, they don't collect it—it's beginning to play a role in location systems. That doesn't mean you knowing your own location—it means a third party knowing your location. For instance, suppose your cell phone could receive GPS signals. It could then relay your position to a 911 operator. If you were stranded somewhere—on a deserted road, for instance—or facing some kind of serious emergency, rescuers would have a much easier time finding you.

> **NOTE** *This may sound a bit Big Brother-ish, but consider the situations in which you'd place a 911 call. You might be injured or panicked and therefore unable to provide the 911 operator with your location. On the other hand, could you be tracked without your knowledge via the phone's positioning capabilities? Well, yes—but that's something to take up with your representative in Congress. Leave me out of it.*

A bit of history here. Years ago, the FCC ordered all U.S. cell-phone carriers to adopt Enhanced 911, or E911, services. According to the FCC's web site, "The wireless Enhanced 911 (E911) rules seek to improve the effectiveness and reliability of wireless 911 service by providing 911 dispatchers with additional information on wireless 911 calls." The carriers were supposed to deploy E911 by October 1, 2001, but not one met the deadline. Part of the problem was that the FCC didn't say how the carriers were supposed to accomplish this goal, only that they had to do it. In other words, "This is the new rule—you figure out how to make it work."

For the carriers, that meant not only upgrades to their own networks, but also offering phones that could transmit the required location data. Many phone makers, like Motorola and Nextel, turned to GPS. And why not? E911 requires a cell phone to know its location, and GPS is already out there providing exactly that information. Just build a receiver into a phone, and presto—problem solved.

> **NOTE** *If a cell phone already provides two-way communication with a network, why can't it "know" its position without GPS? It can, actually, which is why carriers like AT&T Wireless and Cingular originally planned to use a technology called Enhanced Observed Time Difference (EOTD), which uses up to four cellular base stations to pinpoint a phone's location by determining the arrival times of the call signal at various cellular antennas. However, EOTD doesn't work well in rural areas, where often only two base stations are available. EOTD wasn't able to meet the FCC's required level of accuracy. A replacement technology is in the works, but you can see why the E911 delays continue.*

So what's the holdup? Well, adding GPS to phones adds not only cost, but also bulk. Plus, GPS signals can't reach indoors. That's why the majority of carriers seem to be pursuing non-GPS options, at least for E911. However, don't be surprised to find GPS integrated into phones of the future, as there certainly are benefits to mixing GPS data with cellular technology.

One perfect example is the Wherify GPS Locator (see Figure 1-1), a product you may be glad to have but hope never to use. The Locator is a wristwatch with a built-in GPS receiver and CDMA radio. It's designed with kids in mind: in the tragic event that your child gets lost or abducted, the Locator can enable you to pinpoint his or her position. (Like I said, it's something you hope you never need.) You can find out more about these locator products in Chapter 2.

How Businesses Use GPS

As discussed earlier, GPS has long been a popular tool among surveyors. But that's the tip of the proverbial iceberg, as GPS has applications in any business that needs or relies on navigation or location. I'm talking farming, fishing, archeology, trucking,

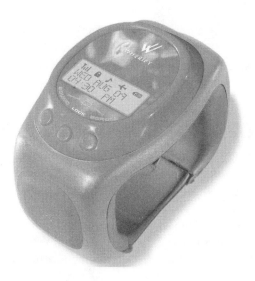

FIGURE 1-1   The Wherify GPS Locator aims to find lost kids by relaying their positions to an emergency center.

Did you know?

The GPS Time Machine

Each GPS satellite has three or four atomic clocks built in and broadcasts the exact time along with latitude and longitude information. Brokerage houses (among other businesses) rely on this so-called "GPS time" for time-stamping trade orders, which must be tracked down to the second. Because the GPS data is so accurate (and costs next to nothing to receive), it has become a kind of informal Wall Street standard.

construction, wine production, shipping, mapping, and fleet management, to name but a few. Several major seaports use GPS to guide robotic cranes in loading and unloading shipping containers. Insurance companies have experimented with GPS to track how far, how fast, and how frequently you drive your car, so they can charge premiums accordingly. (Intrusive though that sounds, I would welcome such a policy, as my car sits in the garage 85 percent of the time.)

In short, GPS is leading a quiet revolution in the way businesses navigate, locate, and even operate. In Chapter 8, you'll learn about some specific business applications for GPS, along with some real-world case studies that should prove interesting to anyone considering adopting the technology.

The Future of GPS

Although the technology has been around for decades, GPS is really still in its infancy. Consider a few of the most recent applications of the technology, all of which demonstrate just how useful GPS can be and how we're only just starting to take full advantage of it.

The first is Meade's LX200GPS telescope, designed for astronomy enthusiasts (affluent ones—it costs a little over $4,000) and equipped with a built-in GPS receiver. That enables automatic telescope alignment, which is half the battle for accurate stargazing.

Next, the Rochester Institute of Technology has developed a new system designed to help combat wildfires. It's called WASP, and it combines advanced GPS equipment with high-tech cameras, all of which are mounted in an airplane's belly. Among other advances, the system will be able to relay a fire outbreak's exact coordinates to GPS-carrying fire crews on the ground.

GPS is even starting to appear in portable pathfinding devices for the blind and visually impaired. Like the man sang, the future's so bright, I gotta wear shades…

An Overview of GPS Hardware and Software

The core component in any GPS-related activity is a GPS receiver—a device that intercepts the wireless signals transmitted by the constellation of GPS satellites. As you might expect, GPS receivers come in many shapes and sizes, with different features and capabilities and a wide variety of price ranges.

Most GPS receivers produce the following raw data:

- Latitude

- Longitude

- Altitude relative to sea level

- Speed

- Heading

- Time

What GPS receivers do with that data and how they present it to the user varies significantly. In some cases, you might see nothing more than the raw numbers: latitude, longitude, and so on. Other receivers keep that data entirely behind the scenes, applying it to beautiful color maps that provide directions to your destinations. In Chapter 2, I explain in detail the different kinds of GPS receivers and help you figure out which one is right for you. In the meantime, let's take a look at the broad categories and then talk a bit about the software side of the equation.

- **Stand-alone GPS receivers**   A stand-alone GPS receiver is exactly that: a product with its own screen and software, and one that's usually pretty mobile (if not mobile by design). These can include marine and aviation products made to go in boats and planes, as well as handheld units built with hiking and other recreational activities in mind. One such handheld, the Garmin eTrex, runs for 18 hours on a pair of AA batteries and measures no larger than a modern cell phone.

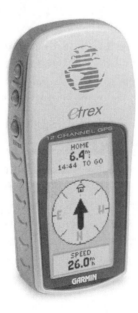

1

■ **GPS receivers for PDAs**   As PDAs have grown in popularity, so have their GPS possibilities. Whether you own an old Palm V or a new iPAQ h1940 Pocket PC, you can probably find a GPS receiver (usually in the form of a plug-in accessory or an add-on "sled") that's compatible with your model. The advantages of going this route are obvious: with their fast processors, big (and in most cases color) screens, and compatibility with a wide variety of software, PDAs make excellent hosts for GPS data. And if you're already carrying one anyway, why not add GPS to its capabilities? In fact, there's even an argument to be made in favor of buying a PDA expressly for GPS. More on that in Chapter 2.

■ **GPS receivers for notebooks**   A notebook computer isn't quite as practical (or portable) as a PDA, but it's certainly capable of running mapping software and receiving GPS data—and you get the benefit of a very large screen. Delorme is one company that makes notebook-compatible GPS products;

its Earthmate GPS Receiver plugs into any notebook's USB port, and even receives power from that port, so no extra batteries are required.

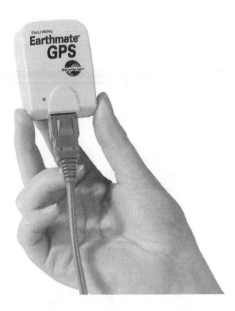

■ **In-car GPS receivers**   More and more car companies are offering in-dash GPS systems in their higher-end models. These tend to be great solutions, as they're built right in and usually come with crackerjack navigation software. There are also third-party aftermarket GPS systems that can be installed in just about any vehicle. Should you consider one? Find out the pros and cons of in-car systems in Chapter 2.

- **GPS cell phones**   E-mail, web browsing, games—is there no end to the features they can pack into a cell phone? Nextel's Motorola-made i88s phone is among the first with built-in GPS, and a third-party service (Televigation's TeleNav) can even add real-time navigation.

- **GPS locator products**   As discussed earlier in the chapter, products like the Wherify GPS Locator squeeze GPS receivers into devices like and wristwatches. Obviously, these have very specific applications; they're not designed for everyday GPS navigation and such.

The Important Role Software Plays in GPS

This is perhaps the single most important section in the book, so please pay attention. Software—be it what's built into a GPS receiver or what's added to a PDA—is the whole enchilada when it comes to GPS navigation. As I noted in the previous section, all GPS receivers collect pretty much the same raw data. But it's the software that determines how that data is presented, used, and leveraged.

For instance, it's the software that supplies the actual maps used for navigation (see Figure 1-2). It's the software that calculates your exact position on the map based on the data from the GPS receiver. It's the software that figures out the best

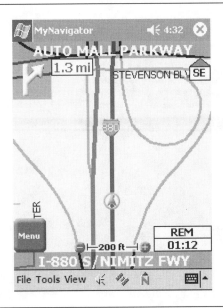

FIGURE 1-2   Mapping software, like this PDA-based program, matches GPS data with latitude and longitude coordinates built into actual map data.

route from point A to point B. It's the software that recalculates your route when you miss a turn or when a road is closed and you can't go the way it wants you to go.

It's also the software that can confuse the heck out of you. Let me be brutally honest: a lot of the GPS navigation software out there is really atrocious—to the extent that it would be easier *not* to use GPS. Fortunately, it's starting to show some improvement, and now you have this book to help you learn and understand it. There are also a few packages I've seen recently that are downright terrific— and believe me when I say that you're going to hear a lot of cheering about them in the chapters to come. GPS navigation is supposed to make your life easier, not more complicated, so I'm going to do my best to steer you clear of the really rotten software.

Following are a few examples of the different kinds of GPS software you're likely to encounter:

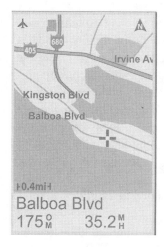

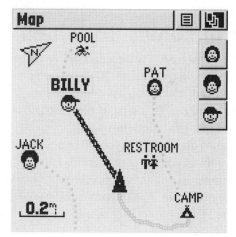

How Does It Know?

So you have an electronic map, which is software, and a GPS receiver, which supplies little more than your latitude, longitude, and heading. How is the software able to apply that raw data to the map? How does it know that N 42° 32.200 by W 083° 30.234 is actually the corner of Vickers and Academy? Simple: the electronic map includes latitude and longitude coordinates (picture them hiding "underneath" the map you see on the screen) and knows which way is north. As a result, the software can match the real-time GPS data to the map's coordinate data and pinpoint your exact location and heading. I'm sorry, but that is just too cool. When you consider just how big the planet is and how early explorers used to wind up hundreds of miles off course, the notion of being able to pinpoint your exact position—to within 30 feet—on a map is just plain magic. My hat is off— I won't even look at another hat—to the clever minds that developed this technology.

GPS Terminology Explained (and Made Simple)

If someone were to create a dictionary consisting solely of GPS and GPS-related terms, it would span about 50 pages and contain hundreds of entries. Actually, someone did, and if you have the patience to type a particularly lengthy web site address, you can find it right here: **http://www.telecom.fh-htwchur.ch/~zogg/ Dateien/the_gps_dictionary.pdf**.

I'm not going to give you 50 pages' worth of GPS definitions (who'd want to read it?), but I am going to identify and explain a few of the terms you're likely to encounter as you delve into the wide world o' GPS. For instance, many modern GPS receivers tout WAAS compatibility. What's the big deal about that, and should you care? Read on.

- **3D Coordinate**   Your position as determined by latitude, longitude, and altitude.

- **A-GPS**   Assisted GPS, or GPS with a little help from cellular technology. Found mostly in the new breed of GPS-equipped phones, A-GPS relies on cellular networks to do some of the tracking. Why? Because GPS signals can't go indoors, and a GPS receiver can't broadcast its own location.

■ **DGPS (Differential GPS)**   A stationary receiver works in conjunction with the satellites to correct errors in the timing signals, resulting in a much more precise measurement of location.

■ **GPS**   Global Positioning System, a constellation of 21 satellites (and three spares) used to determine location, speed, heading, and time.

■ **Latitude**   Imaginary parallel horizontal lines encircling the earth. The line at the equator represents zero degrees of latitude. Latitude lines are measured 90 degrees north and 90 degrees south from the equator (thereby covering the top and bottom halves of the planet).

■ **Longitude**   Imaginary parallel vertical lines running from the North Pole to the South Pole. The prime meridian (zero degrees longitude) runs through Greenwich, England, and serves as the reference line from which longitude is measured east and west (180 degrees total in each direction). Put latitude and longitude together, and you have yourself a grid covering the planet. And from that grid, you can extrapolate the exact coordinates of your position.

■ **NMEA**   National Marine Electronics Association, which specified a standard way to format GPS data. NMEA-compatible GPS receivers can typically work with a wide variety of NMEA-compliant mapping programs on PDAs and notebooks.

■ **Triangulation**   What GPS receivers do to determine their position based on data received from three or more GPS satellites.

■ **WAAS**   Wide Area Augmentation Service, an FAA-funded system that improves GPS accuracy and availability. WAAS was designed with aviation in mind, as it improves GPS accuracy to within about three meters—kind of crucial when you're trying to, say, hit a runway in a blinding snowstorm. Of course, it's not limited to aviation use; many GPS receivers are now compatible with WAAS signals, meaning that they're accurate to within about 10 feet (rather than 30 feet, which is what you get without WAAS).

■ **Waypoint**   An intermediate position on your navigational map. Suppose you want to make three stops en route to your final destination; a GPS receiver considers each of these three stops to be a waypoint. It's the rare (and beneficial) mapping program that supports waypoints in route planning.

Chapter 2

Choosing a
GPS Receiver

How to...

- Identify your GPS goals
- Decide what kind of GPS receiver you need
- Decide whether you need mapping
- Choose a GPS receiver for your PDA
- Choose navigation software for your PDA
- Understand GPS features and tech specs
- Shop for GPS gear online

Now that you know the origins of GPS and all of the cool things it can do, no doubt you're ready to jump in and get yourself some GPS gear. Before you plunk down the plastic and buy so much hardware your spouse files for divorce, remember what carpenters say: measure twice, cut once. In other words, figure out exactly what you need—*then* buy it.

For instance, suppose you're strolling down the aisles of your local electronics superstore one day and you happen to spy Garmin's SporTrak Color GPS. The box shows a pretty color screen with a nifty-looking map on it, so you figure, "Oh, well, here's just what I need for my car," and plunk down your $450.

Wrong!

Different tasks demand different kinds of GPS equipment, and while there's certainly some overlap—GPS receivers aren't generally limited to one job and one job only—you need to identify your GPS goals before making a purchase decision.

NOTE   *This chapter deals primarily with consumer-oriented GPS solutions. If you're interested in business-specific equipment, skip ahead to Chapter 8.*

Identifying Your GPS Goals

Do you hike? Fish? Fly a private plane? Are you a golfer? Do you spend half your day in your car? These are the kinds of questions to start with in determining what kind of GPS receiver you want to buy. And as you learned in Chapter 1, there are lots of different kinds of GPS receivers to choose from: handheld models, add-ons for PDAs and notebooks, and specialized systems for cars, boats, golf carts, planes, and so on.

NOTE *Remember that all GPS receivers provide you with roughly the same raw data: latitude, longitude, altitude, speed, heading, and time. It's what they do with that data and how they present it that varies from device to device.*

Needless to say, if you're just looking for a system to guide you to your favorite fishing spots, this won't be a difficult decision. You'll want a marine GPS, one designed to go in your boat. Ah, but what if you want a GPS that can also accompany you in your car, helping you navigate from home to, say, an unfamiliar boat launch? Are there models that can pull double duty without compromises?

The answer: sort of. Most GPS receivers are designed with a certain category of activities in mind, be it flying, in-car navigation, or outdoor adventure. As a result, they tend not to switch gears very well (though certainly their capabilities can and do overlap). The Garmin StreetPilot, for instance (see Figure 2-1), is really designed for one task: in-car road navigation. It's just not intended for things like hiking and flying.

The Magellan SporTrak Map (see Figure 2-2), on the other hand, doesn't provide door-to-door driving directions (at least, not out of the box—you can transfer street-level maps and routes to the SporTrak with Magellan's optional MapSend software)—

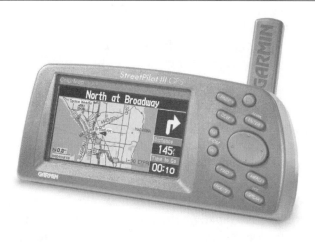

FIGURE 2-1   The Garmin StreetPilot is kind of a one-trick pony (though it does that trick very well), providing door-to-door navigation for drivers.

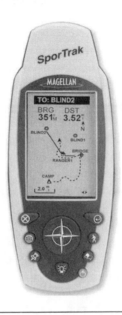

FIGURE 2-2   The Magellan SporTrak Map has basic mapping capabilities, but you wouldn't want to use it for door-to-door navigation.

just major highways, cities, and airports. It's really more of an outdoorsman's GPS. (Outdoorsperson's? Much as I want to be politically correct, that just doesn't sound right.) The StreetPilot and SporTrak have the same underlying capabilities—navigation based on GPS signals—but they produce wholly different results.

Take a look at Table 2-1 for further evidence of the differences among GPS devices.

NOTE   *The products listed in Table 2-1 are examples, not recommendations. They're GPS receivers that happen to fit the stated goal. However, for any given goal you have, there are likely to be several—if not dozens—of models that would do the job.*

Notice the last item in Table 2-1: PDA-based solution. Let me state here and for the record that PDAs are rapidly becoming the ideal GPS platform. Why? Because they have spacious color screens, they do lots more than just GPS, and they're capable of running an endless variety of software—meaning a single PDA can be used for in-car navigation, Geocaching, aviation, golfing, and many other

If your primary goal is...	Then consider something like a...	Which is a...
Boating/fishing	Magellan SporTrak Pro Marine	Handheld GPS with built-in marine maps
Child safety	Wherify	Wristwatch with a GPS receiver and cellular transmitter
Flying	Lowrance AirMap 100	Handheld GPS with extensive airport and flight data
Golfing	SkyGolf SG2	Specialized GPS that calculates your distance to the hole
Hiking, biking, cross-country skiing, snowmobiling, and other outdoor sports	Magellan SporTrak Color	Handheld GPS with a color screen, barometer, and three-axis compass
Geocaching	Garmin Geko 201	Inexpensive, pocket-size stand-alone GPS that supports custom waypoints, backtracking, and so on
In-car navigation	Garmin StreetPilot	Dash-mounting GPS with color screen and door-to-door routing
A little of everything	PDA-based solution	PDA with an integrated or add-on GPS antenna and special software

TABLE 2-1   Choosing a GPS Receiver Based on Your Goals

GPS functions. Do they accomplish these tasks as well as stand-alone, dedicated GPS receivers? Not always—but in some cases, they're even better.

We'll look more at this option in the section "GPS Receivers for PDAs" later in this chapter. In the meantime, let's tackle the tricky area of GPS mapping: the different kinds and how they affect your choice of receiver.

To Map or Not to Map?

Popular as GPS technology has become for hikers, flyers, geocachers, and so on, the killer app is road mapping. As you learned in Chapter 1, a GPS receiver can not only show your exact position on a moving map, but also help you navigate from point A to point B. Believe it or not, there are differences in and among those two capabilities, and it's important that you understand them before choosing a GPS receiver.

 I'm referring here to road maps, not aviation or marine maps. My guess is that if you're a pilot or boater, you're going to want the specific kind of map data that comes with dedicated GPS receivers. See Table 2-1 for examples.

Basic Mapping

Picture a paper road map of your state. It shows the highways, cities, parks, airports, waterways, and so on. Most handheld GPS receivers—models like the Garmin eMap and Magellan SporTrak—have exactly that level of "state map" data, except they usually have it for the entire country, not just one state. As a result, you can use these receivers to track your position while driving—but only on highways and major roads. Let's say you're on I-75 heading south from Detroit; the moving map will show you your position on the highway relative to other major roads and points of interest.

If you leave the highway and head off down some city streets, you'll still see your position relative to I-75, provided you're zoomed out enough to see both. However, you won't see any street data; if you zoom in on your position, you'll see nothing but blank space around you—the map data isn't detailed enough to show individual streets.

Obviously, the usefulness of your GPS device for driving is directly proportional to the amount of map detail contained in your GPS receiver. Most handheld units from Garmin and Magellan include only basic map data (also known as *basemap* data)—and that's if they do mapping at all. That said, you can usually download street-level maps to these units; both vendors offer optional software that allows you to do this. But there's a big caveat here, so keep reading.

Street-Level Mapping

Street-level maps are exactly that: maps that contain every single street in a given area (be it a county, a state, or even an entire region of the country). Not only that; street-level maps usually include address data, thereby making door-to-door navigation possible. Here's what a street-level map looks like on Garmin's StreetPilot:

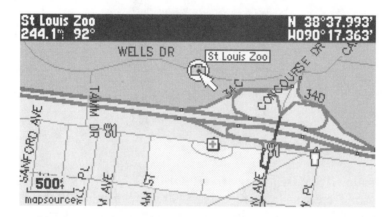

This is where the entire which-GPS-receiver-should-I-buy question comes to a head. If you primarily want this kind of street-level mapping and door-to-door navigation, I highly recommend one of the following solutions:

- **A car with a built-in GPS system**   Though expensive (they're usually a $2,000 to $4,000 option) and obviously not portable from one vehicle to another, most built-in GPS systems offer big screens, easy operation, and the benefit of being built in—no wires strung across the dashboard, no battery drain to worry about. If you have the cash to spare, this is the way to go.

- **A Pocket PC PDA with one of several GPS add-on packages**   I've tested a ton of GPS solutions for both Palm and Pocket PC PDAs, and at the moment there's no question that the best stuff—the best *software—*

appears on the latter platform. You can read more about this in "GPS Receivers for PDAs" later in this chapter.

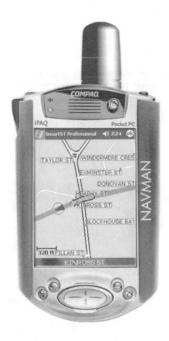

- **Garmin GPS V Deluxe or StreetPilot III** The GPS V Deluxe has a grayscale screen and sells for about $400. The StreetPilot III (see Figure 2-1 earlier in this chapter) is virtually identical but has a color screen and sells for about $700. (At press time, Garmin had just announced a couple new StreetPilot models, each priced well over $1,000. The StreetPilot III is still an excellent choice and should be available in retail/online channels for some time.) Both models are expressly designed to sit atop your dashboard and provide turn-by-turn driving directions—though the GPS V alerts you to upcoming turns with beeps, while the StreetPilot issues voice prompts ("Take next right," and so on).

- **Garmin iQue 3600** This is the first PDA with a GPS receiver built right in (instead of added externally). At $589 it's not inexpensive, but it's definitely one of the most capable and well-rounded navigation solutions you can buy. Find out more in Chapters 3 and 9.

2

■ **Navman iCN 630**   Navman isn't a household name like Garmin (we're constantly talking about Garmin in our house, aren't you? Garmin this, Garmin that…), but the company's iCN 630 gives the StreetPilot III a run for the money. It, too, rides atop your dashboard, employs a beautiful color screen, and delivers voice-prompted driving instructions. List price: $999.

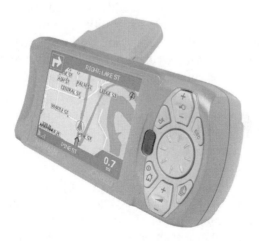

Real-Time Routing: The Killer App

What all of these street-level solutions have in common is this: on-the-fly route generation. In other words, no matter where you are, you can plug in a street address and have driving directions generated on the fly.

You can't do that with a handheld GPS like the SporTrak Color, even if you opt for the desktop mapping software. Can you generate these driving directions—these *routes*—on your PC and then transfer them to the GPS for real-time mapping? Absolutely, but that requires a lot of advance planning and effort, which, in my mind, makes the whole GPS-navigation thing a lot less practical. (Plus, you won't get voice-prompted driving directions, a feature that adds immeasurably to your safety level.)

Thus, my advice is this: if the GPS capability you want above all else is real-time routing (and believe me, that's something well worth having), consider one of the aforementioned options. I'll provide much greater detail on using these options in Chapter 3, which focuses entirely on in-car navigation.

GPS Receivers for PDAs

The idea for this book came to me while tooling up I-70 from Colorado Springs to Denver to see a Rockies game. My good buddy Dave was at the wheel, giving me a chance to tinker with the Dell Axim Pocket PC he'd brought. He'd also brought the Socket GPS Nav Kit, which includes a Bluetooth GPS receiver (more on that in a bit) and the best mapping software I'd ever seen. Scratch that—it was the only *good* mapping software I'd ever seen on a PDA. It was not only attractive and easy to use, it could calculate driving directions on the fly—no PC required.

Did you know?

The Differences Between Palms and Pocket PCs

New to PDAs? If so, I should probably explain that PDA stands for Personal Digital Assistant. I prefer to call them handheld PCs, as that's what they really are, but *PDA* is a little glitzier. Anyway, you've undoubtedly seen these things before—they're pretty popular nowadays. Heck, entire books have been written about them, books like *How to Do Everything with Your Palm Handheld, 4th Edition*, by, ahem, Rick Broida and Dave Johnson. Makes a great gift.

PDAs are like portable extensions of your desktop computer, packed with copies of your documents, contacts, appointments, and other important data. Of course, they're also capable of things like games, e-books, and, oh, I don't know—GPS! All you need is the right software and some kind of GPS receiver.

Ah, but take it back a step: what's the right PDA? There are endless variables to consider, so allow me to shed some light on the key differences between the two main PDA types: Palms and Pocket PCs—or, more accurately, PDAs based on the Palm operating system (or OS, the core software that makes the device work), and those based on the Pocket PC operating system. Palm and Sony are the leading makers of Palm OS PDAs, and HP and Toshiba are the Pocket PC heavyweights.

Fundamentally speaking, all Palm OS and Pocket PC handhelds are capable of the same things. Of the two, I find the Palm OS significantly easier to use, and there's a ton more software available for it. However, much as it pains me to say this (because I have a long and public history of disliking Pocket PC), the best GPS software is available for Pocket PC. I'm referring to products like ALK CoPilot Live, TomTom Navigator, and Socket MyNavigator, which, at press time, were available only for Pocket PC.

There's one exception, and that's the Garmin iQue 3600, a Palm OS–based PDA with built-in GPS capabilities and outstanding navigation software. Thus, you get the benefits of the Palm OS and some top-notch mapping tools, all in a PDA that fits in your pocket. Read all about it in Chapter 9.

Previously, most PDA-mapping solutions I'd used worked like this: load up a woefully confusing mapping program on your PC, manually select a swath of map (or, worse, choose maps by *county*—blech!), and then try in vain to figure out how to transfer the map to your PDA. And if you wanted door-to-door driving directions, you had to first create the route on your PC. Confusing, awkward, inconvenient—three words that, until very recently, described 99 percent of PDA GPS solutions.

But here was Socket's MyNavigator software, with its smart interface, pretty maps, and on-the-fly routing. Suddenly, GPS on a PDA seemed a lot more appealing.

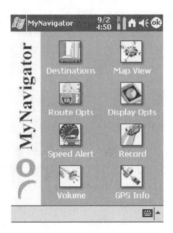

Flash-forward a few months. The book is well underway, and I've unearthed several more PDA solutions that are just as good as MyNavigator, if not better. They say timing is everything, and navigation software for PDAs is just starting to hit its stride.

In this section, I'm going to teach you a bit about PDAs and then explore the many different GPS solutions available for them.

The Upsides to PDAs

PDAs offer some significant advantages over other kinds of GPS solutions, especially where road navigation is concerned. For instance, they can run a wide variety of software. In fact, suppose you've purchased a GPS receiver that happens to come with really crummy mapping software. You don't need to buy a whole new bundle—you can keep the receiver and install inexpensive (relatively speaking) new software.

PDAs also offer unique potential that navigation software is just now starting to realize: integration with your address book. Most people store dozens, if not hundreds or even thousands, of contact names and addresses in their PDAs. Wouldn't it be great if you could tell the mapping software to generate a route to any contact's address? A couple taps of the stylus and you're on your way! (Most mapping software requires you to enter addresses manually.)

2

Finally, let's not ignore the non-GPS capabilities PDAs afford. They're handy little devices to have around. If you're not convinced, pick up a copy of *Handheld Computing* magazine (I'm the, ahem, editor) and check out some of the amazing software and accessories available today.

Should You Buy a PDA Just for GPS?

So you're sold on PDAs—would it make sense to buy one expressly for GPS? That's a tough call. You'd need to spend a minimum of about $600 for the necessary equipment (a fairly robust PDA and a good GPS bundle), though with some careful shopping you could cut that down to around $500. Garmin's StreetPilot III also sells for around $700, and it's a pretty robust in-car navigation system—superior in some ways to even the best PDA setups. Take a look at the previous section and then the next section and weigh the pros and cons.

If I had $700 to spend, I'd go for the PDA option—but that's mostly because I'd use it for lots of other things besides GPS. In fact, I'd most likely get the Garmin iQue 3600 (see Chapter 9), which sells for about $550 (street price) and offers the best PDA-based navigation I've seen yet.

The Downsides to PDAs

Wonderful as I think PDAs are for most GPS applications, there are a few downsides to consider, especially if you're eyeing one for in-car navigation.

- **Batteries**   PDAs are traditionally used in short bursts—a few minutes here and there. GPS navigation requires a PDA to operate for extended periods, and very often to power the GPS receiver as well. As a result, you may have to recharge the device after just a few hours. That means buying and bringing along some kind of external charger.

> **TIP**   *In shopping for a travel charger for my Compaq iPAQ H3850, I found a combination car charger and spare AC adapter selling together for about $12 on eBay. And they were both new, not used. In my experience, there are lots of good PDA-accessory deals to be found on eBay, so start your search there.*

- **Pocket PC OS**   Although the best GPS navigation software is currently available for Pocket PC–based PDAs, the Pocket PC operating system is, in my humble opinion, terrible. It's confusing, crash prone, and often behaves in inexplicable ways. (Sounds kind of like my computer, which also runs a

Microsoft-made operating system.) If you go this route, be prepared to battle a learning curve and contend with some downright wacky problems.

■ **Price**   No one said in-car navigation was going to be cheap, and PDAs offer no exception. The devices themselves are pretty affordable—for about $300 you can get a Palm or Pocket PC with enough horsepower to handle GPS mapping—but the GPS add-on bundle will usually cost you another $300 to $400. Even Garmin's iQue 3600 is $589—not exactly cheap.

■ **Wiring and whatnot**   If your PDA/GPS is going to take up residence in your car, plan on at least one wire hanging from it, if not two or three. Some setups require a wired external antenna that runs from the GPS to the roof of your car. And you're likely to need a charger, so that's another cord. Of course, just about any in-car navigation system—except one built into the car itself—will require charging, so that's pretty much a wash. Finally, you'll need some kind of mounting system to position the PDA at eye level and arm's reach—just one more thing to think about.

What Is Bluetooth and Why Does It Matter for GPS?

Bluetooth is a short-range wireless technology that's starting to become popular in personal devices like PDAs, cell phones, and—you guessed it—GPS receivers. Why choose a wireless GPS receiver over one that plugs right into your PDA? First, because it's wireless, silly! No one wants wires strewn about the car. Second, a Bluetooth GPS receiver is compatible with any Bluetooth-equipped PDA, so you can use it with, say, a Palm OS PDA today, a Pocket PC tomorrow, and just about anything else you upgrade to in the future. If you buy a plug-in (that is, wired) GPS, it may not be compatible with other PDAs you currently own or purchase down the road.

For the moment, Bluetooth GPS products are at the high end of the pricing scale (Socket's excellent GPS Nav Kit sells for $529), and they're not exactly ideal for outdoor activities like hiking and Geocaching. That's because you can't just slip it into your pocket (receivers need an unobstructed line of sight to the satellites, remember?), so you'd have to come up with some creative way to attach it to your backpack, belt, hat, or whatever. (There's also the matter of its battery, which is rechargeable. Lots of luck finding a cigarette lighter for its charger in the middle of the woods.) Thus, a Bluetooth GPS receiver is just about perfect for cars, but not necessarily for all GPS applications.

What to Buy If You Don't Own a PDA Yet

If you've decided to take the plunge and buy both a PDA and a GPS system to go with it, you've come to the right section. My advice is to choose the GPS receiver first and then a compatible PDA. (That is, of course, unless you specifically want a certain PDA make or model, in which case feel free to reverse the order.)

I'm going to recommend three GPS solutions that I've tried and really liked. Needless to say, there are lots more out there, and by now there might even be some that are better than these three. Still, you can't go wrong with any of these.

■   **Garmin iQue 3600**   Yep, it's the much-ballyhooed PDA-and-GPS-in-one. The iQue 3600 gives you the superb Palm OS, a gorgeous high-resolution screen, support for playing MP3 tunes, and absolutely first-rate navigation software. It really is the ultimate solution for someone who doesn't already own a PDA (or who wants a really sweet upgrade). Price: $589.

■   **Socket GPS Nav Kit**   This is a splendid package for two reasons. First, it includes a rechargeable Bluetooth GPS receiver (see "What Is Bluetooth and Why Does It Matter for GPS?"). Second, it comes with MyNavigator, an outstanding Pocket PC mapping and routing program. How good is this bundle? It led me to write an entire book about GPS. Price: $529 (ouch! Visit **PriceGrabber.com** to search for better deals). Recommended PDA to go with it: HP iPAQ h1945 Pocket PC ($299).

■   **TomTom Navigator USA**   I particularly like the software that comes with this Pocket PC package, as it affords not only real-time routing, but also a unique 3D view of the road as you drive. It also comes with three different car mounts (air vent, windshield, and dashboard) and a wired GPS receiver that's compatible with a variety of Pocket PC handhelds. Price: $319. Recommended PDA to go with it: Dell Axim ($199 and up).

What to Buy If You Already Own a PDA

If you already own a PDA, can you just add a GPS receiver and mapping software? Absolutely, though depending on the age and capabilities of your PDA, you may not be able to enjoy the best of what GPS currently has to offer. For instance, older Palm OS handhelds—those running Palm OS 4.x and earlier—aren't likely to have the processing power or audio capabilities to provide real-time routing and voice-prompted directions. You'll probably be able to see your position on a moving map, input waypoints (for things like Geocaching), and possibly even copy preconfigured routes from your PC for real-time navigation. But if you want real GPS-routing muscle, you may want to consider a new PDA.

In Table 2-2, I list a variety of GPS hardware/software bundles for PDAs. Because there are so many bundles and so many PDAs out there, I can't include everything, but all of the mainstream and popular stuff is there.

Product	Platform	Compatible with...	Comments	Where to Find It
CoPilot Live | Pocket PC 4	Pocket PC	Any Bluetooth-equipped Pocket PC	Bluetooth version costs the same as "sleeve" version; solid mapping software can integrate with cell phone for advanced features	**www.alk.com**
Earthmate GPS for Handhelds	Palm OS and Pocket PC	Most newer Palm OS and Pocket PC PDAs	Wired and Bluetooth options available; bundled PDA software supports optional topographic maps	**www.delorme.com**
Emtac Wireless Bluetooth GPS	Palm OS	Palm Tungsten T series, Sony Clié PEG-TG50, and any Bluetooth-equipped Palm OS PDA	Excellent Bluetooth GPS receiver, but bundled Mapopolis software doesn't provide voice directions	**www.palmone.com**
Magellan GPS Companion	Palm OS	Palm m500 series	No real-time routing; bundled desktop mapping software very complicated	**www.magellangps.com**
Mapopolis GPS Bundles	Palm OS and Pocket PC	Most PDAs	Wired and Bluetooth options available; above-average software for both Palm OS and Pocket PC	**www.mapopolis.com**
Navman GPS 3450	Pocket PC	Most iPAQ models	Sleeve-type GPS receiver bundled with windshield mount, car charger, and first-rate software	**www.navman.com**
Socket GPS Nav Kit	Pocket PC	Any Bluetooth-equipped Pocket PC	One of my favorite bundles; includes Bluetooth GPS receiver and top-notch mapping software	**www.socketcom.com**
TomTom Navigator USA	Pocket PC	Most Pocket PC models	Wired and Bluetooth options available; excellent mapping software	**www.tomtom.com**

TABLE 2-2　GPS Add-on Bundles for PDAs

Just the Software

Let's assume for a moment that you already own a PDA and GPS receiver, but you don't like your mapping software (or you picked up a secondhand receiver that didn't have any). You've heard me heap praise on programs like MyNavigator and TomTom Navigator—can you buy them outright without buying a GPS receiver at the same time? Yes! Let's take a quick peek at some worthwhile mapping/navigation packages that you can buy separately and that will work with nearly any GPS receiver you connect to your PDA.

■ **CoPilot Live**   CoPilot Live | Pocket PC 4 is not only the first program ever to have a line down the middle of its name; it's also a robust navigation package that offers features not found elsewhere. For instance, it lets you know in advance which side of the street your destination is on. It enables you to set waypoints in case your destination has stops along the way. And it supports two-way communication (your PDA must have a live Internet connection—no small feat), so you can use it for things like two-way messaging and transmitting your vehicle location to someone back at "home base" (like a family member or coworker). Pretty sweet—and pretty pricey at $229.

■ **Mapopolis Navigator**   Available for both Palm OS and Pocket PC PDAs, Mapopolis Navigator offers spoken driving directions, automatic rerouting, and other nice features. However, the web site is a confusing mess, as is the company's map-purchase system. My advice: download the Mapopolis Navigator software for your PDA (the software is free; the maps will cost you) and a demo map, then see if you like it. I think both the site and software need some serious polish, but Mapopolis Navigator has the distinction of being one of the very few Palm OS programs (so far) to offer real-time routing. Plan on spending around $100 for a full set of maps of North America.

- **MyNavigator** Surprise! MyNavigator, the superb software that comes with Socket's pricey GPS Nav Kit, is actually just a renamed version of Netropa's Intellinav. Why this software isn't available with more GPS receivers is beyond me, but you can buy it separately if you search really, really hard online. I found it for $99 at Semsons & Co (www.semsons.com) masquerading under the name i.Guidance.

- **TomTom Navigator** As I mentioned earlier, the thing I really like about TomTom Navigator is its 3D navigation view, something I've never seen in any other GPS software for PDAs. TomTom also supplies a wealth of customization options, making it a good choice for advanced users and those who like to tinker.

Specialty GPS Receivers

At last, we come to the oddball GPS receivers, the products that don't fit in mainstream categories. These include two-way radios, distance-to-the-pin receivers for golfers, and locator devices designed to help find lost kids (arguably GPS's noblest application). Let's take a closer look at these and other GPS-enabled products.

Two-Way Radio Meets GPS

You've probably seen two-way radios before: they're adult-grade walkie-talkies that have a range of about two miles, which has made them popular among hikers, hunters, campers, and visitors to outdoor flea markets (no joke—that's where I first encountered them). Wouldn't it be cool if these two-way radios had GPS receivers and could beam their locations back and forth? Not only could you talk to your friend, family member, or fellow hunter, you could pinpoint that person's exact location and navigate to the person with ease.

The Garmin Rino 110 (see Figure 2-3) and Rino 120 offer exactly that capability: two-way radio communications and built-in GPS positioning. (At press time, Garmin was the only company to offer such a product. Audiovox had one in the works, but canceled it for reasons the company wouldn't divulge.)

GPS for Golf

If you're an avid golfer, you may already have encountered GPS receivers at courses you've played. The devices have become very popular in overcoming one of golf's biggest obstacles: deciding which club to choose. By providing you with the exact distance from your position on the fairway (or in the rough, duffer) to the pin, GPS receivers enable you to select exactly the right club for your next shot.

FIGURE 2-3   The Garmin Rino 110 looks like a traditional two-way radio but includes
a GPS receiver. It can transmit its position to other Rino radios within
a two-mile range.

GPS receivers for golfers generally take on one of two forms: dedicated products
designed expressly for golfing, and special software designed to work with GPS-
equipped PDAs. Chapter 6 talks about these products and how to use them to
improve your game, so feel free to flip to it if you want to learn more.

GPS for Runners

Here's an envelope-pushing idea: a GPS receiver you wear on your wrist, Dick Tracy
style. The Garmin Forerunner 201 (see Figure 2-4) not only provides the usual
positioning data, but also serves up useful features for runners, such as speed and
distance tracking. For you lap runners, the Forerunner stores helpful data like lap
time, distance, and average pace.

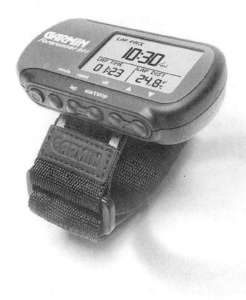

FIGURE 2-4   Designed for runners, the Garmin Forerunner 201 is the first watch with a built-in GPS receiver.

If you hate to train alone, you can take advantage of the Forerunner's Virtual Partner feature, which challenges you to keep pace with a "ghost runner" who, er, lives in the watch. The watch shows you your position relative to your virtual running buddy, so you don't get too far ahead or behind. It even sounds an alarm if that happens. (It's like a high-tech, but mute, drill sergeant. Instead of, "Move your lazy butt, soldier!" you get, "Beep!")

The Forerunner stores up to two years' worth of training histories, shows how many calories you've burned, stores up to 100 locations and enables you to navigate to any of them, and runs on a 15-hour rechargeable battery. The list price is $160. Sounds like a perfect candidate for the avid runner's holiday wish list.

TIP   *Want to use the Forerunner for biking? Garmin offers an $18 handlebar mount bracket. Aha! Fooled you—that's not really the tip. The tip is to be safe if you decide to use the Forerunner this way. You might get so caught up watching its display and fiddling with its settings that you crash into a tree or, worse, bus. As with any GPS technology on wheels, this requires you to be extra careful. What can I say? I'm worried about you. I'm a worrier.*

Child Safety Devices

Just weeks before I began work on this book, I came home after a tennis game to find my wife, Shawna, frantically looking for our three-year-old daughter, Sarah. It was a Sunday morning, and Sarah had just up and disappeared. Shawna had checked with the neighbors, run around inside and out calling Sarah's name, and so on. She was just about to dial the police.

As it turned out, Sarah had gone next door to play with friends, whose parents hadn't heard the doorbell when Shawna first came looking. We wouldn't have been quite so freaked out if she had gone next door without telling us before, but this was the first time Sarah had left the house unannounced.

This kind of thing happens all the time. Kids take an unannounced detour on the way home from school, wander off at an amusement park, get lost at campgrounds, and so on. Then there's the terrifying stuff we see on the news about abducted kids— enough said.

In an ideal world, you'd be able to find your kid at a moment's notice, no matter where he or she was. The Wherify GPS Locator is not quite the ideal, but it's a huge step in the right direction and a potential source of comfort for concerned parents. This sophisticated wristwatch—which has the colorful, bulky, cheap-by-design look of a toy—includes a GPS receiver and CDMA transmitter. (CDMA is the same technology used in many cell phones.) As a result, it can pinpoint the wearer's position and then transmit that data. You can either call Wherify to obtain the location or visit Wherify's web site and view the location yourself on a map. Presto: your lost kid is found.

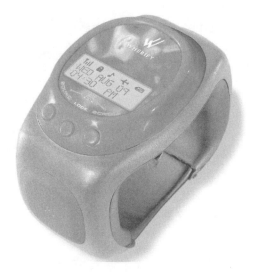

I don't want to sound like a brochure for the product, so I'm not going to regurgitate its various features—you can find all that at the Wherify web site. However, I do want to point out its limitations, as they're important to consider. For starters, the device won't work in shopping malls, cars, houses, and all the other places GPS signals can't reach. Thus, even if Sarah had been wearing one on that scary Sunday, it wouldn't have done us any good (except perhaps to narrow the search to indoor locations). The Wherify also has the usual GPS problems in heavily wooded areas, so if your child gets lost in the woods, you might be out of luck.

Finally, there's the matter of price. The watch itself currently sells for $199 (down from its initial price of $399, thankfully), which is expensive but not prohibitively so. But you have to pay a $35 setup fee and a minimum of $20 per month for the Wherify service, which includes a fixed number of "locates"—actual usages of the service to locate the watch. In an ideal world, the service would be free, or you'd pay just a few bucks for each locate. Actually, in an ideal world, kids would never get lost.

Understanding GPS Features and Tech Specs

Regardless of whether you're looking at handheld, PDA, in-car, or specialty GPS receivers, you're likely to encounter a fair number of confusing terms and features.

Is Wherify Worth It? One Parent's Take

Dave Johnson (this book's tech editor) and I rarely see eye to eye on anything. So it was with some apprehension that I asked him to share his experience with Wherify, the built-for-kids wristwatch locator with integrated GPS technology. Dave's the father of two of my all-time favorite kids: Evan, 13, and Marin, 11. Alas, as usual, he gets everything wrong—20 locates per month should be more than adequate for most users, and the Wherify is really designed with younger children in mind—but he's entitled to his opinion (I suppose).

Personally, I've never been all that worried about Big Brother. Gadgets like Wherify's GPS Locator for Kids, though, raise the specter of pervasive monitoring. Thankfully, it's us parents who are doing the monitoring—not some shadowy government agency.

I was truly ecstatic to try out this gadget. I imagined a million uses for the Locator, and found the thought of knowing where my kids are at any moment—especially now that both of them are approaching their teen years—very reassuring.

Unfortunately, Wherify's first locator product just isn't practical. First of all, my kids simply won't stand for being shackled to—and quite literally locked inside—a wristwatch with all the cool factor of a Happy Meal prize. It's big, bulky, and ugly, and if it is to serve its purpose, it needs to be locked on. How would they explain to their friends that they're wearing a watch that won't come off without their folks' permission? Maybe that's fine for a 5-year-old, but by the time your kids approach the age of 10 or so, such tactics simply won't fly.

Even if you can get past that limitation, I'm not crazy about the service. What if your kid doesn't show up on time after school? Sounds like a job for the watch's breadcrumb mode, in which you can see everywhere he or she has been. But that takes planning—you need to program the watch to record locations to a breadcrumb file ahead of time. All you can do when you know your kid is missing is to ask for the current location. And that works okay, except that the map onto which the positions are drawn is far too small. You can't make it fill the screen or zoom in far enough to distinguish an accurate position.

Finally, keep in mind that you're paying for all your location pings—the $20-per-month plan, for instance, gives you only 20 free locates. After that, they're a dollar each—and that makes the system prohibitively expensive to use regularly. Heck, I burned through 20 locates in a single breadcrumb session one Saturday afternoon. I started out pretty jazzed about Wherify, but it's simply not a practical tool for my near-teen kids. I hope a smaller, cheaper, smarter solution comes along soon.

—*Dave Johnson*

For instance, does it matter if a receiver tracks only 8 satellites instead of 12? What kind of antenna is better: patch or quadrifilar? And what the heck does quadrifilar mean?

Before I dazzle you with the explanations I cut and pasted from a web site (kidding!), I must point out that GPS specs are not unlike modern desktop computer specs: a lot of them are just for show, and understanding them isn't vital to your use (or enjoyment) of the product. Most modern GPS receivers offer certain baseline capabilities that make them more than adequate for their intended purpose(s). That said, you might want to pay close attention to a few features during the GPS-shopping process.

Antenna Type

Some GPS receivers have *patch* antennas. Some have *quadrifilar* antennas (also known as *quad helix* antennas). Is one kind better than another? Generally speaking, patch antennas don't work quite as well as quadrifilar antennas under heavy tree cover, the reason being that the former seek out satellites directly overhead, while the latter scan the horizon.

If you're looking at a GPS receiver for use in your car, you may want one with a connector for a wired external antenna. These are usually magnetic and attach to your car's roof. Some GPS receivers come with said antenna; others require you to buy it separately.

Acquisition Time

Acquisition time refers to the amount of time needed for a GPS receiver to lock onto at least three satellites. When you first turn on the receiver, it performs what's called a *cold start*, meaning that it acquires whatever satellites it can find in the sky at that time. A cold start takes a few minutes—usually anywhere from two to five—which can be inconvenient when you're eager to hit the road/trail/runway/whatever. Thus, look for a receiver that promises a short cold-start time.

Many models also specify a *warm-start* rating, which is the time needed for a receiver to reacquire the satellites it acquired earlier. This process usually takes much less time—sometimes only a few seconds—because the receiver simply has to reestablish signals, not find new ones.

NOTE   *Warm starts are possible only within a few hours of a cold start. Any longer than that and the initial satellites will have moved out of range.*

The warm-start rating is arguably even more important than the cold-start rating, as you're likely to be using your GPS receiver off and on for an extended period, rather than just keeping it running all day. Ideally, a warm start should take just a few seconds, so you can get back to navigating with minimal delay.

Battery Life

Battery life varies widely from one GPS receiver to another, depending in no small part on what kinds of batteries are used, the size and capability (color or grayscale) of the screen, and so on. The good news is that GPS receivers are (surprisingly, if you ask me) judicious in their use of power. Models like the Garmin Geko 201 can last for up to 18 hours on a pair of triple-A alkalines.

Speaking of which, decide up front whether you want a GPS that uses disposable batteries or a built-in rechargeable one. The Socket Bluetooth GPS, for instance, has a rechargeable battery and comes with a cigarette-lighter adapter for cars. That's great for, well, cars, but what if you're using it somewhere else? You can't just swap in a pair of Duracells if the charge runs out.

If you do opt for a rechargeable receiver, investigate your charging options. Can you get a cigarette-lighter adapter for your car? How about an AC adapter so you can charge it overnight?

Finally, if you buy a receiver that's powered by your PDA, make sure you have a spare battery or portable charging solution for that PDA. Plan ahead, people!

NMEA Compatibility

National Marine Electronics Association (NMEA) compatibility is important primarily in marine applications of GPS, as it allows GPS data to be fed to other navigation equipment. Unless you're buying a receiver with boating or fishing in mind, don't be concerned with NMEA compatibility.

Number of Channels

Most modern GPS products employ what's called a *parallel receiver*, which enables them to track multiple satellites simultaneously. This is obviously a vital characteristic, as you need to track at least three to get 3D positioning. Okay, but does it matter how many satellites a receiver can track simultaneously? Or, more accurately, should you care if one receiver can track only 8 while another can track 12? Considering that only 6 GPS satellites are visible in the sky at any given time, the number here isn't that crucial. However, there is one advantage to a higher number:

faster warm starts. The more satellites a receiver can track, the faster it will be able to reestablish signals.

Number of Routes

A *route* is a set of directions, be it from one waypoint to another or from one address to another. Most GPS receivers can store routes for future use, which can be a huge time-saver when you need to navigate back to a spot or address you've already visited. Different models have different capacities for storing routes: some can hold a hundred or so; some can hold a thousand or more.

Tracking Points

Tracking points, or *track points*, are like breadcrumbs: digital markers you leave behind as you hike, hunt, or engage in other circuitous outdoor activities. The idea here is to enable you to retrace your steps, to backtrack the way you came so you don't get lost. Track points are usually found in handheld GPS receivers—I've seen few PDA-based GPS solutions that support this feature (though that's really just a matter of software; see Chapter 4 for details). Some receivers store a few hundred track points; others can store thousands.

WAAS

How important is it that your GPS receiver support WAAS, the Wide Area Augmentation System discussed in Chapter 1? Pretty important. It means the difference between positioning accuracy of around 30 feet (without WAAS) and 10 feet (with it). Whenever possible, opt for WAAS capability.

Waterproofing

The Red Rocks Trail in Colorado Springs is a really cool hike in the early spring, when it's not too hot, the bugs aren't out yet, and there are still patches of snow. Of course, there are also patches of mud and ice. And let's not forget rain. Stuff like that is deadly to a sophisticated piece of electronics like a GPS receiver, right? Not necessarily. Handheld models like the Magellan SporTrak Color and Garmin Geko 201 are waterproof. In fact, the SporTrak actually floats, and the Geko can survive for 30 minutes under a meter of water.

On the other side of the coin, most PDAs are decidedly *not* waterproof, so take care when handling them in any potentially wet outdoor environment. And before you purchase any GPS system, consider what kinds of environments you plan to be in, and whether a waterproof model is important.

Where to Shop for GPS Gear

Most GPS receivers are commodity items, meaning that you can shop around until you find the very best deal on the one you want. Once you've made that determination, I recommend starting with a price-comparison web site like **PriceGrabber.com**. Just enter the name of the model you're after, and you'll find anywhere from a handful to several dozen prices from various vendors that stock the product.

There are also sites that specialize in GPS gear. Among them:

- **www.buygpsnow.com**

- **www.gps4fun.com**

- **www.gpsmarketplace.com**

- **www.thegpsstore.com**

Finally, don't forget to include auction sites like eBay in your search. GPS receivers have no moving parts, so a used one is usually just as good as a new one.

Where to Find It

Web Site	Address	What's There
ALK Technologies	**www.alk.com**	CoPilot Live	Pocket PC 4
DeLorme	**www.delorme.com**	Earthmate GPS
Emtac	**www.emtac.com**	GPS hardware for PDAs
Garmin	**www.garmin.com**	Wide variety of GPS hardware, including Geko and StreetPilot products
Mapopolis	**www.mapopolis.com**	GPS hardware bundles and mapping solutions for PDAs
Navman	**www.navman.com**	GPS hardware for cars and PDAs
Socket	**www.socketcom.com**	GPS Nav Kit for Pocket PC
Thales/Magellan	**www.magellangps.com**	Wide variety of GPS hardware, including SporTrak products

Chapter 3

Driver's Ed: GPS Navigation for Cars

How to...

- Exercise GPS safety
- Enter destinations while driving
- Use voice navigation
- Mount your GPS correctly
- Have a backup plan
- Load maps in your GPS receiver
- Load maps for long trips
- Enter destinations
- Choose a destination from your PDA's contact list
- Set the zoom level
- Deal with GPS flakiness
- Find nearby emergency services
- Understand rerouting
- Use your cell phone for GPS navigation

In the movie biz, producers refer to something called the "money shot," the scene or moment that's designed to push the envelope, create a lot of buzz, or just pack people into theaters. In the GPS biz, map-based navigation is the money shot, the reason most people are attracted to the technology and the most popular application of it. In this chapter, I'm going to show you how to navigate from point A to point B using a variety of devices. Not only that, I'm going to help you understand the concepts of routing, rerouting, waypoints, points of interest, and other important stuff that can help minimize your confusion and maximize your enjoyment of this technology.

As they say, however, safety first. Don't even pick up your car keys until we have a little talk about GPS safety—and I'm not talking about protecting your receiver from a fall. I'm talking about, no joke, saving your life.

GPS Safety (Important!)

There's a reason they don't put TVs in cars (not in the front seat, anyway). When you're behind the wheel of a moving vehicle, your eyes belong in front of you. Wonderful as GPS can be for helping you navigate unfamiliar roads, it's a huge distraction—worse than the radio, worse even than cell phones. That's because a GPS device is not unlike a TV (and just as entertaining as some shows, if not more so), with images that are constantly changing. Plus, it invites interaction: zooming in or out on maps, searching for points of interest, even entering new destinations.

CAUTION   *Never, ever, ever, ever, ever, ever, ever, ever do something as involved as entering a new destination while you're driving. I'm going to say this many times throughout this chapter, so get used to it. I'm not trying to nag or be over-protective—I'm trying to save your life and the lives of others. For your own sake, for the sake of those who love you, and for the sake of other drivers, please heed this warning (see Figure 3-1).*

FIGURE 3-1   Spend too much time looking at your GPS receiver instead of the road, and you could end up like this. Please don't let that happen.

Some states have enacted laws prohibiting cell phone use while driving, because studies have shown that cell phone use is responsible for accidents. There's no data tying GPS use to accidents, but that's because the products are relatively new and not widely used—yet. A few years down the road, though, don't be surprised if a police officer pulls you over and hands you a ticket if you're fiddling with GPS controls while you drive.

In the meantime, I'd like to share some important statistics:

- In 2002, nearly 43,000 people died in car crashes. (Well over half weren't using restraints such as seat belts, which has nothing to do with GPS but boggles my mind all the same. Wear your seat belts, people!) *Source: National Highway Traffic Safety Administration.*

- Drivers talking on cell phones are responsible for about 6 percent of U.S. auto accidents, killing an estimated 2,600 people and injuring 330,000 others. *Source: Harvard Center for Risk Analysis.*

What more can I say? Operating a GPS receiver while driving is inherently dangerous. However, using one doesn't have to be. I hope you'll keep these suggestions in mind before you hit the road.

Enter Directions Safely

Most GPS road-navigation systems work like this: you enter your destination (be it an address, intersection, or point of interest) directly into the device, usually using a slow, unwieldy menu system that requires data entry one character at a time. Even on models like the Garmin StreetPilot III, which was built with in-car navigation in mind, it can take a few minutes to wade through the menus and enter all the necessary information—house number, street name, city, and so on. (My kingdom for a little fold-down keyboard, or some other method to speed up data entry. Maybe someday.) This process can take even longer if, say, the mapping software is unable to match a street name and number—something that happens fairly often (in part because any given city is likely to have a Maple Drive, Maple Lane, Maple Road, Maple Street, and so on—more on this later).

Don't enter directions while driving. Ever. It requires you to take your eyes off the road over and over again, to say nothing of taking one hand off the steering wheel. Instead, enter destinations using one of these three methods:

- *Start in the garage.* Before you leave the house (or wherever), take the time to enter your destination into the GPS. Some mapping software requires an active GPS signal before you can enter a destination, so you may have to pull out of the garage first and wait for a satellite lock. That alone can take a few minutes, and entering a destination can take a few minutes more. Thus, leave five minutes earlier than you'd originally planned. That way, you won't be late getting where you're going, and you won't get frustrated if the mapping software acts flaky.

> **TIP** *Once your destination is logged in and ready, save it—especially if you're using a PDA. If you have to reboot or even just restart the software, you won't have to enter the destination all over again. Many mapping programs save destinations automatically, but not all of them do. In most cases, you should be able to manually save a destination as a "favorite."*

- *Pull over.* If you need to enter a destination when you're already out and about, don't try to do it while driving. That's an accident begging to happen. Find a safe spot to pull over; then you can enter the destination without distraction. It's a huge pain in the neck, I know, but it's cheaper than a new fender—or a funeral.

- *Let a passenger do it.* If someone else is riding in the car with you, let him or her enter your destination. Guys, I know this is the equivalent of letting your wife have the remote, but suck it up. In fact, all GPS users should teach their significant others how to use the receiver ahead of time, so you're not distracted and trying to give instructions with everybody getting all frustrated while you're doing 75.

Rely on Voice Navigation

Part of what makes GPS navigation so potentially unsafe is that you have to shift your eyes from the road to the screen in order to note your position on the moving map and watch for upcoming turns. Fortunately, the latest—and best, in my opinion—navigation solutions include voice-prompted driving directions, meaning that as you drive, you hear a voice issuing instructions like these:

"Turn right in 200 feet."
"Exit onto I-75 north."
"Destination on left."

This is a case where having a "backseat driver" is a good thing. Because the GPS receiver tells you when and where to turn, you needn't spend nearly as much time looking at the screen. No doubt you'll steal glances at it from time to time, but in theory you could avoid the screen altogether and just listen to the directions. That said, there are times when voice prompts can get really annoying, especially if you do a lot of city driving requiring a lot of turns. The first few times you hear your GPS speak, it's a nifty novelty. But it may not be long before you're ready to throw the thing out the window rather than hear "Take next left" again. That's the irony of voice-prompted directions—they make for a safer trip, but they can drive you up the wall.

TIP *Keep the GPS receiver's volume relatively low. That way, the voice prompts won't seem quite so intrusive. You might think you can just mute the voice prompts altogether when you're going to be on the same road for a while, and you can—but then you might miss the prompt informing you of an upcoming exit or turn. Besides, long stretches of highway don't require much instruction, so the GPS probably won't be talking much anyway.*

Every one of my preferred GPS-navigation solutions (see Chapter 2) offers voice capabilities, including those that run on PDAs. Now you know why.

Mount Wisely

Different in-car GPS systems mount differently. The StreetPilot III, for instance, comes with an unusual but effective weighted bean bag that allows the unit to sit atop your dashboard without sliding around. The Navman iCN 630 (see Figure 3-2) comes with a suction-cup mount that attaches to your windshield (it can also mount on your dashboard using an adhesive option). Products like these are fairly straightforward when it comes to mounting: you want to position them so they're as close to your normal field of vision as possible without obscuring it. (I'm not wild about windshield mounts for exactly that reason.)

PDAs require a bit more planning and consideration when it comes to mounting. Some add-on GPS kits come with their own hardware, usually a generic kit for mounting the PDA to an air vent. These can be ideal in that they don't block your

FIGURE 3-2   Some in-car GPS systems, like the Navman iCN 630, mount on your windshield, which can obscure your field of vision somewhat.

field of vision one bit, but they also require you to lower your line of sight from the road, just as you do when adjusting the car stereo. Plus, they block one of your vents, which is not only inconvenient for temperature control, it also means that the back of your PDA is blasted with hot or cold air.

TIP   *If your car allows it, close the vent that's directly behind your PDA. Sounds obvious, I know, but it's easy to forget about stuff like that when you're focusing on proper mounting and entering directions.*

If you do opt for an air-vent mount, make sure the protrusion of the mount and the PDA don't block your normal range of movement when turning the steering wheel.

What You Need Before Hitting the Road

Assuming you're not too scared to leave the house now (it's a jungle out there, isn't it?), you're just about ready to hit the road. I'm also assuming you've already purchased some kind of in-car GPS navigation solution. If not, bop back to Chapter 2 for some recommendations.

Regardless of what GPS hardware you're packing, you'll need two things before you leave the driveway:

- All necessary map data loaded into the GPS receiver or PDA.

- A backup plan.

I'll address the second of these points first.

Have a Backup Plan

Technology is fallible. This is a point driven home when, say, 50 million homes lose power inside of five minutes, or Windows doesn't work right. (Good thing the former doesn't happen as often as the latter, or we'd be spending most of our time in the dark.) Most of the in-car GPS setups I've tried work reasonably well. However, let me posit a few scenarios for you:

- You're running late for a business meeting. You try to enter the client's address into the GPS, but it can't find the street in its map database. You don't know any of the roads or intersections near the destination.

- You're using a Pocket PC PDA and it locks up while you're midway between point A and point B.

- Your destination is in a heavily wooded area, and the GPS receiver loses its satellite lock while you still have five miles to go.

- Your GPS is telling you to go one way, but you *know* you're supposed to go another.

I've experienced three of these situations firsthand—and yet the doctors still can't explain my high blood pressure. Technology is fallible, dear readers, and if you put all your eggs in GPS's basket, you're asking for trouble. I expect things to get a lot more reliable in the years to come, but for now it's essential that you have a backup plan.

That plan is this: MapQuest. You've probably used this web-based service before; it's ideal for generating door-to-door driving directions that you can output to your computer's printer. Assuming you know your destination ahead of time, take three minutes and hit MapQuest before you leave the house or office. Now you have a fallback just in case GPS lets you down.

> **NOTE** *MapQuest is just one of several reliable mapping sites. Others include Microsoft's MapPoint and Yahoo! Maps.*

Loading Maps into Your GPS Receiver

A GPS without maps is like a car without gas: it won't get you very far. All the products featured in this chapter—the Garmin StreetPilot III, Mapopolis Navigator, TomTom Navigator, and so on—rely on map data that must be copied from your PC. Exactly how you go about that is a subject for later sections. For now, let's talk about a few general concepts.

As you might expect, a street map comprises a fair amount of data. Addresses, points of interest, all the graphics needed to depict the visual map—this stuff adds up. In a perfect world, all GPS receivers would have enough storage space to hold all of the street maps for, say, North America. At the moment, however, that's just not an option. As a result, you have to pick and choose what maps to copy—to download—to your receiver. And this requires a little predeparture effort.

> **NOTE** *There is one in-car GPS solution that includes street-level maps for the entire United States: Magellan's 750NAV Plus. It's what's known as an aftermarket solution, meaning it's something a dealer usually has to install (though you can install it yourself if desired). The system includes a hard drive that's large enough to hold all the map data. However, it sells for about $1,500, and it's among the most awkward navigation systems I've ever used. It works well enough, but the learning curve is steep.*

With the exception of built-in navigation systems (those that are actually part of the car) and products like the aforementioned 750NAV Plus, all in-car GPS receivers have a fixed amount of storage space for map data. In some cases they have internal memory; in some cases they have slots for adding memory cards; and in some cases they have both (see Table 3-1 for some examples of car-minded GPS receivers and their storage capabilities). In all cases, there's a ceiling on the amount of map data

GPS	Storage Capabilities	Download Options
CoPilot Live for Pocket PC	Sleeve has CompactFlash expansion slot; Bluetooth option relies on Pocket PC's storage capabilities	Download maps directly to Pocket PC or storage card; can download user-specified radius from any city, all map area visible on the computer desktop, or specific trip data
Garmin iQue 3600	SD memory slot	Download manually selected "map sections" directly to memory card
Garmin StreetPilot III	Internal memory and proprietary memory cards	Connect memory-card reader to PC; download maps based on manual area selection in desktop software
Navman iCN 630	Internal memory and SD/MMC slot for adding more storage capacity	Connect unit directly to PC; download multiple states at once
Socket GPS Nav Kit	Relies on Pocket PC's storage capabilities	Download maps directly to Pocket PC or storage card; download individual states one by one

TABLE 3-1 How GPS Receivers Store Map Data

the receiver can hold. That ceiling varies from device to device, and there are even variations in the actual map data. The state of Michigan might require, say, 40 megabytes (MB) of storage space on one system and 65MB on another. That's because different GPS makers purchase map data from different sources, and many factors can affect the size of map files.

But enough with the FYI stuff. Here, in a nutshell, is how you load map data on any given GPS receiver:

1. Install and run the desktop software that came with the receiver.

2. Select the map area you want to download to the receiver. This area might be a county, a state, a region, an arbitrary swath of map (I'm talking to you, iQue 3600), or a section you select manually by dragging a cursor across it.

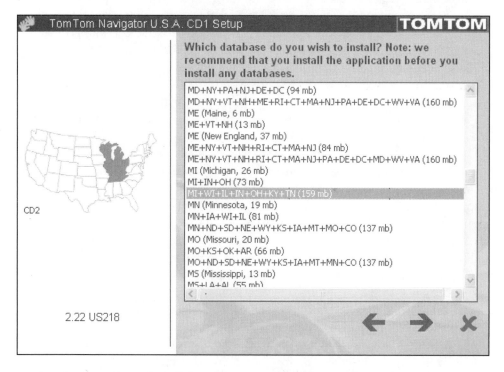

3. Once you've selected the map area, the software will usually tell you how much space it requires and how much space is available on your GPS receiver (and/or its memory card). Obviously, the former must be less than the latter. If not, you'll have to go back and select a smaller area or add a memory card.

4. Follow the instructions to start the download process.

Depending on your driving needs and habits, you may have to complete this process only once. My friend Craig, for instance, spends a ton of time driving

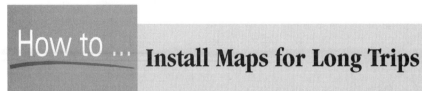

How to ... Install Maps for Long Trips

Let's say you're planning a trip from Michigan to Florida. Because you live in Michigan, you already have its map data loaded on your GPS receiver. But what about all the states between here and there? Do you need to install every one of them? Will your receiver have enough storage space?

There are no simple answers to these questions, only guidelines to consider. For instance, if you consult a road atlas (or desktop mapping software, if your GPS software came with any), you'll see that the majority of your Michigan-to-Florida trip will be spent on I-75. Thus, you don't really need map data for all the states in between—just load Michigan and Florida. If you're planning to stop off in, say, Tennessee, you can add the map for that state or just the area you're going to visit. In other words, you can take a piecemeal approach to map data if you plan ahead.

Ideally, of course, you want full map data for the entire trip. That will ensure that you're covered in case any unexpected detours come up, and at the same time provide a database of points of interest (like restaurants, motels, and sights to see) along the way. However, the longer the trip, the more map data we're talking about, and the more storage space you'll need. That could mean you'll need to purchase a high-capacity memory card—something you don't want to discover five minutes before walking out the door. Copy your desired map data to your GPS receiver a few days before your trip so you'll have time to add any necessary memory.

CoPilot Live, a navigation package for Pocket PCs (see Chapter 2), takes an ideal approach to trip planning. It includes a desktop component you can use to plot your trip in advance, complete with stops and points of interest along the way. Plus, while it provides map data for your entire trip, it minimizes the required storage space by using only a four-mile-wide "corridor" between your starting point and destination. CoPilot Live also lets you enter multiple destinations, a surprisingly rare feature in GPS systems.

between Michigan and Ohio. Thus, he could load the maps for southeast Michigan and all of Ohio, and he wouldn't need to mess with maps again—he'd be covered for all his jaunts around metro Detroit and his frequent journeys south into Ohio. Only if he decided to take a trip to, say, northern Michigan or somewhere other than Ohio would another map installation be required.

Entering Destinations in Your GPS Receiver

Maps? Check. Backup plan? Check. Car keys? Look under the sofa cushions. Now that you're ready for the road, let's talk about using your GPS receiver to get where you're going. That means entering a destination so the software can route you from here to there.

As first mentioned in Chapter 2, this is called real-time routing. You enter a destination directly in the GPS receiver, and it calculates your route—no computer required. (Map data is, however, required; see "Loading Maps into Your GPS Receiver" earlier in this chapter.) Some GPS receivers for PDAs (mostly older bundles) promise "door-to-door navigation," but that's not the same thing. That requires you to create your route on your PC first and then download the resulting door-to-door driving directions to your PDA. Bleh. Real-time routing is where it's at, because it's vastly more convenient and generally a lot more versatile (allowing for things like rerouting, which is discussed in the next section). See Chapter 2 if you need a refresher, and please note for the record that I'm dealing only with real-time routing for the remainder of the chapter. Where in-car navigation is concerned, it's the only GPS technology worth having.

NOTE   *It's possible you won't want to enter a destination at all. There might be times when all you need is the moving map, which simply shows your position as you travel. For instance, suppose you want to find the nearest expressway. Just zoom out a bit at a time until the map shows one. Presto: now you know where it is relative to your current position. By the same token, if your GPS receiver can display points of interest, a moving map can make it easy to spot nearby gas stations, restaurants, and so on.*

GPS receivers vary somewhat in terms of how you enter a destination and what kinds of destinations you can choose. Let's start by looking at the most common kinds of destinations:

- **Address**   Whether you need to find your way to a client's office, a friend's new house, or that hobby shop across town, all you need is the address.

Usually, the street name and number are sufficient, though in some cases you may have to enter the city as well. If you're looking for a specific street but don't know the actual address, you may be able to route to just the street.

■ **Intersection** Let's say you're looking for a bookstore and someone tells you there's one at the corner of Walnut and Main. Some GPS receivers can route you to an intersection, no address required.

■ **Points of interest** Points of interest are exactly that: places along the way that you might need or want to visit. These include rest areas, restaurants, hotels, gas stations, banks, and even attractions like golf courses, movie theaters, and zoos. A point of interest can be your primary destination or a stop along the way.

■ **Favorites** Virtually all GPS receivers maintain a list of favorites—
previous destinations you've entered. (Whether or not they're actually
"favorites" of yours is another story, but that's the terminology.) Favorites
are hugely helpful, as they save you from having to reenter data for a place
you've already been. In fact, the best favorites are usually "home" and
"office," because you can easily route to either one from wherever you
happen to be. That saves a ton of time.

Choosing a Destination from Your Contact List

One of the giant advantages to using a PDA as your GPS receiver is that it already
contains the addresses of people you're likely to want to visit: friends, clients, distant
relatives, and so on. That in itself is an advantage, but some mapping programs go
a step further by offering automatic route generation to any address in your contact
list. A tap here, a tap there, and you're on your way.

On the Palm OS side, the only device that offers this capability is the Garmin
iQue 3600 (see Chapters 9 and 10). Many Pocket PC products offer it, including
CoPilot Live | Pocket PC 4 and TomTom Navigator.

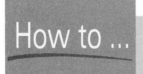 **Enter a Destination Using the Map**

In the old days of paper maps, you'd stick a pushpin where you needed to go and then figure out the best route. With GPS receivers, you usually specify an address or point of interest and then let the software route you there. But what if you don't have any information about your destination except its location on the map? Maybe you just want the receiver to route you from your current position to "riiiiiiiiight…..*there*." Who's got the pushpins?

Some GPS receivers enable you to do this. You simply scroll the map from your current position to wherever it is you want to go, then mark that position on the map and use the software's Route To option. This may require a little zooming out and back in again to get the map to display your desired destination, but the end result is the same: the software guides you from here to there.

Routing Options

Once you've selected a route, you may want to consider modifying a few routing options. These vary quite a bit from receiver to receiver, so one or more of them might not be available on your device.

- **Quickest/shortest**   Do you want the software to plot the route that will get you to your destination as quickly as possible, or the route that covers the least amount of distance? The two can be mutually exclusive.

- **Major/local**   Want to take the scenic route? Some receivers give you the option of traveling entirely on local roads—no highways allowed.

- **Avoid tolls**   If you want your navigation software to avoid toll roads when generating routes, enable this option. Heck, with all the money you'll save, your GPS will pay for itself in no time! (Okay, probably more like in 50 or 60 years, and that's if you drive in an area with a *lot* of toll roads. Still, it's a handy option.)

- **Carpool**   If you live in or are passing through a major city that has carpool lanes, you may want your route to include or exclude them. Some GPS receivers give you this option.

- **Fog mode**   If you're driving in low-visibility conditions, such as heavy fog, this option will instruct the GPS to beep or otherwise alert you when you're approaching an intersection.

- **Speed alert**   Want to avoid speeding tickets and drive more safely at the same time? Some GPS receivers can alert you when you exceed a certain speed.

- **Points of interest**   Most GPS receivers that include points-of-interest (POI) databases allow you to choose whether to display the POIs on the map screen. Why wouldn't you want them? Well, if you're in a metropolitan area, there are likely to be lots of POIs, and the little icons used to represent them can really clutter up the screen. Some GPS receivers let you pick and choose which POIs to display, thus helping keep the clutter to a minimum and helping you zero in on exactly the destinations you want most.

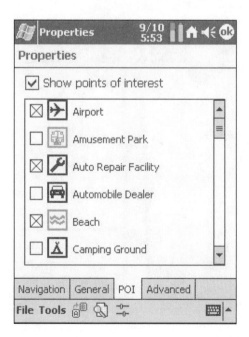

Navigating with Your GPS Receiver

With your destination locked and loaded, you can put the pedal to the metal. This is where the action happens, where you see your position on a moving map, get information about upcoming turns, and monitor things like speed, distance to destination, and the name of the road you're currently driving.

A little caveat before we go any further. You've heard my all-GPS-receivers-are-different disclaimer many times already in this chapter, and that's still true when it comes to certain aspects of navigating. However, most of the core concepts and principles are the same, so for the sake of consistency, I'm going to focus mostly on a single GPS product in this section: Socket's MyNavigator for Pocket PC (see Chapter 2). Your GPS receiver's display and menus may look a little different, but the way they operate is likely to be very similar.

What's on the Display

To paraphrase the old saying, a screenshot is worth a thousand words. Let's take a look at some of the information that's typically presented on a navigation screen.

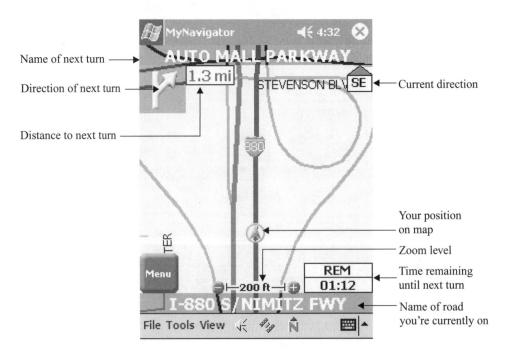

3

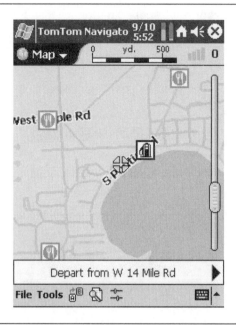

FIGURE 3-3   Most GPS receivers use little pictures, or icons, to represent points of interest on the map.

Some GPS receivers also show your current speed, points of interest (see Figure 3-3), the time remaining until you reach your destination, arrows indicating the direction of one-way streets, and other useful information. Of course, the screen is only so big—you may not be able to see all this information at once. Usually, the device has a setup menu that lets you pick and choose the items you want on the display. The information you choose is largely a matter of personal preference; you'll discover what elements are most important to you based on the kind and amount of travel you're doing.

Turn-by-Turn Directions

When navigation services like MapQuest generate a route for you, they do so with turn-by-turn driving directions. Many GPS receivers can switch between map mode and a "route list" that displays similar turn-by-turn directions. There may be times when it's helpful to see your route spelled out rather than just on a visual map. You can usually switch between these modes at any time.

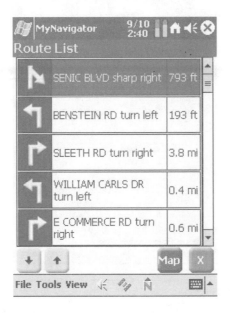

Setting Zoom Level

As I touched on briefly in Chapter 2, a moving map is obviously nowhere near as large as a paper map. That's where zooming comes into play—it enables you to minimize or maximize the amount of map detail you see on the screen. The closer you zoom into a section of map (the section gets smaller the more you zoom, obviously), the more detail (streets, street names, and so on) you see. Zooming out lets you see more of the map at a time, but you lose detail.

Here's an example of zooming in very close—about 500 feet overhead, according to MyNavigator:

3

If we stick with that same section of map and zoom out to 1,000 feet, here's what it looks like:

Notice that the smaller streets are no longer labeled, but the main roads still are. At the same time, you can see more of your route. Finally, let's zoom out to one mile:

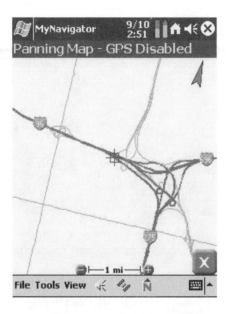

Now the only visible roads are interstates and highways. You might think there's not much value to the map when there's so little detail, but consider: now you know exactly where the highways are relative to your position, and you're getting a "big-picture" view of the area without having to grapple with a giant paper map.

To modify the zoom level on any GPS, look for the little magnifying-glass icons or buttons. (In the case of MyNavigator, you tap a plus or minus sign.)

> **TIP** *On most PDAs running navigation software, you can use the scroll-up and scroll-down buttons (or rocker) to zoom in and out.*

You'll want to experiment to see what zoom level you like best while navigating. Of course, it's not uncommon to adjust it on purpose while you're driving, zooming out when you're on a highway and in when you're in the city and/or close to your destination.

> **NOTE** *Most GPS software automatically zooms in close when you're approaching a turn, simply so you can see exactly where the turn is. Then it zooms back to the previous level after you've made the turn.*

Dealing with GPS Flakiness

If there's one thing I've learned after months of using various GPS navigation systems in my car, it's this: GPS is no substitute for your brain. GPS is also occasionally inaccurate. And if you're using a Pocket PC for navigation, be prepared for software crashes (I speak from experience). In fact, one time I accidentally slid my Pocket PC out of its GPS sleeve, which instantly severed the connection to the satellites and locked up the device. I had to pull over, reboot the PDA, start the software again, wait for satellite lock, enter the destination again, and so on. Bleh.

You can overcome the occasional oddities and inaccuracies of navigating with GPS by following these tips:

- *Study your route in advance.* This harks back to the backup plan I recommended earlier in the chapter. By studying your route in advance, taking note of highways, major road names, and even landmarks, you'll be better prepared in the event of GPS flakiness.

- *Pay attention to your surroundings.* It's very easy to get tunnel vision, to focus entirely on what the GPS is telling you without using your own sense of location and direction. All I'm saying is, remind yourself that the GPS isn't infallible, and that you need to pay attention to where you are and where you're going. Several times a GPS has tried to steer me one way when I know there's a better route. There are several causes for this kind of situation; usually it occurs because the map data is out of date and doesn't include new roads or extended highways. For example, not far from my house is a state highway called M-5 that was recently extended by a few miles. I've yet to see any GPS map data that includes the extension, so very often I'm presented with routes that fail to take into account the extra new road. The next tip can help address such situations.

- *Plan your own alternate routes.* My friend Andrew, a California resident, often laments that he can't force the GPS to route him around a known traffic delay, like a backed-up Golden Gate Bridge. He still needs to travel from point A to point B; he just wants to take the Bay Bridge because he knows it'll be faster. The solution? Just let the software generate a route to point B as it wants to; then drive to the Bay Bridge. By the time you get there (or get close, even), the software will have calculated a new route to point B based on your location. In other words, the path from point A to point B is fluid— you can make your own adjustments as needed, and the GPS will just keep pointing you to your destination.

■ *Ignore turns that aren't turns.* One thing that drives me absolutely nuts is when my GPS tells me to "bear right" or "keep left" when I'm on a straight road and there are no turns ahead. I wish I could explain why this happens or what you can do about it, but I'm stumped on both counts. One time I was on Telegraph Road heading north, and I knew full well my turn wasn't for another two miles, but the software kept telling me to "bear right" every 1,000 feet or so. Talk about annoying. Fortunately, because I'd studied my route in advance, I didn't get flustered or confused—I just waited out the flakiness and continued on my merry way.

Understanding Rerouting

Whoops! You missed an exit. Maybe you didn't hear the GPS's warning, or a big truck was blocking your lane change. Either way, you missed the exit—now what? Have no fear—your GPS is here! Most receivers that can do on-the-fly routing can also do on-the-fly rerouting, meaning that they can calculate a new route if you've

How to ... Find the Nearest Hospital

If the software that drives your GPS receiver includes a points-of-interest database (most do), you can easily find the hospital (or, for that matter, police station or other emergency service) that's closest to your location. I certainly hope you never need to, but it's nice to know the capability is there, especially when you're driving in an unfamiliar area.

1. Use the GPS's controls to bring up the main menu. In most systems, you can access the points-of-interest database from here.

2. Choose Emergency or Hospitals from the list of available categories.

3. In the list of hospitals that appears next, select the one that's the shortest distance; then choose Nav, Route To, or whatever option your GPS presents for navigating to that destination.

4. Follow the route as you would any other.

strayed from the old one. It may take a couple minutes to accomplish this or just a few seconds, depending on the speed of the GPS's (or PDA's) processor. But you shouldn't have to intervene at all—the destination will remain locked in, and a new route (complete with new turn-by-turn directions) will appear.

> **TIP** *Sometimes, before calculating a new route, a GPS receiver will instruct you to make a U-turn. This might be practical in certain instances, but other times you might be better off with a new route. You can "force" the GPS to recalculate just by waiting it out and driving a little farther. Once you get far enough away from the original route, the software will reroute you.*

Stopovers

Suppose you're on the highway, still hundreds of miles from your destination, when nature calls. You can use your GPS's points-of-interest database to find the nearest gas station or restaurant, but if you instruct it to generate a route to it, won't that negate your original destination? It may, depending on whether the GPS software supports stopovers. If it does, it will allow you to choose a new destination and provide an immediate route to it. Once you get there, it will resume the original destination.

If the software doesn't support stopovers, all is not lost. You can still manually reroute to the gas station, restaurant, or wherever and then just regenerate the route to the original destination. Most likely, the software saved it in its Favorites file, so that's where to look for it. If your software doesn't do that, well, you should have saved it yourself. You did read about Favorites back in "Entering Destinations in Your GPS Receiver," didn't you?

Detours

I'm lucky: I work from a home office and rarely have to deal with traffic jams or road construction. But even I take to the streets once in a while, and I don't like those delays any more than you do. Many newer GPS systems can generate alternate routes for you if you run into stopped traffic. (In fact, ALK's CoPilot Live | Pocket PC 4, when used with an Internet-connected PDA, can receive traffic and roadwork updates automatically and then adjust your route accordingly so you never even hit the backups. Someday, all GPS receivers will work like this. Of course, if every driver knows to take an alternate route, then the alternate route will get backed up, and eventually you'll wind up driving from New York to New Jersey by way of Tallahassee.)

Cell-Phone Navigation with TeleNav

My good friend Dave, who also happens to be this book's tech editor (he fixes all the colossal mistakes I make, except the one where I asked him to be tech editor), wrote this stellar review of TeleNav, which turns your cell phone (well, certain kinds of cell phones, anyway) into a poor-man's GPS navigation system, complete with voice-prompted driving directions. With Dave's permission, I give you the review.

Agent 004, MI-6 Mission Report. Classified: Secret.

En route to intercept the Baron and his stolen diamonds, I have found it necessary to navigate my way across the Colonies in a rented Subaru. Lacking my trusty Aston Martin with integrated satellite navigation—which might draw attention in the States—I have instead turned to TeleNav, a GPS navigation service delivered to my Motorola i88 mobile phone.

Q would be impressed. Eschewing PDAs, in-car displays, and other gadgets, TeleNav requires just a Java-capable phone to run the TeleNav application and a GPS receiver. Since my Motorola i88 includes GPS, it's a totally self-contained solution—perfect for those moments when I need to egress the vehicle, fly in my pocket jetpack, and rescue some woman with a ludicrous name. With a non–GPS-enabled phone, though, I could simply plug a GPS receiver into the phone and get the same capabilities, albeit tethered to a puck-like antenna, making derring-do swordfights somewhat awkward.

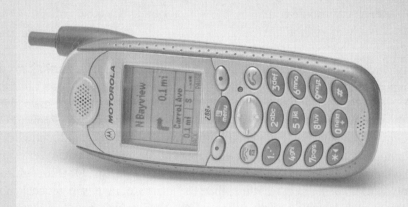

Knowing that the Baron has stashed his diamonds at a warehouse in Denver where he intends to build his weather-control machine, I enter the address into the TeleNav application. It's slow, cumbersome work, using the phone's keypad. The warehouse is a popular point of interest, but that does me no good; TeleNav accepts only complete addresses, intersections, or airport codes—nor can I program a detour around the array of Soviet tanks that the Baron has placed on the highway, blocking my path. Blimey wickets! This is frustrating.

Once entered, TeleNav directs me to my destination with arrows and short instructions on the phone's small screen and reroutes me as needed if I miss turns; a computerized voice echoes that advice, allowing me to keep my eyes on the oil-slicked road and incoming missile assaults. TeleNav may do in a pinch, but I think I shall recommend that Q issue me a Garmin iQue for my next mission.

—Johnson. Dave Johnson.

Where to Find It

Web Site	Address	What's There
ALK	**www.alk.com**	CoPilot Live | Pocket PC 4
Garmin	**www.garmin.com**	IQue 3600, StreetPilot
Navman	**www.navman.com**	iCN 630
Socket	**www.socketcom.com**	Socket GPS Nav Kit
Televigation	**www.telenav.net**	TeleNav

Chapter 4

Go Take a Hike: GPS in the Great Outdoors

How to...

- Choose the ultimate outdoor GPS receiver

- Work with waypoints

- Name waypoints effectively

- Understand tracking

- Retrace your steps

- Use GPS for fishing

- Use GPS for hiking, hunting, camping, and more

- Add topographic maps to your GPS

- Use GPS to explore nature

Before GPS became the road-navigation *tour de force* it is today, its chief consumer application was outdoor activities: hiking, hunting, camping, fishing, and so on. It's still very popular in those areas, and in fact GPS is now used for endeavors like biking, snowmobiling, cross-country skiing, off-road driving, and even botany. If you enjoy the great outdoors, this is the chapter for you.

As with driving, the key benefit of GPS in outdoor activities is navigation from point A to point B. That's true whether you're backpacking in the Rockies, looking for that place where the fish were really biting, or zeroing in on a particularly rare carnivorous plant. However, GPS takes on a new level of importance when you're off the beaten track. It can keep you from getting lost, help you find your way home if you do get lost, and even help others find you in case of emergency. It can direct you to the nearest water source, help you overcome darkness and white-outs, and even steer you safely through rugged terrain.

So what's the best GPS receiver for your preferred outdoor endeavor? That depends on the endeavor, of course. If you're an avid backpacker, you're probably going to want something different than if you're a serious fisherman. As we delve into these hobbies, I'll suggest some equipment and tell you how to make the best use of it. For starters, let me introduce you to a GPS receiver that may just be the ultimate model for your sporting life.

The Ultimate Outdoor GPS?

Okay, so GPS receivers are outdoor devices by definition, but in this case I'm talking about the ultimate GPS for outdoor activities—hunting, hiking, fishing, and so on. Having investigated and fiddled with a huge range of GPS receivers, I can safely say that the Garmin Rino 120 may just be the ideal do-everything model. That's because it combines a solid selection of GPS features with a two-way FRS/GMRS radio. Thus, it not only gives you information on your position and allows you to talk to others, it also enables you to track and navigate your way to others.

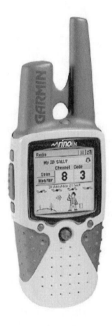

4

> NOTE   *FRS stands for Family Radio Service, and GMRS stands for General Mobile Radio Service. These are radio frequencies designed expressly with family communication in mind. FRS has a maximum range of two miles, and GMRS tops out at five miles. Position-reporting data is limited to two miles.*

Just so you don't mistake me for a Garmin shill, I can tell you that, as of press time, there was no other GPS receiver on the market that included a two-way radio. I just think it's an extremely logical marriage of technologies, and therefore well worth considering for anyone shopping for a GPS. If there's a downside, it's the smaller-than-average screen. But the Rino is also one of the easiest handheld GPS devices I've used, and easy goes a long way in my book. (My book—get it?)

In the sections to come, I'll spotlight some activity-specific GPS receivers, but just about anything those can do, the Rino can do, too. For more information on it, turn back to Chapter 2.

Understanding Waypoints

Rino, hippo, basset hound—whatever GPS receiver you decide to take into the great outdoors, there's one thing you should learn to do with it before you step one foot out of the house: mark and manage waypoints. Waypoints are position coordinates (latitude and longitude, specifically) stored in your GPS. Frankly, I think *waypoint* is a rather confusing term, so I prefer to think of these locators as pushpins—the kind you might use to mark locations on a map.

Waypoints are arguably a GPS receiver's most valuable asset, because they enable you to return to important locations at a later time. A waypoint can be anything from your duck blind to your favorite fishing spot to the place you parked your car. You can set waypoints at the beginning of your excursion, the end, and anywhere along the way. You can also set them in advance.

Indeed, there are two ways to mark waypoints:

■ **Automatically** The receiver displays the coordinates of your current position. You provide a name for the waypoint and then save it in the GPS's memory. This is what you do when you're already out and about and want to store locations for future reference.

■ **Manually** If you have coordinates you want to navigate to, such as those taken from a map or provided by a friend, you can enter them manually and save them as a waypoint.

All GPS receivers can store a fixed number of waypoints. Some limit you to 250; others can hold thousands. Many allow you to assign graphical icons to your waypoints, so you can see at a glance what's near you when you're in map mode. Here's a great example of that, as seen on Garmin's entry-level Geko 101:

The process for marking and managing waypoints varies from GPS to GPS, so I can't really give you instructions here. However, I strongly urge you to familiarize yourself with all aspects of waypoints—marking them, entering them manually, finding them, and navigating to them—before you start your hike, fishing trip, or whatever. GPS menus can be woefully complicated, and you don't want to tackle that learning curve when, say, you realize you haven't seen a trail in two hours.

Effective Waypoint Naming

When the time comes to assign names to your waypoints, you're likely to discover that you don't have a lot of space to work with. Many GPS receivers limit you to just six characters, which means you're going to have to get a little creative with your names. The good news is that you can usually assign icons—little pictures— to your waypoints as well, but those come into play only when you're looking at a map.

GPS to the Rescue: One Couple's Tale

This great story, authored by real-world GPS users "S and L" and provided courtesy of Garmin International, illustrates just how valuable a GPS receiver can be, even if you're not using it for navigation.

My wife and I enjoy exploring the backcountry roads and trails of Arizona in our off-road vehicle. The topography is very interesting and you can drive all day without seeing another person.

We had been traveling for a few hours, and I had not checked our position. Taking a wrong turn we ended up in a large box canyon high in the mountains. At one end was National Wilderness, so no exit, and at the other were a group of trails, none of which looked familiar. We were disoriented and lost.

We drove back and forth through the canyon looking for a way out when suddenly the engine stopped running. It was later determined to be a faulty ignition switch, but we couldn't figure it out at the time. Lost in the mountains, on foot, getting dark and cold, things were getting serious.

This was becoming a scary situation. We looked around with binoculars and climbed a few hills to try to get a sense of where we were in relation to where we had been. Nothing looked familiar and all we could see were more mountains.

We had downloaded quadrants from our MapSource Roads and Recreation and Topo CDs so we zoomed the map in and out until we got a good picture of where we were and where nearby towns and roads were. Even if we had to rough it through the night, we were going to be able to walk out. The relief of having some idea of where we were had a positive physical effect on both of us—we had confidence that we could handle the situation.

We climbed to the top of a razorback ridge and finally got a line of sight with the cell phone to call 911. Reaching the sheriff's office at a nearby town, we gave the dispatcher our position from our eTrex Vista. Within the hour an air-rescue helicopter appeared from below the ridge and took us back to civilization.

When we landed the pilot asked my wife whose toy the GPS was, "yours or your husband's." She told him that I had bought it. He said, "Let him have all the toys he wants. The position you gave us was exactly where we found you." We had never actually used the eTrex Vista before, except around the neighborhood and in front of the TV. We never had to know how far someplace was and in what direction we needed to go. Oddly enough we didn't know if we could trust it. Now we know we can. When traveling in remote areas be sure you have the essentials: cell-phone and food, GPS and water.

Obviously you can use simple words like *home* and *car* as names for key waypoints. But for other waypoints, the key is to come up with abbreviations that are both appropriate to your activity and easy for you to remember. Some examples:

■ **R3 D2**   No, this isn't some distant cousin of R2D2. It might stand for "Ridge 3, Deer 2"—you're on the third ridge, and you spotted two deer.

■ **F4 S12**   You might use something like this to indicate "Fishing spot #4, 12 strikes."

■ **FORKL**   You encountered a fork in the trail and took the path to the left.

■ **H20 FR**   A source of fresh water.

■ **H20 SW**   A good spot for swimming.

■ **H20 WF**   A beautiful waterfall you discovered on your hike.

■ **DUCKB2**   The location of your second duck blind.

■ **RESTR**   Restrooms.

You get the idea. It's easy for waypoints to get totally out of hand, especially if you have a lot of them. It pays to give some thought to how you want to name waypoints so they're easy to find later.

Understanding Tracking

Most GPS receivers are capable of recording a log of their travels—an electronic diary filled with nothing more than dates, times, and coordinates. Each recorded spot in the log—each digital breadcrumb—is referred to as a trackpoint. As with waypoints, GPS receivers are limited in the number of trackpoints they can store: anywhere from a few thousand to 10,000 or more. (Most mid-range and high-end GPS receivers let you adjust the trackpoint interval—the frequency with which trackpoints are recorded—by time or distance.)

As you've probably guessed, the key benefit of tracking is being able to retrace your steps. Many GPS receivers can automatically route you back along your original path—ideal if you've, say, wandered off a trail and can't find your way back to it. Tracking can even help you recover an item you dropped along the way, as it enables you to retrace your steps with incredible accuracy. In most cases, tracking logs work independently of waypoints; they're maintained automatically when you start out, with no need for manual intervention.

Garmin calls its tracking feature TracBack. Here's an example of how it looks on a Geko 301:

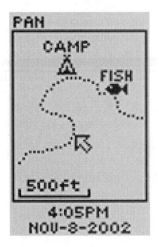

Most GPS receivers can save tracking logs, effectively turning them into routes you can follow in the future.

Downloading, Sharing, and Storing Routes and Waypoints

No man is an island, and neither is your GPS receiver. That's my woefully unclever way of saying that you can export waypoints and routes from your GPS to your computer, while at the same time importing waypoints and routes obtained from friends, fellow outdoorsmen, and web sites. This kind of sharing really opens up a GPS's capabilities.

The key ingredient here is a GPS receiver that can connect to your PC. Most models can, though the cable you need might not have been included in the box. Check with the GPS maker to see about purchasing it. Meanwhile, make sure to investigate the connection method. The majority of receivers rely on 9-pin serial cables, meaning you need a corresponding serial port on your PC (see Figure 4-1). A lot of newer computers don't have serial ports, relying instead on more advanced USB ports. If that describes your system, all is not lost—all you need is a serial-to-USB adapter. The Iogear USB PDA/Serial Adapter is one such product (despite

FIGURE 4-1   Most GPS receivers connect to computers via serial ports. If the necessary cable wasn't included with your receiver, you can usually buy it from the company.

the name, it works with GPS devices as well as PDAs); I found it selling online for about $30.

Here are some examples of how you might want to leverage your GPS's import-export capabilities:

- You're a botanist, and a fellow botanist e-mails you a waypoint file containing the coordinates of a rare orchid. (See "GPS Helps a Hobbyist Find Rare Specimens in the Wild" at the end of this chapter.) You just download the file to your GPS, and you're on your way.

■ You want to climb one of Colorado's famous "Fourteener" mountains, but you don't have the map you need or even know where the trailhead is located. You can download a waypoint for navigation to the trailhead and a route that will guide you right up the mountain.

TIP *A great place to find such travel-related waypoint/route files for downloading is Travel by GPS (**www.travelbygps.com**), home to GPS maps for everything from mountain climbing to scuba diving.*

■ You summited the Fourteener and want to record the date and time for posterity. You use your GPS to mark a waypoint (which includes not only coordinates, but also date, time, and altitude) while atop the mountain and then download it to your PC later.

■ You've stored dozens of routes and waypoints in your GPS and want a backup just in case something happens to the receiver. You can simply transfer them to your PC, where they can be stored indefinitely (and restored on your GPS if needed). You can also use this method to transfer routes and waypoints from one GPS to another, should you decide to upgrade or adopt a second GPS.

■ You want to try the sport of Geocaching (see Chapter 5). Downloading waypoints to your GPS is a heck of a lot easier than entering them manually.

There's an excellent freeware utility for Windows that makes all this importing and exporting possible. It's called EasyGPS, and it's designed expressly to transfer waypoints and routes between your PC and your Garmin, Magellan, or Lowrance GPS (it supports a handful of other lesser-known brands as well). EasyGPS can also be used to create and edit waypoints and routes, which can be a huge time-saver if you're presented with coordinates that aren't already in electronic format. Typing them on your PC is a lot faster than entering them manually on your GPS.

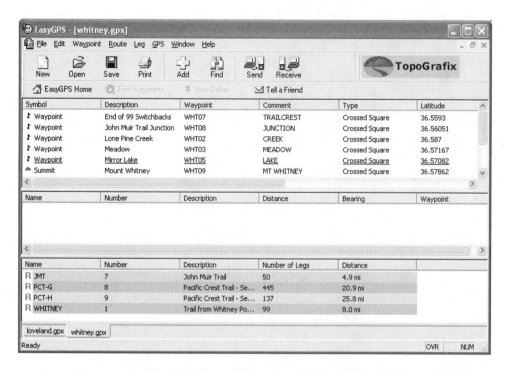

True to its name, EasyGPS is quite easy to use. After you download and install it on your PC, just follow the built-in help to get started. If you're saving waypoints or routes you've uploaded from your GPS, be sure to put them in a folder (such as My Documents) where they'll be easy to find later.

Using GPS for Fishing

I think the last time I held a fishing rod, I was seven years old. (Ironically, that's exactly how mature I am today.) Back then, GPS was a mere glint in the government's eye. Today, it's a major asset to folks who love to fish, as it not only provides much-needed boat guidance, but also helps eliminate some of the guesswork. Let's take a look at some of the gear you might want and how you might want to use it.

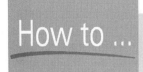 **Download a Mountain-Climbing Map**

California's Mt. Whitney is the tallest mountain in the continental United States and therefore well worth climbing. There's a GPS map all ready to go—you just need to download it, install it, and put on your hiking boots. Here's the process:

1. Download EasyGPS (**www.easygps.com**) and install it on your computer.

2. Connect your GPS receiver to your computer. If you're using a serial cable, make sure the computer is off before you plug in the cable.

3. Follow EasyGPS's setup instructions to add your GPS.

4. Go to Travel by GPS (**www.travelbygps.com**) and search for Whitney. Click the resulting link to view the description page for the Mt. Whitney map. Scroll down a bit to find the "free GPS Map" link, right-click it, and choose Save Target As. Save the whitney.gpx file in an easy-to-find location on your hard drive (such as My Documents).

5. In EasyGPS, click the Open button; then navigate to the folder containing whitney.gpx. Double-click the file to open it.

6. You should see all the route and waypoint info in the EasyGPS window. Click the Send button to transfer everything to your GPS. Now you're ready to hit the trail!

NOTE   *I'm sure there are purists out there who think using any kind of technology sucks the fun right out of fishing. I'm not here to argue that point, only to deliver the information. It's like driving cross-country with bored kids in the backseat: do you give them a portable DVD player so they can watch movies, or do you force them to tough it out because it builds character and they watch enough TV at home? Oh, that is too an apt analogy. Anyway, using a GPS to help you fish is entirely optional. But I'm assuming you want to know how or you wouldn't be here.*

This is a good place to draw a distinction between fishing and boating. While obviously you need to go boating in order to fish, and people often fish while boating, this is the chapter that's focused more on sporting activities, of which fishing is one. If you want to learn about GPS and boating, sail ahead to Chapter 7.

The Right GPS Gear for Fishing

Marine GPS use has become so popular that you'll find entire categories of products devoted to it from major manufacturers like Garmin and Magellan. In fact, Garmin alone offers no fewer than 30 different GPS receivers that are either designed with marine navigation in mind or can be used for that purpose. Magellan, for its part, offers about 15. And companies like Furuno, Lowrance, and Navman have marine-GPS products of their own. What are the differences between all these models? Features, obviously—things like screen size, map-storage capacity, and so on. Here's a list of some of the key considerations for marine-minded GPS receivers:

- **Accuracy**   Most of the marine-GPS receivers available today take advantage of WAAS technology (see Chapter 1), meaning that they're accurate to within about 10 feet. Those that don't support WAAS typically offer accuracy to around 30 feet. How important is that when you're navigating on a lake or the open sea? Not very, but it can make quite a difference if you're looking for fish.

- **Alarms**   Some GPS receivers can audibly notify you of hazards like anchor drag, shallow water, and driving off course.

- **Floatability**   I honestly didn't think floatability was a word, but my word processor didn't flag it, so there you go. Anyway, a few handheld GPS receivers—the Garmin GPSMAP 76 (see Figure 4-2) is a good example— float. Anyone who spends a lot of time on a boat knows the importance of floatation, as you never know when something important—a key chain, a GPS receiver, your beer—is going to fall overboard.

- **Form factor**   Not to be confused with that lame show *Fear Factor*, form factor refers to the size and design of the GPS. In this case, it means do you want a handheld model or something that's going to mount in your boat? Handheld models (see Figure 4-2) offer portability and tend to cost less, but they also have smaller screens. The following photograph shows you what mountable models look like.

4

■ **Mapping features** Even the most rudimentary GPS receiver can be helpful to a fisherman, as it allows you to mark fish-rich hot spots and navigate back to the dock. However, there's definite value in getting a model that comes with built-in maps. The Magellan SporTrak Marine, for instance, includes

FIGURE 4-2 D'oh! You dropped your GPS into the drink! Fortunately, if it's a model like the Garmin GPSMAP 76, you can easily fish it out. It floats.

not only major highway and road data, but also waterways, fog signals, buoys, and lighthouses. It also has enough memory to store more detailed map data, like Magellan's optional MapSend BlueNav Charts. (Garmin offers optional BlueChart and Fishing Hot Spots software.) In other words, look for a model that comes with basemap data, but also has room for additional maps.

- **Screen**   As you might expect, you can choose between color and grayscale screens in both handheld and fixed-mount GPS receivers. That's a personal choice, but consider another feature at the same time: backlighting. Your GPS won't do you a lot of good if it's pitch black outside and you can't see the screen. Backlit screens are visible even in the dark.

- **Sonar**   In the grand tradition of the Ginsu knife, some GPS receivers are two, two, *two* products in one! Garmin, for example, offers the fixed-mount GPSMAP 188 Sounder, which gives you all the GPS goodies, plus traditional fish-finding sonar.

- **Waypoints**   Waypoints, as you learned earlier, are nothing more than stored coordinates, like pushpins on a map. Different GPS receivers have different storage capacities for waypoints. Some limit you to just 500 or so, while others can hold thousands. You might think that even 500 is a lot, but if you're really an avid fisher-person, they can get used up quickly.

How to Use GPS for Fishing

Once you've found the right GPS receiver for your boat or tackle box, what can you do with it? Here are some tips on how to make the most of your GPS in the water:

- *See an outline of the lake.* Using either the receiver's basemap or the marine cartography map you've installed, you can get a bird's-eye view of the lake. This can help you not only with general navigation, but also with finding little out-of-the-way coves or areas of interest you might want to visit.

- *Mark the dock.* Before you head out for the day, fire up your GPS, wait for it to achieve a signal lock with the satellites, and then set a waypoint for your current position. Name it "Dock" or something similarly unmistakable. At the end of the day, set the GPS to route you to that waypoint, and you'll have a blissfully easy time navigating back home.

- *Mark the hot spots.* Ted, an avid fisherman, explains how on a recent fishing trip in unknown waters, he and his buddies spent the first day with a local guide, who helped them scope out all the river's hot spots. Ted used his GPS receiver to mark waypoints for each one. The next day they were able to easily return to those hot spots—no guide required.

- *Find the nearest waypoints.* The Garmin GPSMAP 76 is one receiver that can present you with a list of the 10 nearest waypoints. This may not seem like a big deal, but consider: if you've marked 100 waypoints in various lakes (or even the same lake), how are you supposed to find those that are closest to your current position? Use this feature and you can zip right to where the fish are biting.

- *Follow your drift.* Remember Ted from two bullet points ago? He also uses his GPS to manage drift. Specifically, when he's at a spot where the fish are biting, he marks a waypoint and enables the tracking function. As time goes on, the boat drifts, as boats are wont to do. When the fish stop biting, he can retrace the drift, navigating back to where he started—and very likely to where the fish are still gathered.

- *Calculate your odds.* Many GPS receivers have so-called fish and game calculators, which tell you the best times of the year to fish (or hunt) in your location. You can also view sunrise and sunset times so you can plan your outings accordingly.

Here, Fishy, Fishy: Garmin's MapSource Fishing Hot Spots

If you buy a Garmin GPS receiver that supports optional map data, you may want to check out MapSource Fishing Hot Spots. This software CD contains detailed information for hundreds of lakes (mostly bigger ones, of course) in the United States and Canada. In addition to general cartography for the lakes, Fishing Hot Spots includes suggested fishing areas, lists of facilities (restrooms, campgrounds, and so on), permit regulations, and lake-specific information such as submerged objects and boating lanes. All this gets downloaded from your PC to your GPS receiver.

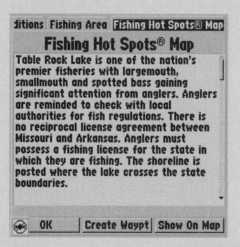

The Fishing Hot Spots CD has a list price of $116.95, which includes an "unlock code" for one of the 15 regions that divide up the U.S. and Canada. If you want to unlock another region, it'll cost you another $93.32 (don't ask me how Garmin came up with a price like that). Or, you can spend $174.98 to unlock all the regions. Meanwhile, Garmin continues to add new maps to Fishing Hot Spots, and if you've already unlocked a specific region, it'll cost you $30 to get the updates for that region. Confusing, no? Yes.

Using GPS for Hiking, Hunting, Camping, and More

GPS might seem an odd companion for activities like hiking, hunting, and camping, which very often take place in heavily wooded areas, where GPS receivers have trouble receiving signals. Certainly, there's that caveat to consider, but I'd still pack a GPS no matter what. Here's why:

- **Winter**   In the winter, the leaves fall off the trees, leaving the skies relatively unobstructed. Presto: GPS works. And on a personal note, I actually prefer cold-weather hiking and camping, as I'm not a big fan of heat, bugs, snakes—pretty much nature in general.

- **Open areas**   Even if you spend the bulk of your time in deep woods, you're likely to pass through an open area here or there. Then you can reestablish a signal lock, note your position, check the direction to your destination, and so on. Furthermore, if you're lost, you can simply make finding an open area your primary goal, rather than focusing solely on "escape."

- **It might still work**   Different GPS receivers fare differently in densely covered areas. Even if you can't lock three satellites, you might still be able to get two, which is better than nothing. Your accuracy might be 50 feet instead of 10, but that's still plenty useful.

TIP	*If you know you're going to be in heavy woods, you can increase your chances of maintaining a signal lock by running your GPS for 5 or 10 minutes at your car or campsite, thereby allowing it to acquire its maximum number of satellites. When things get dense overhead, the GPS will already have a strong lock on its whereabouts and may be able to continue tracking effectively.*

The Right GPS Gear for Hiking, Hunting, Camping, and the Rest

When it comes to land-based outdoor activities like hiking and camping, you really have endless choices for GPS receivers. Most first-generation products were designed with these kinds of activities in mind, so it's no surprise to find a huge variety of them available now. I'm speaking primarily of handheld receivers—models like the Garmin Geko and Magellan SporTrak.

NOTE *Can you use a GPS-equipped PDA for outdoor endeavors? Absolutely (see Chapter 2), so long as you're willing to risk it. The challenge lies in finding software that's suitable to your task, as most of what's available for PDAs centers around road navigation. See "PDA GPS Software for Outdoor Activities" next up in this chapter. And don't forget to check out Chapter 9's and Chapter 10's coverage of the iQue 3600.*

Needless to say, you may want to consider—or at least understand—a few features before choosing a GPS receiver destined for the outdoors:

4

- **Construction**   Some models are better able to withstand the rigors of the outdoors than others. If you're a rough-and-tumble kind of person, look for a GPS that's built to handle drops, knocks, and so on—one that has a rubber bumper around the edges. This is one reason *not* to bring a PDA into the outdoors—one drop and it could be goodbye $500.

- **Waterproofness**   The outdoors is rife with rivers, streams, puddles, snow, and so on, so it makes sense to choose a GPS that's waterproof. Some, like the Magellan Meridian GPS, go a step further: they actually float! You could also consider a ruggedized, watertight case, like those made by Otter (**www.otterbox.com**).

■ **Mapping features**   I highly recommend a GPS that comes with not only a basemap—all the major roads, waterways, and so on in the U.S.—but also free memory for downloading street-level and/or topographic maps (see "Topographic Maps on Your GPS" later in this chapter). In fact, if you plan on using a lot of map data, consider a model with expandable memory, like the Magellan Meridian series. These handhelds have industry-standard Secure Digital (SD) slots for adding loads of megabytes' worth of storage.

■ **Screen**   As you might expect, you can choose between color and grayscale screens. That's a personal choice, but consider another feature at the same time: backlighting. Your GPS won't do you a lot of good if it's pitch black outside and you can't see the screen. Backlit screens are visible even in the dark.

■ **Waypoints**   Waypoints, as you learned earlier, are nothing more than stored coordinates, like pushpins on a map. Different GPS receivers have different storage capacities for waypoints. Some limit you to just 500 or so, while others can hold thousands. You might think that even 500 is a lot, but if you're really an avid fisher-person, they can get used up quickly.

PDA GPS Software for Outdoor Activities

So you've decided to bring your GPS-equipped PDA into the wild. It can be a great travel companion, offering you precision navigation during your adventures and books, music, and games during downtime. The problem is, most PDAs are quite fragile. If you drop one on hard ground or a rock, you might be down one pricey piece of electronics. One solution is to keep your PDA in a padded case, but that might not be possible if the GPS add-on plugs into a slot or piggybacks on the back. The moral of the story: bring your PDA at your own risk.

The other wrinkle lies in software. Most GPS receivers for PDAs come with street-level mapping software, which is great for getting from home to wilderness, but not too helpful once you've left the car behind. The answer lies in third-party software, some of which can give your PDA all the waypoint, tracking, routing, and other features found in handheld GPS receivers.

Palm OS Software   If you own a Palm, Handspring, Sony, or other PDA that runs the Palm Operating System, I recommend visiting PalmGear.com and doing a search for GPS. You'll find dozens of third-party programs that should work with whatever GPS receiver you've connected to your PDA. One of the top products I've found is GeoNiche, a $24.95 program designed especially with outdoor activities in mind.

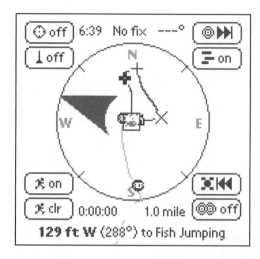

GeoNiche is packed with useful features, including waypoints (which it calls targets), routes, alarms, and tracking. It also includes helpful support for Geocaching (see Chapter 5) in that it can import Geocache data and decode Geocache hints. This program is well worth the $25 registration fee for the outdoor PDA user.

Pocket PC Software   Pocket PC owners should head to Handango.com, home to thousands of Pocket PC programs—including dozens for GPS. I recommend checking out GPSDash, GPS Tuner, and especially VITO Navigator, the latter offering robust waypoint and route support. You can read more about it in Chapter 5, as I also recommend it for PDA-carrying Geocachers.

How to Use Your GPS for Hiking, Hunting, Camping, and the Rest

You already know the value of bringing a GPS into the wild: finding your way back to your car or campground, navigating to duck blinds or mountaintops, and so on. But let's look at some specific examples of using GPS for specific activities:

- **Biking**   Bikers can use GPS to measure their speed, record their routes, and, of course, navigate to a specific destination if biking in unfamiliar territory. As with other activities, you can also find scenic bike routes online and download them to your GPS using a program like EasyGPS (see "Downloading, Sharing, and Storing Routes and Waypoints" earlier in this chapter). Not sure how you're going to carry a GPS so it can receive a signal? Look for a bike mount. They're available for a variety of GPS models at online outlets such as **AdventureGear4Less.com**.

- **Camping and hiking**   This probably goes without saying, but use your GPS to mark the location of campsites, trailheads, restrooms, and other important landmarks. If you're taking a trip with friends or family, I recommend bringing two or more Garmin Rinos (see "The Ultimate Outdoor GPS?" earlier in this chapter). These will let you track not only your own position, but also the positions of your comrades, and stay in voice contact at the same time.

TIP   *Because the Rino uses the standard FRS and GMRS frequencies, it's compatible with other two-way radios that do the same. If you already own a pair, or just want an inexpensive way to keep your group in voice contact, you can mix and match Rinos and ordinary two-way radios.*

- **Hunting**   Obviously, step one is marking the location of your truck so you can find your way back to it. If you're out for deer, you can mark spots where you've found deer signs: tracks, rubs, and so on. After you've marked a few such spots, you can extrapolate patterns to help figure out where the deer are headed.

Topographic Maps on Your GPS

Finally, we come to topographic maps—or topo maps to those of us who like to sound cool. Topo maps—the paper kind—have long been indispensable to hunters,

4

Did you know?

GPS Helps Researchers "Hunt" Troublesome Animals

In August 2003, a group of Japanese researchers began a project using GPS to investigate the behavior of wild boars, which in 2001 destroyed billions of yen worth of crops in Japan. The project, which is expected to take four years to complete, will rely on a GPS tracking system placed on the collars of captured boars. The researchers will then study the behavioral and movement patterns of the animals based on the collected data, with the end goal of placing traps more effectively. I thought this was pretty interesting—hope I didn't boar you.

hikers, fishermen, mountain bikers, and off-road drivers. Unlike street maps, topo maps reflect the topography—the features and elevations and their relative positions—of any given area. Here's what a traditional topo map looks like:

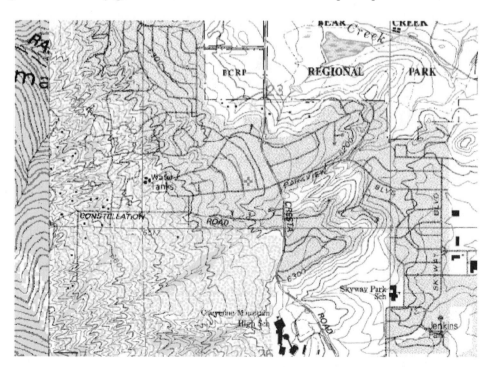

And here's what a topo map looks like on a GPS:

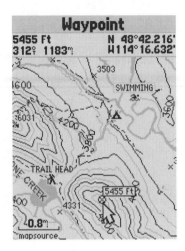

Yep, that's right; it's possible to view topographic maps and data right on your GPS, which could prove invaluable to the avid outdoorsman. Here are your options:

- You can buy a GPS that's expressly designed with topo mapping in mind. The most obvious choice is Magellan's SporTrak Topo, which comes with 100 megabytes' worth of built-in U.S. topographic maps.

- You can buy any GPS that has available storage space for downloading maps. As for the maps themselves, you can buy Magellan MapSend Topo for use with Magellan's products, or Garmin U.S. Topo for use with Garmin's products. Garmin also offers U.S. Topo 24K, National Parks, West, which includes 1:24,000-scale maps of western U.S. parks.

- If you own any GPS that can store external map data, be sure to check out DeLorme Topo USA 4.0. It's an extremely versatile and feature-rich program, and at $99 it costs less than the Garmin and Magellan CDs. Cooler still, it can generate 3D maps. This requires a computer and really has no impact on your mobile GPS, but you can always print some 3D maps in advance of your trip, bring them along, and cross-reference them with the 2D maps on your GPS. This is such a cool feature, I have to show you what it looks like:

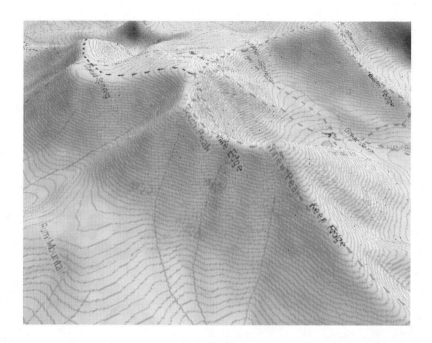

GPS Helps a Hobbyist Find Rare Specimens in the Wild

Stephen Davis spends his days selling ad space for national magazines (and doing a mighty fine job of it, I'm told). His off hours, however, are devoted to two of the more interesting areas of botany: orchids and carnivorous plants. You wouldn't think GPS could play a role in such a hobby, but recently it's become as indispensable as trowels and garden gloves. Stephen offers this report:

I have grown and collected carnivorous plants and orchids for nearly a decade. One of the joys of studying plants as a hobby is seeing them in their natural habitat. Finding a plant in an open meadow, one that you've grown in a pot for years, is akin to seeing a lioness playing with her cubs on a safari after seeing them sleeping at your local zoo. Well, maybe not that exciting, but it's a lot cheaper to do, and they grow all over the world, so some probably grow near you.

Only three times have I seen carnivorous plants in the wild. They're rare, and finding them is time-consuming. Most sites have been destroyed as we fill in lowland wet places for our shopping malls and condos, so the ones left are remote and difficult to find.

Admittedly, fellow enthusiasts have told me about sites, but my eyes glaze over when they try to explain how to find them. "Then you will see an old fence with a break in it about 100 yards from the fiftieth turn down steep trails past the old oak tree, in the middle of nowhere," they might say. After the third turn, I'm lost, and I haven't even left yet. Often, sites are far from roads, and you could never find them without a guide.

GPS solves this problem. After hearing that I was going on a camping trip with my family, a friend from the Bay Area Carnivorous Plant Society sent me coordinates to some sites of the rare Darlingtonia, or Cobra Lilly, in the Butterfly Valley Botanical Preserve in northern California. As the sites were close to some dirt roads, I was able to use Microsoft Streets & Trips to import the data from an Excel spreadsheet. I then exported the map of Butterfly Valley to my iPAQ Pocket PC, which already had Streets & Trips installed.

After a long drive to the site, following the dirt roads to get as close as possible, we parked the car on the side of the road and hiked the rest of the way. You couldn't see anything from the road, but after checking the map on the Pocket PC and following the moving marker to the coordinates I had loaded earlier, we found it. We walked into a meadow, and there they were, like a nest of cobras rearing up out of the grass, tongues tasting the breeze. Even my wife and daughter, non-CP folks, were excited. This was a small site. I've seen pictures of sites with tens of thousands of Cobra Lillys covering a hillside, but this was still well worth the trip.

Later, I used software called RoboPhoto that looks at the time I took pictures with my digital camera, compares it to the GPS tracking file, and produces results that I can use to nearly pinpoint where pictures were taken on the trail. This combination works great for wildflower buffs as well. You can compare the times on your photos to the coordinates in the tracking file and find, with a fair degree of accuracy, the location of the flowers the next time you go on that hike. If you use a Garmin device, you can use RoboPhoto to do this comparison automatically.

Most GPS receivers can record something called a tracking file, which simply logs where you are at any given time. After my trip, I used RoboPhoto to match the pictures I took with my digital camera with the data contained in the tracking file and then had RoboPhoto generate a web page containing a thumbnail gallery of the photos, complete with time, date, and other information. The page can even include a variety of maps (street, topo, nautical, and satellite) that show where each photo was taken. The catch is that the software supports only those tracking files generated by Garmin GPS receivers. It's my hope that RoboPhoto will someday support standard tracking files so more people can use this feature.

Although GPS makes it easy to navigate to and record exotic plant life, you shouldn't publish locations on the web or give them out indiscriminately. Not everyone is interested in the preservation of plants in the wild, and some are so consumed by their hobby that rational thought goes out the window, and they collect plants they shouldn't, possibly endangering the long-term survival of the plants. Some sites have been completely wiped out by plant poachers.

There is a certain etiquette you must follow with plant people. If someone takes you to a site, especially a ranger or a preserve manager, ask if you can mark the site with your GPS unit. There are stories of people exploding in anger when they have taken a small group to a precious site, one that they were already a little tentative about taking people to, and someone pulls out a GPS unit. You probably won't be shown another site after doing something like that.

Where to Find It

Web Site	Address	What's There
DeLorme	www.delorme.com	Topo USA 4.0
Garmin	www.garmin.com	Rino 120, various other GPS receivers, and mapping software
RayDar LLC	www.nwlink.com/~raydar/ GeoNiche/index.html	GeoNiche for Palm OS
Magellan	www.magellangps.com	SporTrak Topo, various other GPS receivers, and mapping software
RoboPhoto	www.robophoto.com	RoboPhoto
TopoGrafix	www.easygps.com	EasyGPS
VITO Technology	www.vitotechnology.com	VITO Navigator for Pocket PC

Chapter 5

Geocaching and Other GPS Games

How to...

- Decide whether you want to try Geocaching
- Choose the right equipment
- Locate Geocaches in your area
- Create and hide your own GPS
- Use GPS to find any given Geocache
- Enter coordinates into your GPS
- Play by the rules
- Geocache responsibly
- Play other GPS games

Every kid dreams of buried treasure—usually the pirate variety packed with gold doubloons. Unfortunately, that can be hard to come by. So many kids, so few doubloons unaccounted for. But the yearning remains, the deep-seated desire to follow the dotted line on a tattered old map until it leads you to a giant X and something precious hidden beneath it.

Small wonder, then, that Geocaching has become an overnight sensation.

As you've probably deduced, Geocaching (also known as Geostashing, GPS Stash Hunting, and Navicaching) is a kind of high-tech treasure hunt. In place of worn parchment, you have GPS as your "map." Instead of a chest filled with riches, you find a box (or Tupperware, possibly) packed with trinkets. No fame, no fortune, but all the fun of searching for hidden booty.

This chapter tells you everything you need to know about Geocaching: what it means, how it started, what you need to enjoy it, and where to get started (hint: it might be closer than you think). You'll also find information on other games played with GPS, such as Geodashing and MinuteWar.

What Is Geocaching?

The word *Geocaching* comes from two separate words: *geo*, for geology; and *cache*, which means a hidden store of goods or valuables. Oh, and just so you don't sound silly when describing this to others, cache is pronounced "cash," while Geocaching is "Geo-cashing." If you go around saying "catch" or "caché," people are going to snicker at you.

Interestingly, the sport wasn't conceived as a sport. In 2000, shortly after the permanent deactivation of SA (see Chapter 1), someone in a celebratory mood hid a container of goodies outside Portland, Oregon. A man named Mike Teague found the container (which included a logbook), logged his visit, and created a web site to document this and other hidden treasures. The rest, as they say, is history.

A fellow named Jeremy Irish picked up the baton from Teague and developed **Geocaching.com**, which is Ground N 0° W 0° for all things Geocaching. The site is home to detailed instructions on getting started, a cache search engine (which lets you filter by state, country, or zip code), a message forum, and information on what kind of gear to buy and even where to buy it. You can also set up a personal account to keep track of caches you've found and receive notifications of new ones in your area.

What's in the Box?

So what can you expect to find in a cache, and what do you do with it once you've found it? The goal of Geocaching is neither riches nor thievery. A cache is usually a box, tin, or some other container (see Figure 5-1) filled with one or more bits of

FIGURE 5-1 This cache, a camouflaged piece of PVC pipe, contained various trinkets and a logbook, all secured in plastic bags.

"treasure": a spool of thread, a tennis ball, a Smurf doll, and so on. You can take something from the cache, but only if you leave a different item behind. Taking the whole cache just isn't done, as it kills the spirit of the game and leaves nothing for the next Geocacher. You're also likely to find a notebook inside the cache, where you can record your name for posterity.

You may even find a camera inside the cache. The idea here is to snap a photo of yourself (or your group) so the keeper of the cache has a visual record of visitors—and so there's proof of your visit (which is often posted to a web site). Using the camera is entirely optional.

Is Geocaching Really for You?

I'll admit it: I'm not a big fan of the outdoors. My ideal environment is a sealed, temperature-controlled indoor room, preferably one with a giant window so I can scoff at nature's inability to reach me. If you share these feelings, Geocaching might not be the sport for you. It is by definition an outdoor activity, and more often than not it involves tromping through the woods—sometimes thorny, bug-infested woods (see "My Dinner with Geocaching" later in this chapter). Of course, as with other outdoor activities, you can stay safe and happy via careful preparation and proper gear.

I also urge you to try Geocaching a few times even if you don't care for the outdoors. It's fun and challenging and gives you a great distraction from the things you perhaps don't like about the outdoors.

For example, when I lived in Colorado, my wife and I would occasionally go hiking in the mountains. I loved the scenery, but tended to get really bored by the activity. If I could have combined Geocaching with it, I would have eagerly taken to the trails. Alas, now we live in the concrete jungle that is suburban Detroit, which barely has sidewalks, let alone hiking trails.

How to Get Started

Ready to plunder for treasure, matey? Arrr! (I have to admit to an embarrassing fondness for speaking like a pirate. My favorite *Simpsons* character is the Sea Captain.) The first thing you'll need, natch, is a GPS receiver—can't Geocache without one. Then you'll need to choose an actual cache, which is accomplished at web sites like Geocaching.com. Finally, you'll want to bring along some important gear like water and sunscreen.

Choosing a GPS Receiver for Geocaching

In Chapter 2, you learned about the different kinds of GPS receivers and how to choose one that best suits your needs. Where Geocaching is concerned, just about any GPS will do—provided it allows you to download from your PC or manually enter latitude and longitude coordinates (a.k.a. waypoints). Some products, particularly those designed with road navigation in mind, don't offer this capability.

If you're new to GPS, don't own a receiver yet, and don't want to spend big bucks, I recommend something like the Garmin Geko 101. It sells for just $99.95, fits easily into a pocket, offers all the features you need for Geocaching (and then some), and looks rather cute. (You can't tell from the picture, but the case is a happy yellow.)

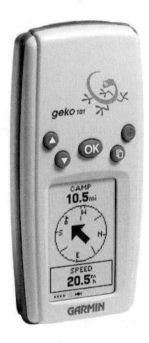

The Geko is truly ideal for Geocaching, as it includes a feature called TracBack that helps you retrace your path from point B (the cache) back to point A (the car). If you've spent any amount of time tromping through unknown terrain, you've no doubt been looking forward, not back, and paying more attention to the GPS than the surroundings. When the time comes to head back to the car, you might discover that you haven't a clue how to get there. That's where a feature like TracBack can prove indispensable.

TIP *You can accomplish roughly the same thing with any GPS receiver. Before setting off from your car, fire up the GPS and note the coordinates of your location. Write them down or set them as a waypoint. This won't help you retrace your exact steps, but it will make sure that you know the direction of your car during the return trip, and that's half the battle. Plus, you can mark additional waypoints as you proceed to the cache coordinates, thereby creating a kind of electronic breadcrumb trail.*

On the other hand, the Geko—like many handheld GPS receivers I've tried— can be extremely complicated to use, at least until you get accustomed to its menu system and terminology. I'll tell you how to perform specific setup and operation functions a bit later in this chapter.

What About a PDA?   If you already own a PDA and have been thinking about buying a GPS for it (or already have one), you're probably wondering if you can use the pair for Geocaching. The answer is a qualified yes. In most cases, the GPS hardware that's available for Palm OS and Pocket PC handhelds comes with street-level mapping software, which usually doesn't allow for entering latitude and longitude coordinates. (Destinations are based on addresses, intersections, points of interest, and so on.)

Fortunately, you can usually work around this shortcoming by installing additional software on your PDA. (You're not limited to the software that came with the GPS bundle.) Users of Palm OS devices, for instance, can try ThatWay!, a simple $10 utility designed expressly to give you the heading and distance to specific coordinates.

Pocket PC users can check out VITO Navigator, a $16 program that works similarly.

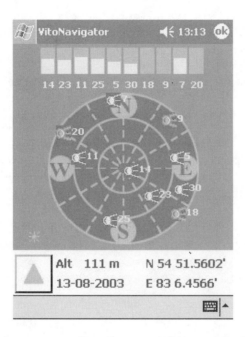

So that answers the question, *can* you use a PDA for Geocaching. But *should* you? There are pros and cons. Obviously, some PDAs are quite expensive, meaning you wouldn't be too happy if yours got lost or damaged in the wilderness. Plus, PDAs are not exactly rugged. On the other hand, if you're Geocaching as part of an extended trip, say camping or backpacking, it's nice to have your PDA along for games, e-books, and even music.

In fact, consider buying the do-everything Garmin iQue 3600 (see Chapters 9 and 10), a Palm OS–based PDA with built-in GPS. It even allows you to enter coordinates, so it's ready for Geocaching right out of the box.

> **TIP** *You can buy a Handspring Visor (a Palm OS–based PDA) and Magellan GPS Companion (a plug-in module for the Visor) for under $100 on eBay. That's a pretty solid GPS setup for a low price, and you get a downright decent PDA out of the deal as well.*

Seven Questions for Geocaching.com's Cofounder

Bryan Roth is the vice president and cofounder of Groundspeak, the company that owns Geocaching.com. Despite his insanely busy schedule, he took the time to answer these seven questions about the site and the sport.

RB: What's your definition of the ultimate Geocache?

BR: There is no ultimate Geocache. Since each Geocache is placed by an individual, each one offers a unique challenge or experience for the finder. What some might consider to be an easy cache might present exciting challenges for others. I personally have a Geocache near my home. It is considered to be an easy-to-find cache and one that is great for beginners. For the more experienced, however, it is probably too easy. Nevertheless, yesterday it was found by three tourists from Germany!

RB: If someone is shopping for a GPS solely for Geocaching, what should he or she look for?

BR: Fortunately, the basic GPS models have all the functionality required to find a cache. All you really need is the ability to enter a waypoint (latitude/longitude) and have the GPS direct you to that waypoint. Some of the more advanced models have integrated mapping that can route you to the Geocache using local roads. Others can show you where the local restaurants and other travel-related facilities are located. The basic [models] will do the job, but sometimes it is nice to have some of the more advanced features.

RB: Why is Geocaching so popular? What's the core appeal?

BR: Geocaching is popular for a number of reasons. Anyone can play, from older retirees to families with young children. All it takes is a GPS and a desire for adventure. Geocaching provides people with the opportunity to visit great places and enjoy a variety of new and exciting experiences. You can find a local park that you never knew existed just because someone else thought it'd be a cool place for a cache. You can basically go out treasure hunting (almost anywhere in the world) with a $12 billion satellite system.

RB: Do you think environmentalists are right to be concerned about Geocaching's impact?

BR: Yes and no. In many ways, the impact of Geocaching is very positive for the environment. It brings people with a love of the outdoors outside and, through caching experiences, provides them with a greater appreciation for the environment. Also, the Cache In Trash Out policy has been very beneficial. Now you have Geocachers around the world going out with trash bags and cleaning up the local areas as they seek out caches. This kind of exposure, especially for children, teaches a very positive lesson and helps us to develop the environmentalists of tomorrow. Geocaching.com works with park services and landowners all the time to make sure that caches are placed properly. In the event a cache needs to be moved or removed, Geocaching.com will contact members of the community to make sure that it is done. Many parks and conservancies are using Geocaching as a tool to create awareness for their local resources and parks. An example: **www.lancasterconservancy.org/Geocaching.htm**.

RB: What's your definition of "responsible Geocaching"?

BR: Responsible Geocaching involves having a respect for the environment, staying on trails, proper cache placement, and especially Cache In Trash Out. Responsible Geocaching involves passing on the lessons of environmentalism and outdoor enjoyment to others who are just getting started and providing further education within the Geocaching community.

RB: What's the most memorable thing you've ever found in a cache?

BR: Actually, it was an event cache for Washington State that took place [in 2002]. I met/found my current girlfriend at the cache site! Also, some of the Travel Bugs I've found have been amazing. Each one bears its own tales of travel around the area and some even around the world. There is a Darth Vader Travel Bug that was picked up by an air force pilot and even flew on combat missions over Afghanistan.

RB: What will Geocaching be like in five years?

BR: This is a tough question. Geocaching has changed drastically in the first three years. Over the next few years, we expect to see parks and landowners take notice and further develop policies that permit environmentally friendly Geocaching. We expect to see organizations develop around the world to support the sport and guidelines further developed for the placement and maintenance of Geocaches.

Choosing a Cache

Once you have a GPS receiver, you're ready to select a cache. First stop: Geocaching.com. Using the tools in the upper-right corner of the page (see Figure 5-2), you can locate caches in your area based on zip code (the best method), state (if you're looking for new caches), or country (if you live outside the U.S.).

Let's walk through this process so you can get a feel for how Geocaching.com works and what kind of information it supplies. Enter your zip code in the appropriate field; then click Submit. In a moment, you'll see a page that looks like Figure 5-3. This is the first page of cache listings in your area, starting with those closest to you. Odds are there's at least one—if not dozens—pretty close by, because at press time the site had catalogued about 65,000 caches worldwide.

Enter your zip code here to immediately find caches in your area.

Choose your state from this list to find caches that have been added in the last seven days.

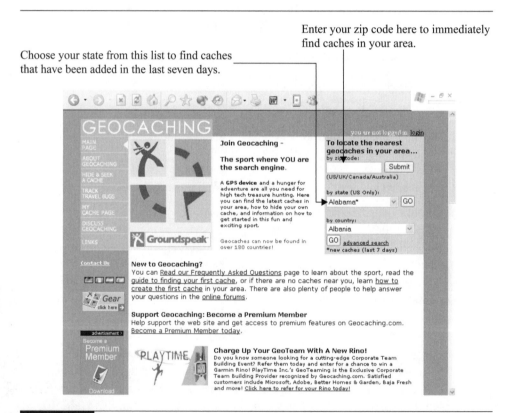

FIGURE 5-2   The Geocaching.com home page is where you can enter your zip code to find caches in your area.

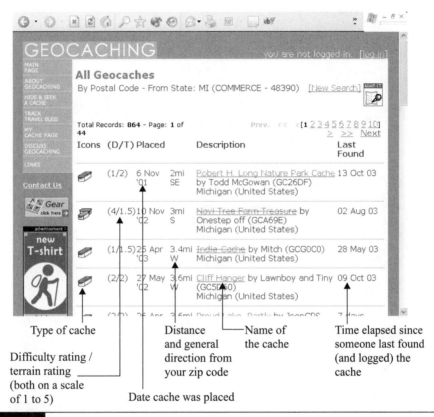

FIGURE 5-3 Caches are listed based on proximity to your zip code, starting with the nearest.

Click the description for any given cache that sounds interesting. From there, you'll be taken to the page containing complete information about that cache: coordinates, description, clues, and messages left by others who have found the cache. See Figure 5-4 for a look at one of these pages.

TIP   *Be sure to print the page(s) for any cache you plan to visit, especially if you're new to Geocaching. It's not enough to simply enter the coordinates into your GPS and hit the road. You'll want the description, the clues, and especially the information on where to park. Another tip: click the link marked "Make this page print-friendly (no logs)." This will send you to a printer-friendly version of the cache listing, one that omits the logs of other visitors. Why do that? Because they often reveal the location of the cache or key clues that spoil the surprises.*

Universal Transverse Mercator
(UTM) coordinates

Latitude and longitude coordinates

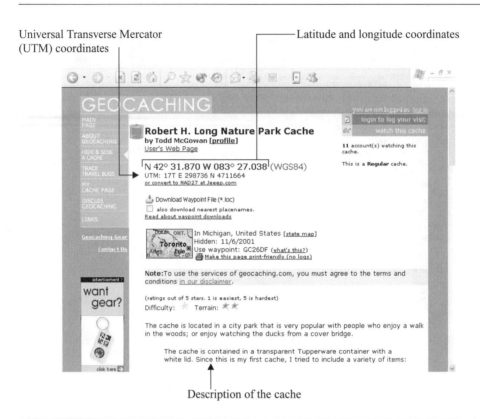

Description of the cache

FIGURE 5-4 The cache information page includes coordinates, a general-area map, and loads of other important stuff.

That's it! Once you've chosen a cache that sounds appealing, you're ready to go. Well, almost. Make sure to read the next section, "Other Things to Bring," before you depart. You'll also want to peruse "Working with Geocaching.com" later in this chapter, which explains the finer points of the web site, including different kinds of caches, downloading waypoints to your GPS, and premium memberships (you knew *someone* was going to have a hand out at some point, right?).

Other Things to Bring

GPS receiver—check. Cache information—check. Car keys—check. Hold it, don't open the garage yet—you're still not quite ready for Geocaching. Anytime you're dealing with the outdoors, it pays to prepare. Here's a checklist of other items you should seriously consider bringing:

Did you know?

Universal Transverse Mercator

Below the latitude and longitude coordinates for caches listed at Geocaching.com, you'll find an additional set of numbers labeled UTM. This stands for Universal Transverse Mercator, another kind of global coordinates. The UTM grid is measured in meters, and UTM lines are orthogonal: always at right angles to each other. Many GPS receivers include a UTM option, but there's no particularly compelling reason to use it.

■ **The Geocache instructions**   Once you've selected a cache at Geocaching.com (or a similar site), be sure to print the instructions so you have a hard copy of the coordinates, parking instructions, hints, and so on.

- **Sunscreen**   You know the drill: apply it 30 minutes before getting into the sun, apply it generously, and reapply it often. A hat is probably a good idea, too.

- **Bug spray**   If you're Geocaching in the summer, you'd be foolish not to apply bug spray. I say this as someone who went Geocaching in the summer and didn't apply bug spray. The skeeters had me for lunch.

- **Water**   This probably goes without saying, but make sure to pack at least one water bottle. You never know how long you'll be away from civilization.

- **First-aid kit**   I never made the leap from Cub Scouts to Boy Scouts, but I still know well enough to "be prepared." That means not venturing into strange woods without basic first-aid supplies.

- **Extra batteries**   GPS receivers are surprisingly frugal when it comes to power, but you should always pack an extra set of batteries just in case.

- **Cell phone**   You probably don't need much convincing to carry your phone—most folks are loathe to go anywhere without one—but it's definitely worth having in case of emergency.

- **A friend**   Sure, you can go it alone, but why? Geocaching is an activity that's best shared. One person can monitor the GPS, another can watch for bears, and so on. So bring your spouse, a buddy or two, your nieces and nephews—anybody who enjoys a nice trek in the outdoors. Oh, it's a heck of a lot safer, too.

Working with Geocaching.com

At its most basic level, Geocaching.com works like this: enter your zip code, find a cache in your area, print the details, and go. But the site offers a lot more features and flexibility to those serious about the sport. Let's take a look at some of the nooks and crannies of Geocaching.com and why you'd want to visit them.

Other Cache-Finding Options

You already know you can search for caches by zip code, state, and country. Those options are right there on the main Geocaching.com page. However, if you click

Geocaching Doesn't Sound All That Hard, But...

If GPS is accurate to within 10 feet, it shouldn't be that hard to find a partially hidden item, should it? That's the initial stigma associated with Geocaching: it sounds like a walk in the park (or, more accurately, the woods), and therefore none too challenging. However, there are three factors to consider.

First, the person who hides the cache will be recording its coordinates based on information from his or her GPS receiver. That information itself will be accurate only to within 10 to 30 feet, depending on the accuracy of the receiver and whether or not it has precision technology like WAAS.

Second, anyone seeking the cache will likely have a different GPS receiver, which means there could be a slight variance in that 10- to 30-feet accuracy (imagine two overlapping but slightly offset radar circles). Now you might be looking at a search area of, say, 45 feet, or even 60 or 75 feet. That's a fairly sizable area.

Finally, there's the topography. Caches are usually partially obscured, if not completely hidden. One might be eight feet off the ground in the crook of a tree branch. Another might be covered in a pile of leaves or disguised to look like part of the terrain.

Thus, the hard part of Geocaching usually isn't reaching the coordinates of the cache, but finding the cache itself. Fortunately, both parts are lots of fun.

the Hide & Seek A Cache option in the left toolbar, you can expand your search possibilities considerably. Options here include latitude and longitude (in either degree or decimal format), telephone area code, username (if you want to find caches hidden by a specific Geocaching.com user), and keyword. The latter option is nice because it allows you to search by specific place names. For instance, I live close to the wonderful Kensington Metro Park. A zip code search certainly isn't going to help me locate caches there, but a keyword search on "Kensington" will.

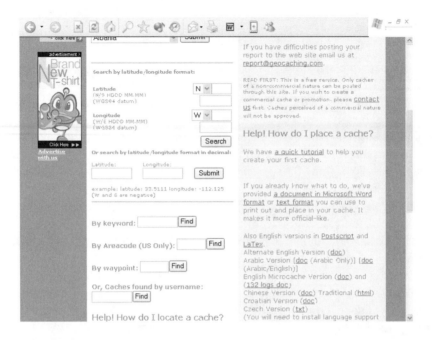

Different Kinds of Caches

Notice in Figure 5-5 that Geocaching.com employs different icons to reflect different kinds of caches. Like any good sport, Geocaching has already witnessed variations on the theme—slight twists on the original concept. Three examples:

- **Offset cache**   Instead of finding the actual cache at the provided coordinates, you find something like a historical landmark, plaque, or benchmark. The actual cache is "offset" from there, accessible either via instructions at the coordinates or included with the Geocache listing you printed.

- **Multi-cache**   The cache you find is just the first. A multi-cache may have two, three, or even more total caches, the first providing instructions for finding the second, the second for the third, and so on.

- **Virtual cache**   The cache is not an item but a landmark, such as a statue or tombstone. To prove your visit to this cache, you must answer (via e-mail) one or more questions posited by the cache creator.

Hitchhikers (a.k.a. Travel Bugs)   Wouldn't it be cool if you left an item in a cache and it "traveled" all over the world? That's the idea behind hitchhikers, also known as

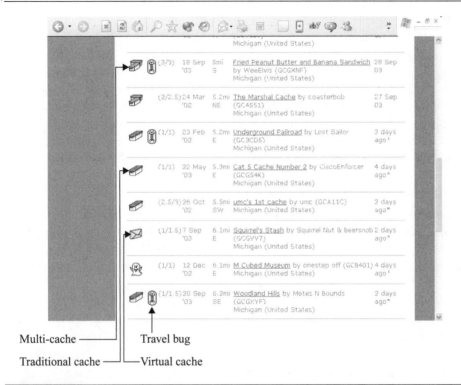

Multi-cache ——

Traditional cache ——

Travel bug

Virtual cache

FIGURE 5-5 The results of your Geocache search will include icons representing the various kinds of caches.

Travel Bugs. These items move from cache to cache, carried there by one Geocacher after another. (Example: I take an item from cache A to the next cache I find, cache B. The next person to visit cache B removes the item and takes it to cache C, and so on.) What's particularly cool is that the hitchhiker's whereabouts are logged on the Geocaching.com site, so you can track its movement.

Said tracking is best accomplished through the use of Travel Bugs, which are like bar-coded dog tags. The Geocaching.com web site sells them by the pair for $5.99. You can learn more about hitchhikers and Travel Bugs by clicking the Track Travel Bugs link on the home page.

By the way, if you specifically want to seek out caches that have hitchhikers in them, look for this icon in the Geocaching.com listings.

Premium Membership

If you really get serious about Geocaching, you may want to consider a Premium Membership to Geocaching.com. Priced at $3 per month or $30 per year (payable via PayPal or by mailing a check), this membership entitles you to a few extra perks, such as predefined cache queries (searches, basically) that are e-mailed to you in e-book format for viewing on your PDA. With these, you can access cache details while out and about, without having to visit the Geocaching.com site. You'll also gain access to member-only caches (which may or may not be any better than public caches, but they sound enticingly elitist).

Creating and Placing Your Own Cache

Once you've enjoyed the thrill of the hunt, you might decide you'd like to make and place a cache of your own. (Consider: you can fill it with all the junk from your junk drawer.) You can find all the information you need by clicking the Hide & Seek a Cache link at Geocaching.com. The site is home to an excellent set of guidelines (things like "respect private property" and "don't put a cache on railroad tracks"), which I'm not going to repeat here. Needless to say, if you want to get in the cache-creation game, you should read the material thoroughly. Geocaching is a sport that could easily be tarnished by cruel or careless people, so please act responsibly.

Treasure in Geocaching.com's Message Area

Got questions? Need help? The Geocaching.com site maintains an extensive and heavily trafficked forum—a collection of message boards where you can post questions and comments and read the posts of others. There are boards devoted to Travel Bugs, GPS hardware, organized Geocaching (where the game becomes a team sport), and lots more.

Entering Coordinates into Your GPS

Before you even think about going on a stash hunt (that's what cool people call Geocaching—which is why I haven't called it that for the entire chapter), make sure you know how to enter coordinates into your GPS receiver. The last thing you want to do is hit the road with visions of troll dolls and key chains dancing in your head, only to discover that you can't figure out how to create a waypoint. That'll end your Geocaching expedition right quick.

> NOTE
>
> *Terminology check: from here on, I'm going to refer to latitude/longitude coordinates as waypoints, because that's how they're identified on the GPS receivers themselves. A waypoint is simply a spot, a location—a set of latitude/longitude coordinates. And they're arguably the most valuable and important tool in the Geocaching arsenal.*

As you recall from Figure 5-4, the location of any given cache is expressed in latitude and longitude. When you enter these numbers into your GPS receiver, they become your destination waypoint. However, the input process is what I consider to be Geocaching's only major hassle, solely because most of the stand-alone GPS receivers I've tried (like the Garmin Geko and Magellan SporTrak) are woefully confusing.

The SporTrak, for instance, requires you to navigate to the Mark menu—not exactly what you'd expect for entering a waypoint. After you've entered the latitude and longitude, select Go To Route to tell the GPS that you want to navigate from your present location to the waypoint. Assuming that the GPS has locked onto at least three satellites, you'll now see your precise distance and bearing from the waypoint—the Geocache.

On the Geko, the procedure is somewhat similar, but still rather counterintuitive. Cycle through to the Menu screen and then select Mark. (This option is normally used to "mark" the coordinates of your current position, which is why it's so confusing to realize that it's also used to create waypoints.) You immediately see a little guy with a flag:

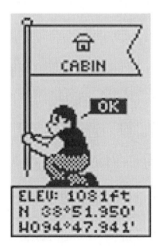

You see your current latitude, longitude, and elevation at the bottom of the screen. The only apparent next step is hitting the OK button, which seems logical given that OK is highlighted on the screen. However, if you use the Geko's arrow buttons, you can select any of four other options:

- **Icon** The Geko includes dozens of icons (or symbols) designed to make waypoint recognition easier. In the case of Geocaching, you might want to choose the little treasure chest.

- **Name** Just below the icon is a field for creating a six-letter name for the waypoint. I strongly urge you to do this step, as it'll make finding the waypoint later much easier. You may have to get a bit creative with your abbreviations, but at least you already have the icon to indicate that it's a cache (as opposed to some other kind of waypoint, like a river or campground).

- **Elevation** This isn't too relevant for Geocaching, but you can enter the waypoint's elevation (represented here as ELEV) if you know it.

- **Coordinates** Finally, the most important field of all: where you enter the cache's coordinates. Once that's done, use the arrows to scroll back up to OK; then press the OK button on the Geko.

Because there are roughly 8.1 gazillion different GPS receivers out there, I can't demonstrate how to enter waypoints into each one. However, now that you understand what you need to do and why, hopefully the instruction manual that came with your device will make a little more sense.

Downloading Waypoints

Entering coordinates manually is a chore, to be sure, which is why you may want to consider downloading waypoints from your computer to your GPS. Most handheld receivers have this capability; some come with the necessary cable, others require you to purchase it separately. Fortunately, once you've made the connection (just follow the instructions in the manual), it's a relatively simple matter to download the coordinates you get from Geocaching.com. Here's the process in a nutshell:

1. At Geocaching.com, click the Log In link to create an account. This involves nothing more than choosing a username and password, and it costs nothing.

2. Once you're logged in, point your browser to **www.geocaching.com/ waypoints**. You'll see some information about downloading waypoints,

starting with a Groundspeak License Agreement. Click the link; then follow the instructions to accept the agreement.

3. Return to the Geocaching.com home page and enter your zip code to see a list of caches in your area (see Figure 5-3). At the far right of the screen, you'll see a check box next to each cache. Click the ones you want to download; then scroll down to the end of the list and click the Download Waypoints button.

4. You will be prompted to save a file called geocaching.loc. Save it to your hard drive, making sure to note exactly where you're saving the file. (My Documents is always a good choice.)

5. Now you need to download and install a terrific freeware program called EasyGPS (**www.easygps.com**). Once it's installed, run the program, click Open, then find the geocaching.loc file. Presto! You should now see your selected caches in the EasyGPS window. Make sure that your GPS is connected to your PC, then click the Send button to download the cache coordinates.

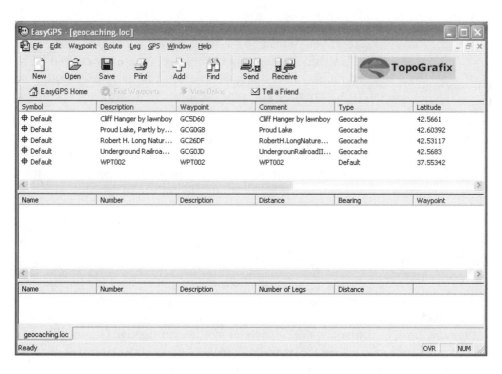

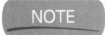 *On subsequent occasions, you'll need to perform only steps 3 and 4 and then run EasyGPS. Also, EasyGPS lets you upload from your GPS any waypoints or routes you created manually—great for saving them for posterity or sharing them with others.*

Fair and Responsible Geocaching

I'm not your parent, your conscience, or even your deity (hard to believe, I know), but I do want to take a moment to be the voice of reason and fair play. Geocaching is not a right, it's a privilege, and for the sake of everyone who wants to participate, please consider the following guidelines:

■ *Play by the rules.* That means leaving the cache in exactly the same spot where you found it, with exactly the same camouflage or positioning. If it was partially obscured by leaves, pile the leaves back on top when you're done. If it was masquerading as a fence post, put the post back in place. You want the next person who comes along to enjoy the same experience you just had.

■ *Consider what you leave behind.* Part of the fun of Geocaching is discovering the trinkets inside. If you're planning to leave something behind, make sure it's appropriate. Kids and families will be looking in there. Also, absolutely no food! You may think you're doing Geocachers a favor by leaving, say, a roll of LifeSavers, but animals will come out of the woodwork and disturb— if not destroy—the cache.

■ *Respect the environment.* It's easy to get caught up in the thrill of the search— at the expense of tree branches, flower beds, and other elements of nature. Be considerate of the environment you're invading, and remember that if you upset the area around the cache too much, you could ruin the search for subsequent Geocachers.

My Dinner with Geocaching

One of my early Geocaching experiences sheds some light on both the fun and foibles of the game. At the tail end of a recent weekend getaway, in which three buddies and I holed up in a Kentucky lake house for wine and wakeboarding (not at the same time, of course), we decided to do a little investigative Geocaching. I needed more field research for the book, but it took a little cheerleading to convince my skeptical comrades, James, Craig, and Doug. "Doesn't sound like much fun," they opined. Finally, they agreed to try a cache located just a few miles out of the way: Old River Mill, White Mills, Kentucky.

Armed with two printed pages from Geocaching.com, two handheld GPS receivers—a Magellan SporTrak Map and Lowrance AirMap 100 Plus (the latter belonging to Doug—he's a pilot)—and a pitiful lack of bug spray, we plugged in the coordinates and piled into the minivan. As with most Geocaches, the instructions for this one explained where to park once we got near the destination, though we did use a paper map to help find the actual town.

Navigating solely by coordinates—both GPS receivers told us exactly how far we were from the cache, first in miles, then in feet—we drove until we were within 200 feet—and then realized we were on the wrong side of the river. A little backtracking took us across a quaint old iron bridge, after which we found ourselves in the parking lot of a youth camp, as described in the Geocache instructions. Distance to coordinates: about 0.15 mile. We left the bug-free sanctity of the van and began wending our way along the riverbank.

And, oh, the bugs. The gnats and mosquitoes descended on us with a fury, despite the time of day (around three in the afternoon) and weather conditions (hot and sunny). Lesson learned: when the Geocache instructions say "Bug Spray recommended: yes," respect those instructions. For me, the flying circus all but ruined the experience.

As we narrowed in on the destination coordinates, my WAAS-enabled SporTrak started acting a little flaky. I'd be standing still, but the Distance measurement would continue falling. The likely culprit was the increasingly dense foliage overhead. Although the SporTrak still showed anywhere from three to six satellites locked in at any given moment, I suspected that accurate readings were getting harder to come by.

Then we reached an impasse: a narrow but inhospitably dense thicket of woods. Between the bugs above, the poison ivy below, and the man barreling toward us in a golf cart, I began to think the hunt was about to come to a premature end.

Man in a golf cart?

Across the freshly cut camp grass rode a groundskeeper who pulled up alongside our crew, grinned, and said, "I know what y'all are looking for."

He then explained that the camp was private property, no one had gotten permission to put anything there, and, by the way, he knew exactly where the thing was. Before I could start pleading my book-author-doing-field-research case, he said—to our surprise and relief—that the camp didn't mind the activity; they just wanted visitors to stop in at the front desk first.

So now the question became, were we willing to plunge into the thorns and ivy and certain loss of GPS signal to find the cache? Intrepid, dedicated book author that I am, I bravely allowed Craig and Doug to continue on while James and I stayed behind to guard the perimeter.

When the rescuers found my two friends several days later, they were confused and dehydrated but otherwise unhurt. Kidding!

What happened was, Craig and Doug managed to get within 20 feet or so of the cache and then had to utterly ignore the GPS (which felt odd, given our total reliance on it up until then) and actually hunt. That's Geocaching in a nutshell: use technology to navigate to an X, one that marks not the spot but the general vicinity, and then use your brain to find the treasure. That we'd chosen a seriously overgrown, bug-infested Geocache sucked some of the fun out of it, to be sure, but there was no debating the intrinsic appeal. I say that as someone who *didn't* get his legs bloodied by thorns and forehead covered in welts.

A few points worth noting. First, the person who placed the cache probably didn't know the camp was considered private property (we saw no sign to that effect), and the locale was probably deserted at the time. That's because he placed it in March, when the camp was likely shut down. Likewise, there were probably few bugs and no foliage, both of which would have improved the experience considerably.

Lesson learned: some Geocaches are best explored in the late fall or early spring, perhaps even in winter. The thick of summer can make for some nasty run-ins with nature.

Other GPS Games

Geocaching is both a company name and the generic description of the activity. However, it's by no means the only way to have fun with a GPS receiver. The capability to navigate to specific coordinates lends itself to many other intriguing adventures, and I'm sure it's just a matter of time before they invent more ("they" being the clever people who think up stuff like this). Here's a sampling of the current variations:

- **Geko Games**   One reason I'm particularly fond of Garmin's Geko 201 is that it comes with four built-in GPS games. They're played outdoors, naturally, requiring an open area ranging in size from a roomy backyard to a football field. In all four games, you're the player, the "game piece" that moves in accordance with what you see on the GPS screen. My favorite is Virtual Maze, in which you have to navigate a virtual maze and collect virtual flags. Kinda silly, sure, but great fun for kids and juvenile adults like me.

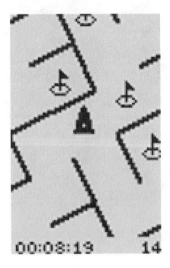

- **Geodashing**   Take Geocaching, make it a team sport, scatter the waypoints across the planet, and you've got Geodashing, which is much more of a game than a hunt. There are no physical caches to find, only randomly selected places to visit and log. This is a game for people with lots of free time and a yen to travel far and wide.

- **MinuteWar**   From the same folks who brought you Geodashing comes MinuteWar, another GPS game played on a global scale. The best description I can give you is the one found on the web site itself: "MinuteWar is a game of capture-the-flag using the whole world as the playing field and GPS receivers for navigation. Every player in the world uses his own local map, but all the maps are combined so that all players compete against everyone else at the same time no matter where they live."

Where to Find It

Web Site	Address	What's There
Garmin	**www.garmin.com**	Geko 201 and other GPS receivers
Geodashing	**www.geodashing.org**	The GPS game Geodashing
Magellan	**www.magellangps.com**	SporTrak Map and other GPS receivers
MinuteWar	**www.seaotters.net/~scout/ MinuteWar/**	The capture-the-flag game MinuteWar
Navicache	**Navicache.com**	More Geocaching sites
TopoGrafix	**www.easygps.com**	EasyGPS cache-management program
VITO Technology	**www.vitotechnology.com**	VitoNavigator

Chapter 6

Fore! GPS Goes Golfing

How to…

- Use GPS on a golf course
- Decide between dedicated and PDA systems
- Find GPS software for Palm PDAs
- Find GPS software for Pocket PC PDAs
- Share golf course data with other users

When faced with a par-5 dogleg and a stiff headwind, it's only natural to look for help from above. Specifically, about 11,000 miles above, home to those amazing GPS satellites I've been doting on for a hundred-odd pages now. It's rather ironic that a satellite system originally developed for the military could play a role in the game of golf, but believe me, it's a hot property nowadays on the fairways. (Come to think of it, astronauts took golf clubs to the moon, so maybe it's not so surprising.)

In this chapter, we're going to look at how GPS is being used by golfers and golf courses to help you improve your game. I'm not saying you're going to shave six strokes or anything, but if you do manage to lower your scores, I get all the credit.

Indeed, given the increasing number of products devoted to leveraging GPS technology on the fairways, it's safe to say this could be the best thing to happen to golf since the Big Bertha. So if you're serious about improving your game, just look to the heavens. On second thought, keep your eye on the ball.

GPS on the Golf Course

As any golfer knows, choosing the right club is half the battle. And knowing which club to choose when you're on the fairway is largely a matter of guesswork. Armed with a GPS receiver, however, you can determine your exact distance to the hole (within about 10 feet, anyway), thus simplifying club selection and, theoretically, cutting strokes off your game. And unlike other range-finder solutions, such as lasers, GPS requires no direct line of sight to the green, no precision aiming. Maybe they should call it the Golf Positioning System.

Yep, I made that one up myself. Copyright 2003 Rick Broida. Anytime you say "Golf Positioning System," you have to send me $5. Cash is fine.

You might wonder if using this kind of technology sullies the game somehow, or if it provides an unfair advantage. In my humble opinion, it's really no different

Did you know?

How GPS Works on a Golf Course

A GPS receiver can tell you how far it is to the green? No way!

Way. How does GPS work this particular bit of positioning magic? You already know that a GPS receiver can determine its own position—its own latitude and longitude—by triangulating signals from orbiting satellites. So if the receiver—and, by proxy, you—knows where it is, the only other tidbit of information it needs is the coordinates of the green. Those coordinates are easy enough to determine; all someone has to do is walk on the green and mark a waypoint. Presto: instant coordinates.

Now it's up to the software, whether it's in a dedicated receiver or a PDA, to calculate the distance between your coordinates and the coordinates of the green. Usually, the distance between two points is given in miles, tenths of a mile, or feet, but it's a simple matter to convert it to yardage. Boom: you're 112 yards from the green, so grab your seven iron. (I have *no* idea what club to use at 112 yards, but you do, and you're the one who matters. Fore!)

than a club that promises farther drives or one of those gadgets that finds the sweet spot on your ball. People are always looking for ways to improve their games. The difference is, GPS actually *works*. Heh, heh.

I kid—I'm a kidder. Golf really isn't my game—you're more likely to find me on a tennis court or in a kickboxing ring—but my dad's a fanatic, and I appreciate the sport's popularity. That's why I'm devoting an entire chapter to it. Let's start by looking at the different kinds of gear used to bring GPS to the fairways.

GPS Gear for Golfers

As you learned in the first few chapters, GPS receivers come in many shapes and sizes and with a wide variety of features. Some provide street maps, others incorporate two-way radios, and so on. Where golf is concerned, however, you effectively have two choices:

- A dedicated GPS receiver built expressly for golf

- A PDA outfitted with a GPS receiver and special software

Dedicated GPS Receivers

It's called a dedicated GPS receiver because it was built with a specific purpose in mind—in this case, golf. Examples of such products include the GolfLogix xCaddie (see Figure 6-1), a cell phone-sized receiver preloaded with specific information about any given course, including playing advice for each hole and real-time distancing to major hazards.

Another product, XY Golf's Color Portable Unit, ups the ante with a spacious color screen, graphics representing each hole, score tracking, and even food and beverage ordering. It can store graphics for up to 30 golf courses and provides two-way messaging between you and the pro shop. ("Hey, could you send a new five iron to the 12th hole? I just broke mine in half.")

FIGURE 6-1   The GolfLogix xCaddie relies on a Garmin-made GPS receiver to provide distance information to major hazards and the green.

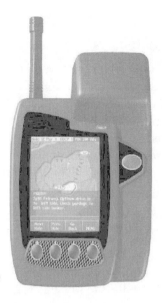

Speaking of the pro shop, that's not the place to look for products like the xCaddie and Color Portable Unit. That's because they're sold directly to golf courses and rented or loaned free to players. Some are installed directly in golf carts.

If your favorite courses don't offer GPS, you can bring your own. One option is a personal dedicated receiver like the SkyGolf GPS SG2 Personal Digital Caddie, which sells for $329.95. Unlike the other models, it doesn't come with any built-in course data—you either have to map your favorite courses yourself (usually

Did you know?

xCaddie on the Job at Pebble Beach

In case you're thinking this whole GPS thing is a flash in the pan, I thought you'd be interested to know that the GolfLogix xCaddie system has been adopted by Pebble Beach Golf Links in California—a somewhat well-known golf course. The devices are mounted in golf carts, but they can be carried right up to the ball as needed.

Of course, the real question is, does Tiger use one? I'll ask him the next time we do lunch.

GPS on the Golf Course: One Golfer's Take

Stuart McCarthy, an avid golfer who runs a small public relations firm, has sampled dedicated GPS systems at various courses and finds them "quite convenient. They speed up decision making on club selection by immediately [providing] yardage to the pin, green, hazard, or other feature," he says. "Without them, golfers who use carts waste a lot of time wandering around looking for a sprinkler head with a yardage marker on it, or pacing off distance from the standard 100-, 150-, 200-, and in some cases 250-yard markers."

accomplished by recording various latitude and longitude points for each hole, which you can do the next time you play 18) or subscribe to the SkyPlayer service. Starting at $19.95 per year, SkyPlayer allows you to download course data to your PC and then transfer it to the device. Needless to say, this is a far more convenient option, as all the legwork is already done.

The other option is a PDA.

PDAs on the Golf Course

As you learned in Chapters 1 and 2, most Palm OS and Pocket PC PDAs are compatible with add-on GPS hardware. You can buy golf-minded GPS bundles that include both the hardware and software, or opt for just the software if you already own a GPS receiver for your PDA. (The software usually isn't particular about the hardware; nearly any receiver should work.) SkyGolf GPS, for instance, offers not only the aforementioned SG2, but also the Personal Digital Caddie for PDAs, a combination of golf software and a GPS receiver for the Handspring Visor, Palm V, or Palm m500 series. As with the SG2, you must subscribe to SkyPlayer to get course data, but you also get the benefit of your PDA's larger screen—to say nothing of stat-, score-, and shot-tracking capabilities.

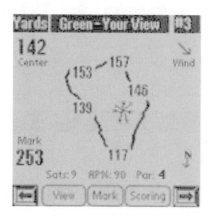

GPS on the Golf Course: Another Golfer's Take

Peter Schollenberg, who uses SkyGolf GPS with his Palm m515, regards the technology as nothing less than revolutionary. "It's a great product [that] will change the way amateurs golf," he gushes. "I'd say it has reduced about six or seven strokes from my round. This is primarily because when you do stray from the fairway and are taking a second shot to the green, you know exactly what the yardage is and begin to focus on the other things: lie, wind, trees, and so on."

Golf Position Solutions offers a similar solution for Pocket PC users in the form of the Pocket Caddie. You can buy a complete bundle—GPS hardware and software, plus charging and mounting accessories—for $299, or the software alone for $99.95. You'll need to purchase course data separately, with prices ranging from $19.95 for one to $89.95 for 10.

StarCaddy (see Figure 6-2) makes one of the most economical packages. StarCaddy for Pocket PC includes a CompactFlash-based GPS receiver (thus ensuring its compatibility with a broad range of models), the StarCaddy software, and a free course map (additional maps cost $19.95 each). StarCaddy for Palm OS includes the same items, save for the GPS receiver: a sled-type accessory that's compatible with the Palm m series, i705, and a handful of older models. Both bundles sell for $249.90, which is about what you'd pay for a GPS receiver alone. Alternately, if you already own GPS hardware, you can buy the StarCaddy software—free map included—for $49.95. Not sure you'll like it? You can download a trial version of the software to see if it performs as advertised.

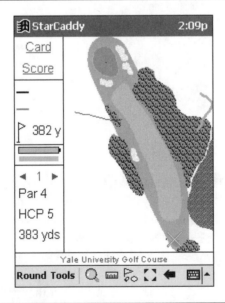

FIGURE 6-2   StarCaddy offers a variety of GPS-and-software and software-only bundles for Palm and Pocket PC PDAs. The Pocket PC version is shown here.

If you own a newer Palm OS handheld, such as a Tungsten T or Zire 71, or one of Sony's Clié models, you may have noticed that none of the aforementioned GPS bundles offers compatibility with your device. That's because, as of this writing, few GPS receivers are available for those newish PDAs. However, you're not without options; you can simply shop for a compatible GPS receiver (start with **Mapopolis.com**) and then take your pick of the various software options. These include products like the aforementioned StarCaddy, which offers an extensive database of course maps, and GolfViaGPS, which requires you to enter course info manually.

Which Is Better: A Dedicated Receiver or a PDA?

6

Now that you have the facts about dedicated GPS receivers versus PDAs equipped with GPS and software, what should you buy? Needless to say, if you already own a PDA, it probably makes sense to investigate the GPS options available for it (see Chapter 2). As I've said before, the nice thing about PDAs is that they can run a variety of software, so you're not necessarily limited to golf applications. You can also use it for Geocaching, street mapping, and so on.

That said, there are pros and cons to dedicated receivers and PDAs alike. The key thing to look for is WAAS support (see Chapter 1 for a refresher), which improves the receiver's accuracy to around 10 feet (or 3 yards, to use golf parlance). If it doesn't support WAAS, it'll be accurate only to around 10 yards, and that can mean the difference between one club and another. Thus, your choice of club won't be quite so cut and dried.

Coming Soon: New Golf Products for PDAs

At press time, two companies were putting the finishing touches on GPS products for both Palm OS and Pocket PC PDAs. The first, Karrier Communications' IntelliGolf, has already gained worldwide popularity as the ultimate golf scorecard program. The latest version includes GPS positioning capabilities, meaning it will provide distances to fairway markers and the front, center, and back of each green. You can also add custom coordinates for sandtraps and other hazards (which, obviously, become useful only the *next* time you play that course).

```
┌─────────────────────────────────────┐
│  Hole 1  GPS Distances        ⓘ     │
│ To Green                             │
│ 241 back   227 center  203 front     │
│ To Markers                           │
│ 27   200   77  150   127  100        │
│ To Objects  ▼ From Whites            │
│ 101 Carry water        214           │
│ 163 Bunker left                      │
│ 189 Oak Tree                         │
│ 47°39'95.93"N   122°9'53.13"W        │
│ ( OK ) (Record) (Record Tee)         │
└─────────────────────────────────────┘
```

Two things you should know about IntelliGolf: first, it's a software-only product (priced at $39.95), meaning it's up to you to supply a GPS receiver for your PDA (see Chapter 2 for some options); and second, the course data (all the positioning information for the markers, greens, and so on) comes not from the company that makes IntelliGolf, but from other users. What happens is that another IntelliGolf user will visit any given golf course, record the marker and green information while playing a round, and then upload the data to Karrier Communications' web site. The company maintains a shared database that's accessible free of charge to anyone who purchases IntelliGolf. The only downside, of course, is that course data may not be available for the course you plan to play. If it isn't, you can record it yourself and upload it for others to use!

iGolf Technologies' iGolfgps is a similar golf-scorecard product that works in a similar fashion: course data is gathered by golfers and distributed online via a shared database. One key difference, however, is that iGolf also offers a GPS receiver: one that's compatible with Palm and Pocket PC PDAs. At press time, iGolf's SD GPS was the first receiver built on top of a Secure Digital (SD) expansion card. That's significant because most of the latest and greatest PDAs, like the Hewlett-Packard iPAQ h1935 and Palm Zire 71, have SD slots. The iGolf bundle is a pretty good deal at $349, because it includes not only the GPS receiver and iGolf software, but also Mapopolis Platinum for street-level mapping (see Chapter 3).

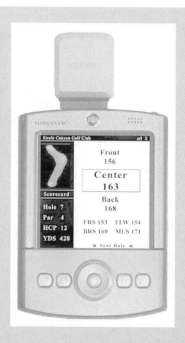

IntelliGolf and iGolf are compelling products because they include scorecard capabilities, not just positioning. Aren't PDAs the greatest?

Where to Find It

Web Site	Address	What's There
GolfLogix	**www.golflogix.com**	xCaddie
GolfViaGPS	**www.golfviagps.com**	GolfViaGPS for Palm OS
iGolf Technologies	**www.igolftech.com**	IGolfgps
IntelliGolf	**www.intelligolf.com**	IntelliGolf
Pocket Caddie	**www.gpsgolf.net**	Pocket Caddie GPS and PDA software
StarCaddy	**www.starcaddy.com**	StarCaddy GPS and PDA software
SkyGolfGPS	**www.skygolfgps.com**	SkyGolf SG2 and PDA software
XY Golf	**www.xygolf.com**	Color Portable Unit

Chapter 7

GPS for Pilots and Sea Captains

How to...

- Use GPS in aviation
- Leverage GPS's capabilities in the sky
- Simulate a panel-mount GPS on your PC
- Choose a GPS receiver for aviation
- Use a PDA for in-flight GPS
- Use GPS for boating
- Choose a marine GPS
- Use a PDA for marine GPS

You can get only so lost on the ground. Eventually you run into street signs, gas stations, other people, even topographical landmarks. But when you're at sea or in the air, figuring out where you are and where you need to go are entirely different propositions. Fortunately, those are two places where GPS signals come through loud and clear, as they're generally free of trees and other overhead obstacles.

It should come as no surprise, then, that GPS now plays a significant role in aviation and open-water boating and fishing. For pilots (specifically private pilots), this means access to the kind of precision accuracy normally available only in airline jets. For sea captains, it means a more versatile and precise alternative to LORAN, the ground-based beacon system. In this chapter, we're going to see how GPS works in the open water and the open sky.

GPS in Aviation

I love flight. I'm not wild about flying, mind you, and commercial aviation is not my idea of a fun way to travel. But once you're up there in the clouds, preferably in a window seat, you get a chance to do something truly remarkable: scoff at birds. ("I'm higher than you, nyah, nyah!") Oh, and the scenery's nice, too.

Commercial airliners are pretty well set when it comes to navigation technology (I hope), but so-called general aviation (GA) stands to benefit tremendously from GPS. From $400 portable receivers to panel-mount models that cost, well, considerably more, GPS has taken to the skies in a big way.

Did you know?

GPS Has Landed in Microsoft Flight Simulator

Call it art imitating life: Microsoft Flight Simulator 2004, the latest version of the company's best-selling PC program, incorporates Garmin 500 and 295 series GPS. In other words, you can activate a window that displays a "real" GPS receiver, one that looks and functions just like its real-world counterpart. (The data it receives correlates to the action within the game, of course.) It shows color moving maps, airport information, GPS approaches, approach transitions, and more. Take a look:

If you haven't tried FS 2004, I highly recommend it, as it enables you to fly everything from Charles Lindberg's Spirit of St. Louis to a Boeing 747-400— and in real-world weather conditions, too. If you happen to have access to an

LCD projector (or can borrow one from work), do yourself a favor and hook it to your PC for some big-screen flying. Trust me: you'll dig it.

By the way, if you don't consider a videogame to be art, you haven't seen Flight Simulator 2004. Check out this actual screenshot from the game:

How GPS Promises to Transform Aviation

Something fairly momentous happened just as I was getting underway on this book: the Federal Aviation Administration (or FAA, to those of us who prefer snappy abbreviations) certified WAAS for aircraft use. As you may recall from previous chapters, the Wide Area Augmentation System accomplishes something that's seemingly minor—improving GPS accuracy from 30 feet to 5 to 10 feet—but where aviation is concerned, it's all the difference in the world.

NOTE   *Pilots have been using GPS technology for well over a decade. The FAA's certification of WAAS means that in the future, pilots will have access to more accurate GPS data and, therefore, safer flights.*

Did you know?

Only a Handful of Airports Have Radio Beacons

Radio beacons, the kind traditionally used to help pilots reach runways in poor weather, cost more than $1 million per runway, which explains why so few airports have them. However, pilots who bring GPS receivers into their cockpits will be able to land safely just about anywhere, as the airport itself needn't provide any additional equipment.

Indeed, the better accuracy dramatically expands the number of airports where planes can land in adverse weather conditions. Right now, just over 300 of the United States' nearly 5,300 public airports have the radio-beacon systems necessary to guide pilots to runways in poor-visibility conditions. Armed with even an inexpensive GPS receiver, a pilot can land on any runway in the country.

WAAS-enhanced GPS allows pilots to obtain the same quality of flight information—the same vertical guidance to a runway—as a traditional instrument landing system (ILS), according to the Aircraft Owners and Pilots Association (**www.aopa.org**).

At the same time, pilots can more accurately report their positions to controllers, which will help ensure air-traffic safety and allow for a greater number of flights. This won't happen overnight, of course—industry experts say it could be 10 to 20 years before enough aircraft use GPS to improve air traffic. But there's no question that GPS has earned its wings—so to speak.

What Does GPS Offer a Pilot?

Some of the benefits of aviation GPS may seem obvious; others may not. Let's take a look at a few of those benefits in detail.

- **Alarms**   Many GPS receivers can issue alarms when you cross into an airspace, near your destination, veer too far off course, and come in proximity to a set waypoint.

- **Altimeter**   According to *USA Today*, accidentally striking the ground is the most common killer in aviation. GPS provides a backup (or even primary) altimeter that's accurate to within 5 to 10 feet (assuming it supports WAAS, that is). Indeed, a GPS receiver is like a redundant system for important flight tools.

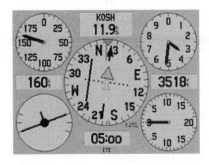

■ **Course and heading** By far the most valuable (and obvious) advantage to having GPS in the cockpit is its ability to provide course and heading information. Find the airport you want to fly to, choose the Route To option, and presto—your course and heading are ready to go.

■ **Groundspeed indicator** As any pilot knows, an aircraft's airspeed indicator looks at how fast the wind is blowing—rarely an accurate measurement of the aircraft's actual speed. A headwind or tailwind can affect the results considerably. A GPS receiver provides a totally accurate groundspeed indicator.

■ **Location awareness** This probably goes without saying, but a GPS receiver in the air works just like a GPS receiver on the ground, giving you your exact position on a moving map. The difference here, of course, is that you're not seeing your position relative to city streets and points of interest, but rather to airports, airspaces, runways, and standard basemap elements (like cities and major highways). Of course, some portable models (like the Garmin GPSMAP 196) can double as automotive navigators, giving you turn-by-turn driving directions on either the basemap or optional street-level maps. It's like two, two, *two* GPS receivers for the price of one! (Actually, the GPSMAP 196 is like three in one, as it includes a marine mode as well.)

■ **Logbook** Many aviation GPS receivers include electronic logbook features that automatically record your departure airport, arrival airport, and flight time—information that can be downloaded to your PC for easy logbook management.

■ **Nearest airport** As Doug Luzader points out in "A Pilot Takes to the Skies with GPS," receivers like the Lowrance AirMap 100 can be lifesavers in emergency situations. With the push of two buttons, it can guide you to the nearest airport.

GPS Receivers for Aviation

GPS receivers for aviation fall into two main categories: panel-mount models that are installed in an aircraft along with its other avionics, and portable models that can be moved from plane to plane—and sometimes even to cars and boats. Garmin and

Lowrance are the two major makers of consumer-level GPS receivers built with flying in mind. Here are some examples of the two varieties:

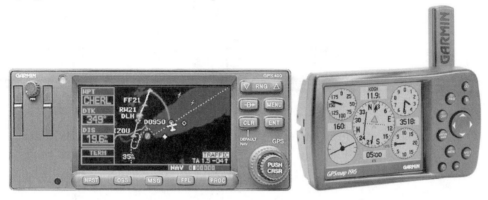

I'm not going to get into much detail regarding panel-mount systems, other than to say that they undergo more rigorous testing than portable models, and they're generally more reliable and practical because they tap into information about the aircraft. There's not much how-to information I can give you here that would supercede what you'd get from flight and instrument training.

As for portable models, they're just about ideal for casual fliers and those who rent airplanes, as they can easily go from one plane to another. Even if you're flying a plane that has a panel-mount GPS, a portable GPS can be a great backup. In fact, once you land at your destination, you can take the receiver from the plane to, say, a rental car (assuming it doesn't already have that Hertz NeverLost system you've probably heard about) and use it to find your way around. That's provided, of course, that its basemap includes highway and major road data, or it has memory available for downloading street-level maps.

Two models worth checking out:

- **Garmin GPSMAP 196** This highly versatile GPS sells for around $1,000 and offers aviation, land, and water modes, meaning it's equally well-suited to flying, driving, and boating. Its copious features include a roomy screen (3.8 inches diagonally) and extended runway centerlines to help orient you to the runway.

- **Lowrance AirMap 100** I've seen this one selling online for as little as $229, making it the bargain of the century for pilots. It's available with an optional yoke mount and, like the Garmin, offers extended runway centerlines and support for optional land and marine maps.

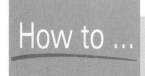

Try an Aviation GPS Simulator on Your PC

Want to see how a fancy-schmancy panel-mount GPS receiver looks and works? Garmin offers a software-based simulator you can download to your PC. It includes the full Jeppesen database of airports and pretty much all the features and functionality of the real deal. Plus, it allows you to "fly" various scenarios to get a feel for how the system works. You can find the 13.5-megabyte emulator at Garmin's web site (**www.garmin.com/products/gns530**).

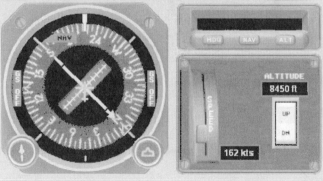

Can You Use a PDA for Airplane GPS?

In other chapters, I've extolled the virtues of using a PDA for GPS navigation. They can be quite effective for street mapping and driving directions, and they're adept at outdoor activities like hiking and Geocaching. So what about flying? Can you trust your airborne safety to a PDA? Should you?

At the very least, it's a proposition worth considering. As you know from earlier explanations, the combination of a PDA and GPS receiver can be a potent one, provided the software is competent. Aviation requires a level of sophistication and capability that exceeds the boundaries of most PDA-based mapping solutions. However, I recommend checking out two options: one for Palm OS handhelds, the other for Pocket PCs.

PathAway for Palm OS   PathAway is perhaps the most powerful third-party GPS software available for Palm OS PDAs. (By *third party,* I mean software that doesn't come bundled with built-in or add-on GPS hardware.) It has just about all the basic GPS features you could want, including moving map, waypoints, routing, backtracking, and customizable screen views.

TIP   *PathAway is one of the first third-party GPS programs I've seen that works with Garmin's iQue PDA (see Chapters 9 and 10). Thus, if you were hoping to leverage that model for use in an airplane, now you can.*

However, the way it works with maps is a little different than the way most GPS systems work. While it does provide a moving map, the map itself is essentially a fixed image—one that you've obtained online or from a software-based mapping program. While PathAway lets you import maps from a variety of sources, it's important to understand that you won't be able to interact with those maps the way you can with maps on, say, a portable or panel-mount GPS. Specifically, zooming in or out won't change the level of detail shown by the map, because the map is not dynamic—it doesn't change depending on zoom level. It's just an image—a photo of a map, really.

With that in mind, PathAway has lots of advanced features (I wouldn't recommend it for novice PDA users) and can even switch between multiple maps automatically, zooming into the one with the most detail when appropriate. Say you're flying from Ann Arbor, Michigan, to Louisville, Kentucky. You could load highly detailed maps of the two cities and a larger, less-detailed map of the area in between. PathAway will switch between the maps as you travel, effectively giving you the map data you need when you need it.

You can download a 15-day trial version of PathAway, but keep in mind that its GPS connection time is limited to 10 minutes. Thus, try it on the ground before you try it in the air. You may just find this $50 program to be your perfect GPS companion. To find out more about GPS options for Palm OS PDAs, see Chapter 2.

TIP *If you're really an advanced user and want to try a freeware alternative to PathAway, check out GPS Master. It supports a similarly broad range of GPS features: routes, waypoints, downloaded maps, and so on. You can find this nifty freebie at **PalmGear.com**.*

TeleType for Pocket PC   TeleType offers one of the most powerful and versatile GPS solutions for Pocket PC handhelds. I haven't mentioned it much in previous chapters because I find the software—both on the desktop and the PDA—to be annoyingly complicated, and I don't like complicated. That said, TeleType's aviation capabilities are second to none on the Pocket PC, so it's a package worth considering.

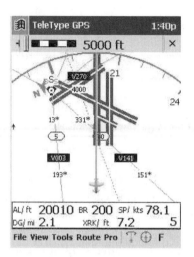

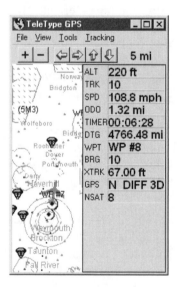

TeleType GPS is available as a software-only package ($195) or with various GPS hardware bundles. The latter include CompactFlash (CF) GPS receivers that will work with any Pocket PC with a CF slot, and Bluetooth GPS receivers that will work with any Pocket PC equipped with Bluetooth.

NOTE *The TeleType software is compatible with third-party Bluetooth GPS receivers, but works only with TeleType's CF receiver. That's something to keep in mind if you already own, say, a sled-type GPS for your Pocket PC and want to add just the software. No can do.*

A Pilot Takes to the Skies with GPS

Doug Luzader is a Fox News television reporter whose credits include live coverage of Kuwait and Baghdad during the war in Iraq. He's also a private pilot who recently added a GPS receiver to his cockpit. In this report, he extols the virtues of the technology—especially in a post-9/11 world—while cautioning against over-reliance on it.

"Cessna 139, report the field in sight."

For a private pilot, the task once would be simple. Find the airport. Land. Not now. In the world since September 11, pilots of small planes are watched with enormous scrutiny. What once were leisurely weekend flights from one rural airport to another can be filled with anxiety for pilots, air traffic controllers, and law enforcement.

"139, report field in sight, did you copy?"

Particularly in the areas surrounding New York City and Washington, D.C., all aircraft, regardless of size, are now tracked on a continual basis. Slight deviations from course can bring a reproach from an air traffic controller; inadvertent turns can find you with F-16s off either wing.

"Approach, 139 is looking for the field."

I began flying planes two years before September 11 and, like many private pilots, enjoyed flying in relatively unrestricted airspace. I could come and go as I chose. Since September 11, I have moved to Washington, D.C., and nothing has been the same. Private pilots here now have most of the same radio and navigation procedures as airline pilots. It may be the most scrutinized, secure airspace in the country.

I learned to fly using a chart and a compass. They are, after all, the same tools that got Lindbergh across the Atlantic. But given the stakes, I've decided they are no longer enough. Like many pilots, I now fly with the flight controls in one hand and a GPS unit in the other.

"Approach, this is 139, having difficulty finding the field. Can you give a heading, please."

The first time I went up with my Lowrance Airmap 100, I was amazed. The small plane in the center of the screen was sitting on a runway, with a course line plotted to my intended stop for the day. In the air, it provided instant analysis of nearly all aspects of flight. What's my ground speed? Altitude? Heading? If the engine dies, I press two buttons simultaneously, and it guides me to the nearest airport for an emergency landing.

These are all wonderful tools for a pilot to have at his disposal, but, for me, the wonder of the GPS is still its most basic function: Where am I? Knowing that can be the difference between an uneventful landing and an armed escort.

Student pilots still learn to find their way around the old-fashioned way, and their final exam test flights do not allow GPS use. That's as it should be. My compass never runs out of batteries, and my paper chart can't lose a signal. GPS in the cockpit is simply another tool, but for safety it offers insurance and reassurance. There's never a question where the field is. You know where. Exactly.

"Approach, Cessna 139 has the field, 5.2 miles northeast."

Marine GPS

So there you are, miles offshore in your new sailboat, and your motor conks out. The wind stops blowing. Pop-Tart rations are growing dangerously low. Armed with even a $100 GPS receiver, you can radio your exact position to the towing service so it can pull you back to port.

Say, couldn't you do that with old-fashioned LORAN (Long Range Navigation) systems, too? Yes, but not with nearly the same accuracy. LORAN is out; GPS is in (and has been for many years now). It is without a doubt the perfect tool for open-water navigation, as you have endless open sky from which to receive signals and no pesky streets or restricted airspaces getting in your way. And, obviously, it's good for a lot more than just reporting your position to the tow boat.

 If you're interested in GPS's fishing applications, see Chapter 4. This chapter deals more with navigation, particularly on major waterways and oceans.

Oh, it's also a tool that could save your life, as grippingly illustrated in "Man Overboard! GPS Saves a Life at Sea." In this section, we look at how boaters can use GPS receivers to their advantage and discuss the various hardware options, including PDAs.

What Does GPS Offer a Mariner?

It's amazing how far marine navigation has come. From compasses and sextants to LORAN and GPS receivers, we've gone from navigating by stars to navigating by satellites. Needless to say, satellites work better.

Let's take a look at some of the key benefits to using a GPS chartplotter (the marine term for mapping).

■ **Autopiloting**   Higher-end GPS systems can link directly to a boat's navigation systems for sophisticated autopiloting.

■ **Course and heading**   As with so many other GPS solutions, the number-one benefit of marine GPS is being able to plot a course and steer to it. This capability is ideal for everything from fishing (finding your way to fish-rich spots) to pleasure cruises ("I know the most beautiful spot to watch the sunset") to just finding a port when traveling by boat.

■ **Fish finding**   Some marine-minded GPS receivers have built-in sonar capabilities, thus giving you a kind of 3D positioning system—complete with the same kind of fish-finding capabilities found in stand-alone sonar devices. The difference here, of course, is that once you find the perfect spot, you can easily navigate to it again by marking a waypoint.

■ **Location awareness**   A GPS receiver in the water works just like a GPS receiver on the ground, giving you your exact position on a moving map. The difference here, of course, is that you're not seeing your position relative to city streets and points of interest, but rather to land masses, obstructions, navigation buoys, and other water stuff. If you purchase and install optional maps, you can enjoy the electronic equivalent of traditional paper charts, complete with shaded depth zones, shipwrecks, shoals, and more.

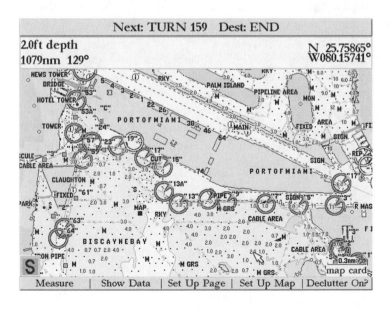

7

- **Nearest gas station**   Running low on gas? Just as an aviation GPS can guide pilots to the nearest airport, so can a marine GPS direct you to the closest filling station.

- **Shipwreck locations**   Enjoy scuba diving? With optional marine maps, a GPS receiver can guide your boat to shipwreck sites with precision accuracy.

- **Speedometer**   Boat speedometers aren't terribly accurate. GPS receivers are great for monitoring your exact speed, be it in knots or miles per hour.

Man Overboard! GPS Saves a Life at Sea

This story, reprinted here courtesy of Garmin International, was just too good to pass up. You might think about using GPS to backtrack only in the wilderness, where the terrain and foliage can get you good and lost, but at sea you really just think about going forward, getting from point A to point B. As this story proves, it's a good thing even marine GPS receivers let you backtrack.

Every good mariner has a boatload of fish tales and stories that'll set your neck hairs on end. Reese Ward and Steve Leasure have a whopper. And a leading character in their real-life adventure just happens to be a Garmin chartplotter.

When Leasure, 35, of Charleston, South Carolina, purchased his 29-foot sport fishing boat along with a business partner, he insisted that they spend a little more money on a GPS system. He chose a Garmin GPSMAP 230. Turns out that was a life-changing decision.

Memorial Day weekend, 1999, Leasure, Ward, and four other friends spent a day fishing in the Gulf Stream off Charleston Harbor. After hauling in a sizable catch of mahi-mahi and wahoo, they turned around the *Summer Girl* and headed home.

Ward, 30, will never forget what happened next. As he walked to the boat's stern to relieve himself, he was pitched overboard. Ward yelled for help, but no one heard his cries over the noise from the boat, now speeding away at a 23-knot clip.

Shirtless and without a life jacket, Ward spent the longest 45 minutes of his life bobbing in the warm Gulf Stream waters.

"I'll tell you, a lot of things went through my mind," Ward recalled. "And I was talking to the man above—talking out loud."

As he treaded the warm waters, Ward worried about getting cramps. Then, a scarier thought crossed his mind... sharks.

"But I put that out of my mind real quick," Ward said.

Back on the boat, Leasure woke up from a short nap in the cabin and asked where Ward was. Nobody knew. At first, he thought it was a joke. But it didn't take long to search the boat.

Leasure immediately radioed the Coast Guard. Then he spoke the words every captain hopes he'll never have to: "I'm missing one of my crew members. I need some assistance."

While still on the radio, Leasure started fiddling with the GPSMAP 230. He switched to TracBack mode, a feature that shows the boat's previous course on the moving map display. Leasure turned the boat around and started to backtrack.

"At first, I thought we would find him in two or three minutes. I had total confidence we would find him," he said.

After about 10 minutes, his confidence began to slip. After 30 minutes, his heart sank. *There's no way he could tread water for this long, he thought.*

But the man overboard kept treading, and when Ward spotted a dot on the horizon that seemed to be coming toward him, he found the strength to keep going.

Aboard the *Summer Girl,* Leasure was the first to spot Ward, bobbing in the two- to three-foot waves. He radioed the Coast Guard. "We have him in sight... I can't believe it."

Amazingly, Ward was right on the [GPSMAP] 230's course plot. "He hadn't drifted a bit, which was unusual," Leasure said. "If we hadn't seen him, we would have run right over him."

Safe on board, Ward hugged everyone and said he was sorry for ruining a good day of fishing.

Ruined a good day of fishing? Nah. These guys netted a whopper of a story and took in some valuable seamanship lessons as well. New rule aboard the *Summer Girl:* No one goes to the back of the boat unless someone's been notified.

You can bet Reese Ward follows the buddy system. And he's darn glad his buddy was an experienced captain who had insisted on buying first-rate navigation equipment.

7

Marine GPS Receivers

Unsurprisingly, marine GPS receivers come in many shapes and sizes, and with a wide variety of features. Some models are designed to mount inside boats; others are portable—nice if you want a system that can go from boat to car and back again. Even if you spring for the fanciest fixed-mount GPS on the planet, there's still something to be said for keeping a portable, battery-powered handheld model as a backup.

Garmin, Magellan, Lowrance, Navman, and Raymarine are among the leading makers of marine GPS receivers.

Can You Use a PDA for Marine GPS?

You can! In fact, the same two products I spotlighted in the aviation section work for marine navigation as well. See "PathAway for Palm OS" and "TeleType for Pocket PC" earlier in the chapter for details. (You can just about substitute "marine" for "aviation," and everything will still be accurate.) In the meantime, here's a sample of what a marine map looks like in TeleType:

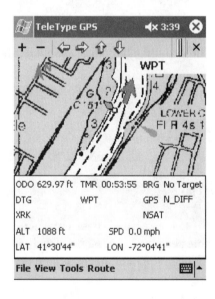

Did you know?

Even GPS Can't Beat Nature

All this talk about GPS saving lives at sea got me thinking about the *Andrea Gail*, the doomed fishing boat that became the subject of Sebastian Junger's gripping 1998 book, *The Perfect Storm* (which later became a movie starring George Clooney). It had been a while since I'd read it, but I knew the tragedy occurred in 1991—long before GPS receivers had become popular for marine navigation. I wondered if things might have turned out differently if the crew had had access to GPS technology. So I asked Mr. Junger.

"No, they knew exactly where they were," he told me. "They had a LORAN system that was almost as good [as GPS]. So I don't think anything like that could have helped them."

That's pretty much what I'd thought. The sad moral of the story is that technology is no match for Mother Nature. Be careful out there.

7

Where to Find It

Web Site	Address	What's There
Aircraft Owners and Pilots Association	**www.aopa.org**	Information for pilots and aircraft owners, plus articles on GPS in aviation
Garmin	**www.garmin.com**	Aviation and marine GPS receivers
Lowrance	**www.lowrance.com**	Aviation and marine GPS receivers
Muskokatech	**www.pathaway.com**	PathAway software for Palm PDAs
Navman	**www.navman.com**	Marine GPS receivers
Raymarine	**www.raymarine.com**	Raychart GPS receivers
TeleType	**www.teletype.com**	TeleType GPS for Pocket PC PDAs

Chapter 8

GPS in Business

How to...

- Leverage GPS cell phones
- Use GPS in fleet management
- Use GPS for dispatching
- Decide between GPS cell phones and vehicle mounts
- Monitor employee whereabouts and billable time
- Use GPS for team building
- Use GPS in vineyard management

Until now, we've looked almost exclusively at GPS's consumer applications: road navigation, outdoor fun, the great game of Geocaching, and so on. But GPS is also becomingly increasingly popular in business, where it's used for everything from dispatching to fleet management to vineyard management. Yes, vineyard management.

Consider GPS's core benefits:

- Location mapping
- Navigation
- Tracking

Now consider how any business might be able to leverage one of those benefits. Off the top of my head, I can think of a dozen examples, including:

- A plumber, painter, or any other kind of contractor uses GPS to find the way to a customer's home.
- An ambulance driver uses GPS to navigate to an intersection where an accident has occurred.
- A delivery service uses GPS to quickly and efficiently move from one drop-off location to the next.
- That same delivery service uses GPS to track trucks in the field. When someone requests a pickup, the dispatcher routes the truck that's closest to the pickup location.
- Surveyors use GPS to achieve much more precise results than they could with traditional surveying equipment, and for a fraction of the cost.

■ Company employees engage in a GPS treasure hunt as part of a team-building exercise.

GPS in the Cellular Market

The marriage of GPS and cell phone promises to bear some interesting fruit. Ashu Pande is director of product marketing for SiRF Technology, a company that makes GPS chips for use in cell phones and other mobile devices. I asked him to explain how GPS-equipped phones will affect consumers and businesses. Here's his report.

As the world becomes more mobile and less wired, consumers and businesses alike have begun to turn to GPS technologies and products to figure out where, location-wise, they are. GPS, once the domain of government agencies such as the United States Army, has now entered the mainstream, conferring location awareness—the ability to pinpoint location—to millions of consumers worldwide.

In 1995, the need for location awareness for cellular phones got a boost from the United States Federal Communications Commission's Enhanced 911 Mandate—more commonly known as the E-911 mandate—requiring carriers to pinpoint cellular callers within 10 meters to aid in emergency relief. While the initiative served to popularize the idea of location, it has limitations. It is applicable only to the United States market and carries no revenue-generating mechanism. As a result, carriers and wireless device manufacturers worldwide have sought to capitalize on the commercial potential for GPS with a wide variety of location-based services. These include personal navigation, location filtering of web content, concierge services, and enterprise applications such as asset tracking and fleet management—along with dozens of others. The results have been promising; consumers by the thousands have come to rely on the ability to know their location and take advantage of the myriad convenient location services. Meanwhile, carriers are realizing significant productivity gains from mobile resource management applications—not to mention substantial revenue gains.

Examples include geolocation provider Kivera, which recently deployed North America's first location-aware Yellow Pages service, allowing GPS-enabled cell-phone users to search Yellow Pages listings for their current location. The Avis Assist phone-based navigation system, developed by Motorola, lets Avis rental-car customers rent Nextel phones that literally talk them through street directions while driving. Finally, on the enterprise side, Reeve Trucking runs a web-based mobile resources management application, @Road's GeoManager Pocket Edition, to monitor the location and speed of trucks and drivers in real time.

8

Put simply, GPS can be invaluable for any business or service in which getting lost costs valuable time, and in which being found can improve the bottom line. Plus, as the last example illustrates, even the fun side of GPS can have a practical application.

To help give you a closer look at the what, why, and how of GPS in business, I asked several industry insiders to share stories and case studies. Please don't consider them product endorsements on my part, but rather relevant insights that happen to center around a specific company or product.

Fleet Management and Dispatching

In the wonderful world of *Star Trek* (okay, it was wonderful until *Star Trek Enterprise* came along—now it's just dreck), Starfleet Command always knows the precise location of its starships. The Enterprise is in the Denari System, the Defiant just left Deep Space 9, and so on. Here on 21st-century Earth, it's not so easy to keep track of a fleet—especially when you're talking about a fleet of trucks or other vehicles. That's too bad, because there are considerable gains that come from fleet tracking: employee monitoring, improved routing efficiency, defense against Klingon invasion, and so on.

Companies like FleetBoss, Minorplanet USA, Televigation, and Xora offer fleet-management products and services based on GPS technology. One obvious question that crops up immediately is, how does GPS enable fleet managers to track vehicles in the field when GPS is a one-way technology? Ah, you remember your studies, grasshopper—well done. As you no doubt recall from previous chapters, a GPS receiver only receives signals—it doesn't transmit them. In other words, you could stick a GPS receiver inside a truck (or implant it in, say, a driver's shoulder, which would be much cooler), but it would have no way to relay the received positioning information. Hmmm.

The answer lies in a marriage of technologies: GPS and cell phone. The GPS receives positioning data, and the phone (or a device that uses cell-phone networks) relays it wherever it needs to go. The advantages here are significant, especially in terms of driver accountability:

- **Service stops**   A company can determine exactly how long an employee (technician, driver, or whoever) or vehicle spends at a customer's location.

- **Speed control**   Drivers who exceed the speed limit consume more gasoline, risk their safety and the safety of others, and so on. Some fleet-management systems can notify the central office when a vehicle exceeds a predetermined speed limit. As a result, companies can save money on both gasoline and insurance premiums. In fact, in one case study, a company was able to prove in an insurance claim that the driver was not responsible for an accident during icy conditions. The GPS data proved he'd been driving at a safe speed.

■ **Route tracking**   Fleet managers can monitor each truck's location and heading and see that information relative to customer locations. Thus, routing can be handled more efficiently, and managers can tell customers when vehicles are due to arrive.

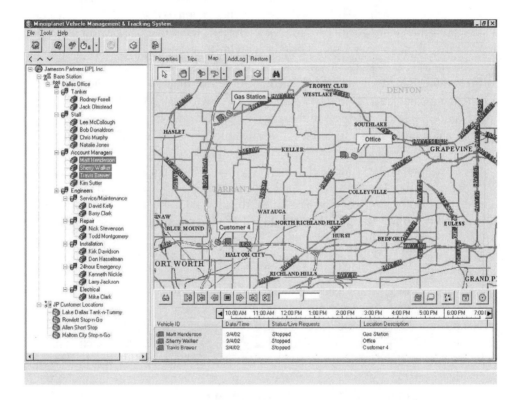

■ **"Geo-fencing"**   Don't want your drivers going hither and yon? Some systems can notify the central office when a vehicle goes outside a predefined geographical area. Sounds like Big Brother, but it's hardly different than keeping certain employees from entering restricted areas within a building.

■ **Overtime management**   GPS tracking prevents employees from padding their overtime reports. You know precisely when they arrive on the job and when they leave.

Dispatching

Part and parcel with fleet management is dispatching—sending a vehicle to a customer or jobsite location. Here's an example: your car has broken down, and you've called your motor club for a tow truck. The problem at your club's end is finding the fleet's closest truck and dispatching it to your location. Instead of waiting, say, 15 minutes, now you're waiting an hour.

AAA-Atlantic has found a solution in the form of Kivera's D/2000 AutoDispatch Location Engine, which uses GPS and mapping integration to automatically determine which tow vehicle is closest to a stranded motorist's location based on mileage and accessibility impediments such as bridges and railroad tracks.

"Our traditional dispatching process was very labor-intensive, involving repetitious calls to numerous trucks and a significant amount of manual follow-up by our dispatchers," said Art Lemke, Managing Director, ERS Delivery, AAA Mid-Atlantic. "Kivera eliminated repetitive labor and guesswork from our dispatch systems by giving us fast and precise location-based information and the ability to use it for real bottom-line results."

GPS-enhanced dispatching also has the potential to save lives. For example, England's London Ambulance service handles over one million calls per year and serves an area of roughly 620 square miles. In July 2003, the service deployed a system that combines not only GPS (for in-vehicle street navigation), but also WiFi, GSM (global system for mobile communication, Europe's prevalent cell-phone technology), and GPRS (general packet radio service, a high-speed wireless data system).

In the event of an emergency, ambulances are notified by the sound of a bell in the cab while detailed instructions appear simultaneously on their in-vehicle touch-screen device. Following the initial notification, vehicles receive detailed driving directions via an in-vehicle navigation unit, which is attached to the touch-screen PC. Meanwhile, the control room is also receiving GPS navigation data back from the vehicle every 15 seconds. A map is also displayed on the PC, which enables the crew to see where the vehicle is in relation to their destination.

Like fleet management, dispatching can rely on either phone-based GPS or vehicle-mounted systems. In the next section, I'll clue you in on the pros and cons of each.

Cell-Phone GPS or Vehicle Tracking?

Products like Televigation's TeleNavTrack and Xora's GPS TimeTrack rely on GPS-enabled cell phones, while FleetBoss and Minorplanet rely on dedicated systems mounted inside vehicles. Which is better? That depends on the business, of course. Let's look at the advantages and disadvantages of the two options.

GPS-Enabled Phone

■ It's a GPS receiver and a cell phone in one device. That means one piece of equipment to buy instead of two.

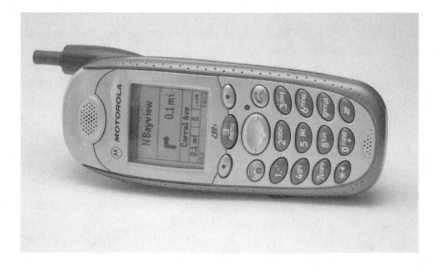

■ It's mobile, so it can go from vehicle to vehicle and person to person. On the other hand, it can also be easily lost.

■ It enables personal tracking, which obviously makes sense for employees who spend a lot of time away from their vehicles.

Vehicle-Installed GPS

■ It's a security system for the vehicle itself and all the equipment stored inside it. If the vehicle is stolen, it's easily tracked. That could lower a company's insurance premiums and, of course, save money on lost equipment.

■ Some models can be moved from one vehicle to another, but by and large they're not portable. They're certainly not designed for personal tracking.

Case Study: Fleet Management Floors 'Em

True to its name, Xora GPS TimeTrack tracks employees' timesheets, jobs, and locations. The software leverages GPS-enabled phones, which can not only provide their users with positioning information, but also relay that information back to a main office. Ananth Rani, Xora's vice president of Products and Services, shares this story of how GPS TimeTrack is used by a typical business.

Another day, another process improvement. That's the story at Butler-Johnson Corporation, a distributor of flooring and surfacing products to more than 5,000 retail establishments, fabricators, and installers in Northern California. Since implementing Xora GPS TimeTrack in the spring of 2003, Butler-Johnson has improved service to customers and increased the accuracy of its payroll calculations. The result: Butler-Johnson is on pace to save more than $140,000 in overtime expenses in the next year.

As warehouse distribution manager at the company's San Jose facility, Jon Bujuklian (otherwise known as JB) is responsible for supervising the activities of 20 delivery drivers. Seeking to continue a longstanding company tradition for providing excellent customer service, JB selected Xora GPS TimeTrack, an easy-to-use and affordable solution for locating and managing mobile workers. Now JB knows where his drivers are at all times.

"When a customer calls with a question about the status of their delivery, I can use the Xora service to pull up a map that displays the location of each of my drivers in real time," says JB. "Within minutes, I can tell the customer the precise location of their shipment and make a credible prediction as to when it will arrive."

Each of JB's delivery drivers carries a GPS-enabled mobile phone from Nextel that runs the Xora service. Therefore, JB can keep track of his workers whether or not they are in their trucks. This suits JB just fine. "Sure, we looked at those location-based services that use devices which are hard-mounted to the vehicle, but they were too expensive. Xora GPS TimeTrack costs much less than competitive products and allows us to locate workers, not vehicles."

With Xora, JB knows the exact time his drivers started and finished their work each day. This allows him to more accurately calculate payroll, in particular the amount of overtime each driver earns. Prior to implementing Xora GPS

TimeTrack, JB's drivers were putting in at least 30 hours of overtime for each two-week work period. Since the company began using Xora, total overtime hours have been cut in half.

"Xora GPS TimeTrack will help us reduce overtime expenses by more than $140,000 this year," remarks JB. "Even after we take into account the cost of the Nextel phones and Xora service, we will still save well over $100,000. I can't say that about any other product or service I am using."

JB is also using Xora GPS TimeTrack to ensure that his drivers are traveling at safe speeds. Because JB has set up the Xora service to update driver status every five minutes, he can quickly determine if a driver is exceeding the speed limit. "This helps to ensure the safety of our drivers and other motorists, while protecting our customers' shipments. And, if our drivers have better driving records, we can keep insurance costs down."

8

Navigation

Just as GPS can be a major asset for everyday motorists trying to navigate from point A to point B, so can it aid independent contractors, delivery drivers, and other small-business users. Consider the plumber who spends every day going from one job to another and has to call each customer (perhaps more than once) to get directions. With a GPS system and the destination address, he can quickly and easily get an accurate route from his current location, and without pestering the customer. Same goes for painters, builders, electricians—heck, even pizza-delivery drivers.

The key question to consider here is whether you can use stand-alone gear— such as any of the products described in Chapter 2—or you need something that's going to link to a central office. In case of the latter, check out the products and services mentioned in "Fleet Management and Dispatching" earlier in this chapter.

My guess, however, is that the vast majority of small-business owners and employees will need nothing more than a moving map and door-to-door driving directions. For that, I highly recommend something like the Garmin iQue 3600 (see Chapters 9 and 10), which offers not only first-class mapping, but also something else every field worker needs: a solid PDA.

Team Building

Corporations are very big on team-building exercises these days; they give employees a chance to get out of the office, do something fun, and, most important, learn the benefits of teamwork. Perhaps you recall the classic *Simpsons* episode in which Mr. Burns organizes an outdoor retreat for the nuclear plant, randomly pairing off employees who must work together to reach a cabin deep in the woods. It's that kind of thing—only usually without the avalanches.

You may also recall Chapter 5, which was equally classic and hilarious. What if you could somehow combine Geocaching with team building? You could call it, oh, I don't know, Geoteaming. Instead of a single individual using GPS to locate a hidden cache, you could create teams of coworkers and turn the hunt into a friendly competition—one that requires teamwork to succeed.

That's the idea behind PlayTime, Inc.'s Geoteaming (can you believe someone already took my name?). Teams cooperate to find the caches, which contain puzzles or challenges. Then each team must work together to solve the next clue, ultimately leading to a final surprise cache. Sounds like a pretty fun time to me—wish I worked for a corporation. (Nah, come to think of it, no I don't.)

Did you know?

How the Mapmakers Make Maps

Which came first, the chicken or the egg? While you ponder that imponderable, let's try another one: how can GPS be used to make GPS maps? The folks at Navigation Technologies (a.k.a. NAVTECH) know the answer; they're driving millions of miles to create accurate digital maps. This struck me as fairly ironic, seeing as the company relies on GPS technology to make road maps it will turn around and sell or license to GPS hardware makers. This is a great story, one I'm grateful to Navigation Technologies for sharing.

It's just after 10 p.m., and Todd Anderson and John Utich are stumbling bleary-eyed into their hotel rooms near Jackson, Mississippi. They've just returned from logging 10 bone-crunching hours behind the wheel of their company car. They're tired, they're sore, and they're thrilled with the roadway they have managed to cover on this day: 120 miles in all.

Okay, so 120 miles isn't much to your average road warrior, but Anderson and Utich are not your garden-variety road warriors. They don't cruise roadway as much as scrutinize its every inch: every road sign, highway exit, speed restriction—the whole gamut of legal driving maneuvers. As field analysts for Navigation Technologies, their mission is to make the road warrioring of other road warriors that much easier. Using all manner of high-tech gear, they ride the nation's roadways, mapping every element of the roads they drive. For them, the journey *is* the destination. And yeah, 120 miles is a good day.

You may not recognize the name Navigation Technologies, but chances are you've used their flagship product, and maybe you've even come to rely on it. The company's digital maps are ubiquitous among location-based products and services; they enable every in-car navigation system in the U.S. and the lion's share of those in Europe, as well as online mapping solutions like AOL/Mapquest.com and handheld solutions from Motorola, Whistler, and Garmin, among others. Indeed, Navigation Technologies' maps drive virtually every location service launched in the last two years, among them services from Microsoft, Vindigo, Webraska, and Rand McNally.

Navigation Technologies creates and maintains digital road maps for North America and Europe and also for such far-flung regions as South Africa and parts of the Middle East and Asia. In the U.S. alone, field analysts have been known to be on the road for as long as two months at a time, collecting data sun

8

up to sun down, dealing with everything from swarms of bees to machine-gun-toting survivalists to constant inquiries by locals about whether they're lost.

Last year, the company's mapmakers drove 3.5 million miles to collect and maintain its map data, a staggering sum on its own, but one that becomes truly breathtaking when you consider the scrupulous process that governs the creation of a map representing a targeted stretch of road.

The process starts by procuring and analyzing source material to plan the road trips that field analysts will inevitably embark upon to create and qualify a NAVTECH map. Staff call local sources to get a sense of variances before dispatching soldiers from a 400-plus global army of field analysts, among the world's largest array of privately employed digital mapmakers, to drive the roads.

Armed with a battery of high-tech tools, including differential GPS equipment to ensure accurate positioning to an absolute five-meter accuracy standard, the field analysts collect more than 150 attributes for every road segment they drive: legal, logical, and physical turn restrictions; the functional class of the road (superhighway versus feeder road versus local street); access restrictions; gates and toll booths; speed information; lane information; and so on. The map data is put through a coded process and field tested again to ensure accuracy.

Field analysts then populate the collected road data with points of interest that travelers commonly need to know, from the significant (airports, hotels, and tourist attractions) to the more mundane (gas stations, parks and recreation centers, ATMs). Mile by mile and layer by layer, NAVTECH maps are built, checked, and rechecked regularly, a process so painstaking that one customer dubbed NAVTECH the world's most detail-minded company.

Founded in 1985, the company was the first to create a navigable map—that is, a map with the level of detail needed to enable turn-by-turn driving directions. It was the first to initiate a global network of offices to build its maps, the first to employ a uniform standard for its data. It historically has developed methods and tools to enhance its core product—its digital maps—over the years, evidenced most recently by an emerging set of options paramount to the convergence of voice, data, and Internet technologies.

8

A PDA, a GPS, and Thou...

Given the huge increase in the popularity of wine in recent years, it's no surprise to find vineyards turning to the latest technology to help improve their crops—and that includes, believe it or not, GPS. Armed with a Palm PDA, GPS receiver, and ScanControl's CropTrak software, a vineyard can easily record important field data.

"A number of grape growers and vineyard management companies are using our product to track plant phenology, disease instances, pest infestations, and field treatments," says ScanControl general manager Robin Wood. "The system provides an interface where the user simply keys in the type of data that should be recorded in the field. This could be as much or as little data as you want, and it could be related to specific pest counts or something as subjective as a flavor assessment."

Don't laptops usually handle field-data gathering? Wood says PDAs are more robust and more resistant to dust. "Not to mention less bulky and power hungry," she adds. "The form factor is ideal for use in agricultural, inspection, logistics, and many other environments where a semi-wearable device is even more convenient than a clipboard." After you're done recording data, you can synchronize the PDA with CropTrak's desktop database software simply by pressing a button on the PDA docking cradle.

Another CropTrak advantage over traditional laptop systems is the presence of GPS technology, which allows you to cross-reference latitude and longitude with every field record. Translation: you'll know the precise location of, say, a pest infestation or diseased plant. No more guesswork in retracing your steps.

CropTrak costs $299 per PC—it's up to you to supply the Palm PDA and GPS receiver. Best bet: the now-discontinued Palm m500, which you can find online for around $125, and the Magellan GPS Companion, which sells for roughly the same price. Try eBay for both.

Where to Find It

Web Site	Address	What's There
FleetBoss	www.fleetboss.com	Vehicle management systems
Garmin	www.garmin.com	iQue 3600 PDA
Geoteaming	www.playtimeinc.com	Geoteaming
Minorplanet USA	www.minorplanetusa.com	Minorplanet vehicle management
ScanControl	www.scancontrol.com	CropTrack
Televigation	www.telenavtrack.com	TeleNavTrack
Trimble	www.trimble.com	GPS surveying products
Xora	www.xora.com	GPS TimeTrack

Chapter 9

How to Do Everything with Your Garmin iQue 3600

How to...

- Enter data on the iQue
- Work with Graffiti
- Use the onscreen keyboard
- Work with menus and icons
- Use the buttons and toolbar
- Understand synchronization
- Select maps for transfer to the iQue
- Create and modify routes
- Improve battery life
- Charge your iQue while traveling
- Beam contacts and programs
- Work with memory cards

Throughout the book, you've heard me mention the Garmin iQue 3600. It's a PDA built around the Palm Operating System (OS), which itself isn't all that unusual. Palm, Sony, and several other companies also make Palm OS PDAs. But the iQue is the first PDA with a built-in GPS receiver, and that alone makes it special. What's more, it offers by far the best implementation of street mapping and navigation I've seen on any PDA. Plus, thanks to new third-party software (programs created by companies other than Palm and Garmin), it's now possible to use an iQue for marine and outdoor navigation instead of just street mapping (though there are caveats associated with doing so, which I'll discuss later in the chapter).

The iQue is such a uniquely capable device, it deserves its own chapters. Whether you've just taken the shrink-wrap off your iQue or you've been thinking seriously about buying one, you'll find plenty of helpful information in the pages to come.

NOTE   *I'm not going to regurgitate the setup and basic-operation information that's contained in the iQue manual. Instead, I'm going to explain certain key features and why they're important, give you tips on using the iQue to navigate to your destination, and introduce you to the endless capabilities afforded by the Palm OS.*

TIP   *Haven't purchased your iQue yet? At press time, the unit had a list price of $549.99, but I found it selling online for almost $100 less. Visit* **PriceGrabber.com** *and search for iQue—you may be able to save big bucks.*

Introduction to the iQue

Is the Garmin iQue 3600 a GPS receiver with a PDA attached, or is it the other way around? I tend to look upon it as the latter: a PDA that also has splendid GPS capabilities. Thus, let's start by discussing the iQue's role as a PDA: what this functionality means, why it's important, and how you can use it.

Put simply, a PDA is a pocket-sized electronic organizer that enables you to manage addresses, appointments, expenses, tasks, and memos. If you've ever used a Franklin Planner or similar kind of paper-bound organizer, you get the idea.

However, because a PDA—in this case, the iQue—is electronic, there's no paper or ink involved. Instead, you write directly on the device's screen, using a small plastic stylus that takes the place of a pen. A key advantage here, of course, is that you're able to store all of your important personal and business information on a device that's much smaller and lighter than a paper planner.

What's more, you can easily share that information with your Windows-based computer. The iQue is not self-contained: it can *synchronize* with a desktop computer and keep information current on both sides. This is an important advantage, because it effectively turns your iQue into an extension of the computer you use every day. Changes and additions made to your desktop data are reflected in the iQue, and vice versa (see Figure 9-1).

9

TIP   *Although the iQue doesn't support Macintosh systems, a third-party solution is available that does: The Missing Sync for iQue 3600. This $30 utility enables the iQue to synchronize with Macs. However, there's a major caveat: it doesn't include map support, meaning that you won't be able to download maps from your Mac to the iQue.*

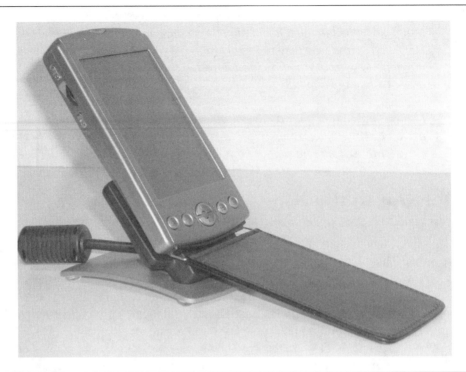

FIGURE 9-1 The iQue connects to a PC via its HotSync cradle, which allows data to be synchronized on both devices. It also charges the iQue.

Saying that an iQue is an extension of your PC is only a half-truth; in reality, it's more like a pocket computer. That's because it's capable of running software written by parties other than Palm and Garmin, and those parties (known as software developers) number in the tens of thousands. There are literally thousands of programs and databases that extend your iQue's capabilities, from spreadsheet managers and expense trackers to electronic-book readers and web browsers. Got five minutes to kill? You can play a quick game of the classic *Bejeweled*. Need to check your e-mail while traveling? Just plug in your cell phone for wireless connectivity.

What makes all this possible is the Palm Operating System, or Palm OS for short.

Did you know?

What's an Operating System?

Windows is an operating system. Mac OS X is an operating system. The core software that drives any computer is an operating system. Hence, when I refer to the Palm OS, I'm talking about the software that's built right into the device—the brains behind the brawn. The Palm OS itself not only controls the iQue's fundamental operations, such as what happens when you press a button or tap the screen, but it also supplies the built-in applications (the address book, memo pad, date book, and so on—all of which I'll discuss in detail later in this chapter).

The Palm OS is the key ingredient that links many PDAs, whether they're manufactured by Palm, Handspring, Sony, or one of the other companies licensed to use the Palm OS.

> NOTE   *These licensees have been granted permission by Palm to use the Palm OS in hardware of their own design. It's kind of like the arrangement that allows PCs from a hundred different companies to all run Windows. The iQue is a Palm OS-based model that happens to offer GPS as its major attraction.*

An iQue looks quite a bit different than, say, a Palm Zire 71, but on the inside they're fundamentally the same. They both use the Palm OS, and therefore operate in a similar fashion and are capable of running all the same software.

> NOTE   *The exception to this rule, of course, is Garmin's mapping software, which runs only on the iQue. Other Palm OS PDAs can run other mapping software, as discussed in other chapters.*

In case you're wondering, the iQue employs Palm OS version 5.2.1, which is virtually identical to the version used in the latest PDAs from Palm and Sony. As you start to fill up your iQue with extra software (which I'll get to later in the chapter), make sure you choose programs that are compatible with that version of the OS.

9

The iQue's Key Features

You already know about the iQue's claim to fame, of course—its GPS receiver.
Flip up that antenna in the back and you're going from here to there in style, baby.
But the iQue sports some other key features that are well worth discussing—and
understanding. Check out Figure 9-2, then meet me at the next paragraph.

- **The screen**   The iQue sports a 320-by-480-pixel *touchscreen*, meaning
  that you can tap or write on the screen and the OS will recognize your
  input. The screen's high resolution and support for 65,000 colors make it
  ideal not just for viewing maps, but also for viewing digital photos, playing
  games, and even reading e-books.

- **The jog dial**   Located on the left side of the iQue, the jog dial is a little
  black wheel that you can rotate up and down. The wheel also acts as a
  button, as you can press it straight in. The key benefit of the jog dial is that
  it enables one-handed operation of the iQue. When you're viewing a map,
  for instance, you can use the jog dial to zoom in and out. In other instances,
  you can use it to launch programs, scroll through and select records, and
  flip e-book pages.

- **The expansion slot**   The iQue includes a Secure Digital (SD) expansion
  slot, which was built primarily with memory expansion in mind but can
  also be used for accessories like WiFi networking cards and even digital
  cameras. Although the iQue has quite a bit of internal memory—32 megabytes
  (MB), to be exact—that gets used up fairly quickly as you begin to load
  maps (and third-party software) on the unit. A map of southeast Michigan,
  for instance, consumes about 13MB. If you want to keep a lot of map data
  on hand, you'll want to invest an SD memory card. My advice: always buy
  the largest one you can afford.

TIP   *One of my favorite spots to shop for SD cards is* **eCost.com**. *At press time,
  I found a 128MB card selling for about $50, and a 256MB card for about
  $67. See "What Price Memory?" later in this chapter for more details.*

- **The IR port**   All Palm OS PDAs, the iQue included, have an *infrared (IR)*
  communications port. This enables you to *beam* information wirelessly from
  one PDA to another. What kind of information? Any record stored in your
  address book, calendar, memo pad, and so on. In fact, you can even beam
  your "business card" to other PDA users. You can also use the IR port to
  beam actual programs and play two-player games. Pretty cool stuff. You
  haven't lived until you've beamed.

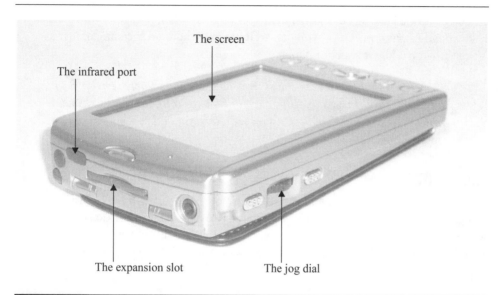

The screen

The infrared port

The expansion slot

The jog dial

FIGURE 9-2   It's helpful to have a clear understanding of some of the iQue's non-GPS features, like its jog dial and expansion slot.

9

A Guided Tour of the Hardware

The iQue is pretty simple device. It has a screen, a handful of buttons, that flip-up GPS antenna in back, and the various items discussed in the preceding section. Tour's over, right? Wrong. Let's take a quick look the buttons and screen, which play a huge role in your use and mastery of the iQue.

When you use a desktop computer, you use a mouse to navigate and a keyboard to enter data. With an iQue, you use a plastic-tipped stylus for both navigation and data entry. If you want to access, say, the To Do List program, you tap the To Do List icon that appears on the screen. If you want to remind yourself to buy milk, you write the words on the screen.

NOTE   *Many novice users think they have to double-tap the application icons, just like double-clicking with a mouse. Not true! A single tap is all you ever need when working with an iQue.*

The Difference Between Tapping and Writing

Tapping the screen is the equivalent of clicking a mouse. You tap icons to launch programs, tap to access menus and select options in them, and tap to place your cursor in specific places. Writing on the screen is, of course, like putting a pen to paper. However, most writing you do on an iQue takes place in a specific area of the screen, which we discuss in the next section. But when you're working in, say, a sketchpad or paint program, you can scribble anywhere on the screen, just as though it were a blank sheet of paper.

 *Don't press too hard with the stylus. The screen is fairly sensitive, and light pressure is usually all it takes to register a tap or stylus stroke. If you press too hard, you could wind up with a scratched screen—the bane of every iQue user.*

The Graffiti Area

Ladies and gentlemen, boys and girls, I give you…the *Graffiti area.* This is a special portion of the screen that's used exclusively for entering text and numbers. Graffiti is the handwriting-recognition software that's built into the Palm OS, and therefore into the iQue. However, whereas some other PDAs have "silkscreened" (that is, permanent) Graffiti areas, the iQue has a virtual Graffiti area, meaning that it appears and disappears as necessary. Take a look:

 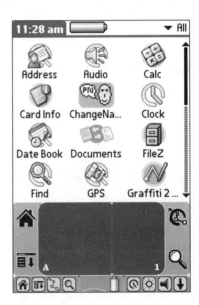

Virtual Graffiti is really slick, as it lets you enter data when you need to and then tucks out of the way to give you extra screen estate for icons, text, movies, and so on. To show or hide the Graffiti area, tap the arrow in the lower-right corner of the screen.

NOTE *While most of the Garmin's built-in programs support the virtual Graffiti area, some—most notably Documents To Go—do not. That means the aforementioned show/hide arrow appears dimmed, and that the Graffiti area can't be hidden. By the time you read this, however, DataViz (the makers of Documents To Go) may have a software patch available that remedies this issue. As for other programs, look for those that specifically say they support 320 by 480 pixel screens.*

Graffiti makes it possible to enter information using the stylus, but you can do so only within the confines of the Graffiti area (shown in Figure 9-3).

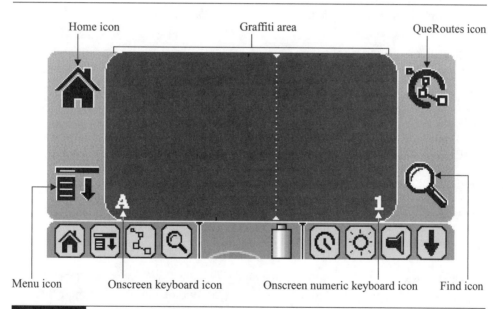

Home icon   Graffiti area   QueRoutes icon

Menu icon   Onscreen keyboard icon   Onscreen numeric keyboard icon   Find icon

FIGURE 9-3   The Graffiti area is where you write data into your handheld device and access various options like menus and "home base."

NOTE   *I'll tell you more about Graffiti—how to use it and alternatives to it—later in the chapter. For now, we'll focus on the Graffiti area itself.*

What about those icons on either side of the Graffiti area? They serve some important functions. Here's an overview.

The Home Icon   Represented by a picture of a house and located in the upper-left corner of the Graffiti area, the Home icon is the one you'll tap more often than any other. From whatever program you're currently running, the Home icon (see Figure 9-3) takes you back to the main screen—home base, as it were (hence the house picture).

TIP   *When you're using any program, tapping the Home icon returns you to the main screen. When you're viewing that screen, however, tapping the Home icon cycles through the application categories, which are designated in the top-right corner of the screen. You can accomplish the same cycling effect by pressing the Esc button on the side of the iQue.*

The Menu Icon   Tapping the icon in the lower-left corner of the Graffiti area— a.k.a. the Menu icon (see Figure 9-3)—gives you access to the drop-down menus that are part of the Palm OS. These menus vary somewhat from program to program in the options they provide, but they're fairly consistent within the core Palm OS applications.

TIP   *The Menu icon works like a toggle switch. If you accidentally tap it or just want to make the drop-down menus go away, simply tap it again.*

TIP   *Another way to access menus is by tapping the title bar in the top-left corner of whatever program is currently running—not unlike the way you use a mouse to access menus on a PC.*

The QueRoutes Icon   As you might have guessed, the QueRoutes icon (see Figure 9-3) isn't a standard Palm OS feature. (You won't find it on Palm or Sony PDAs, that's for sure.) When you tap it, you gain access to the iQue's various routing features, which vary depending on whether you already have a route established. We'll talk more about routing and this button later in the chapter.

NOTE   *The toolbar also includes a QueRoutes icon (see "The Toolbar" later in this chapter), which functions identically. In fact, you can access the QueRoutes menu in yet a third way: by pressing the Que button repeatedly until the menu appears.*

The Find Icon   Finally, we get to the little magnifying glass in the lower-right corner. Because an iQue can store such vast amounts of information, and because sifting through all that information to find what you're looking for can be tedious, it offers a handy little search feature called the Find icon (see Figure 9-3). When you tap it, the QueFind menu appears. Tap Palm OS Find, write the name, number, or other information you're looking for, and then tap OK. (I'll tell you about the rest of the QueFind menu later.)

9

> **NOTE**   *As with QueRoutes, the Find icon is duplicated down on the toolbar. That's handy, as it enables you to access the feature even when the Graffiti area is hidden.*

The A and 1 Buttons   The lower-left corner of the Graffiti area (see Figure 9-3) contains a little *A*. The lower-right corner contains a 1. You use these to bring up the onscreen keyboards (which you can use in place of—or in addition to—Graffiti for data input). Tapping the A launches the QWERTY keyboard; tapping the 1 brings up the numeric keyboard.

> **NOTE**   *You can't access either keyboard unless there's a cursor in a data-entry field. If you're viewing the main screen—the one with all the icons—and tap either keyboard button, you'll just hear a beep. Try starting a new memo and then tapping one of the two buttons.*

The Toolbar

Across the bottom of the screen, below the Graffiti area, lies the iQue toolbar (see Figure 9-4). The first four icons, from left to right, duplicate those found in the Graffiti area. Why? Because those are features you'll want easy access to when the Graffiti area is hidden. They function exactly the same way in both places, and it doesn't matter which one you use or when you use it.

In the middle of the toolbar is an arc that looks like, oh, say, the top edge of a planet. When the GPS receiver is active, you'll see little animated satellites flashing around it. You can also tap this GPS Status icon (whether the receiver is active or not) to gain immediate access to the QueGPS screen, which shows the satellite acquisition status and other basic information:

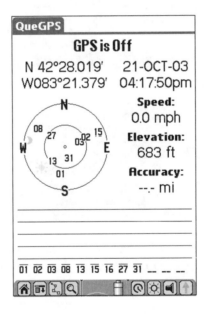

Next comes the Battery Gauge icon, which you'll want to keep an eye on. The iQue's only significant shortcoming is battery life.

TIP   *You can improve battery life significantly by reducing screen brightness, which I'll be discussing three or four sentences from now.*

The icon that's fourth from the right and looks like a little clock is, in fact, a clock. Tap it to see the time and date. Next comes the Brightness icon, which pops up a little onscreen slider you use to, well, adjust brightness. You can crank this

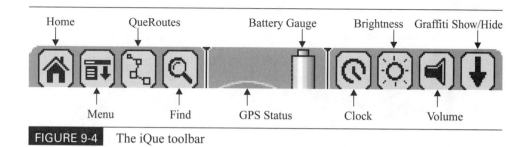

FIGURE 9-4   The iQue toolbar

way down when you're outdoors (or turn off the screen's backlight altogether by holding down the power button for two seconds), or crank it up when you're in the car and need maximum brightness.

Finally, there's the Volume icon, which you can use to adjust eight different volume settings:

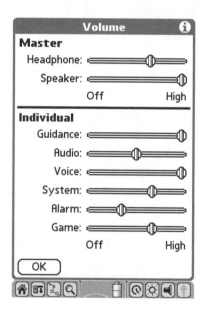

The Buttons

The iQue's buttons may seem self-explanatory, and for the most part they are. But let's take a quick peek at them so I can teach you a few tricks. Figure 9-5 shows the four main ones—Date Book, Address Book, To Do List, and Que—plus the scroll controls.

Date Book button   Scroll Up button   Que button

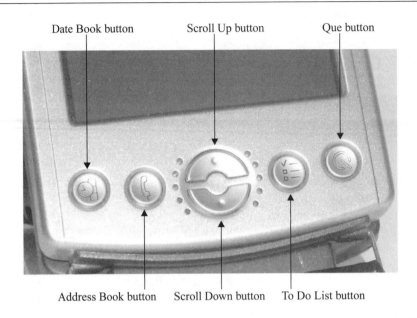

Address Book button   Scroll Down button   To Do List button

FIGURE 9-5   Learn the iQue's buttons, young Jedi. They will serve you well. (Yes, I'm that big of a geek.)

You use these so-called application buttons to instantly launch the core applications. Let's say you want to look up a number in your address book. You can turn on your iQue, tap the Home icon to get to the main screen, and then find and tap Address. Or you can take the much faster way: simply press the Address button, which is represented by a picture of a telephone handset. This single button press serves the dual function of turning on the iQue *and* loading the Address Book program.

The same holds true for the three other buttons (see Figure 9-5), which launch Date Book, To Do List, and whatever Que screen you viewed last. You can use them at any time, whether the iQue is on or off, to quickly switch among the four core programs.

As for the scroll buttons, they're the two half-moons located between the two pairs of application buttons, and they're used to cycle through multiple screens of data. If you're looking at, say, a memo that's too long to fit on the screen in its entirety, you can use the Scroll Down button to move down to the next section—not unlike turning pages in a book. The Scroll Up button simply moves you back a page.

How to ... **Reprogram Your Handheld's Buttons**

Want the To Do List button to load your e-book viewer? Or the Routes button to load the built-in calculator? You can reprogram an iQue's four hardware buttons and Routes button to run any installed program. On the Home screen, just tap the Prefs icon, then select Buttons from the drop-down list in the top-right corner of the Preferences screen. Now assign your desired applications to the various buttons. That's all there is to it! If you ever want to undo these changes, just return to the same screen and tap Default.

NOTE *In many programs, onscreen arrows and scroll bars serve the same function. Instead of having to press the scroll buttons, you can simply tap the arrows or slide the bar with your stylus. The approach you use is largely a matter of personal preference; try both and decide which you like better.*

TIP *You can skip the scroll controls, both onscreen and off, altogether and just use the jog dial to scroll within documents. It's more convenient and usually much more comfortable, and it doesn't require two hands.*

9

Getting to Know the Operating System

I'm not exaggerating when I say working with an iQue is roughly eight gazillion times easier than working with a traditional computer. There's no confusing menu system to wade through, no accidentally forgetting to save your document, no clicking the Start button to turn the thing off (don't get me started on that one). Following are some of the fundamental—but still important—differences between an iQue and a PC:

- When you turn on a PC, you have to wait a few minutes for it to boot up. When you turn on an iQue, it's ready to roll instantaneously. Same goes for shutting it off: just press the Power button, and the screen goes dark. There's no lengthy shutdown procedure. And no data is lost, ever, unless you erase it yourself.

- On a PC, when you're done working with a program (say, your word processor), you must save your data before exiting that program. On an iQue, this isn't necessary. Data is retained at all times, even if you, say, switch to your to-do list while in the middle of writing a memo. When you return to Memo Pad, you find your document exactly as you left it. This holds true even if you turn off the iQue!

> **NOTE** *There are a handful of exceptions to this rule. In the office suite Documents To Go, for instance, you do have to save the open file before exiting.*

- In that same vein, you don't "exit" an iQue program so much as switch to another one. This is a hard concept for seasoned computer users to grasp, as we've all been taught to shut down our software when we're done with it. There's no exit procedure on an iQue, and you'll never find that word in a drop-down menu. When you finish working in one program, you simply tap the Home icon to return to home base or press one of the application buttons.

> **NOTE** *We strongly encourage experimentation. Whereas wandering too far off the beaten track in Windows can lead to disaster, it's virtually impossible to get "lost" using an iQue. So tap here, explore there, and just have fun checking things out. Because there's no risk of losing data or running too many programs at once (impossible in the Palm OS), you should have no fear of fouling anything up. Play!*

The Icons

Icons are, of course, little pictures used to represent things. In the case of the Palm OS, they're used largely to represent the installed programs. Thus, on the Home screen, you see icons labeled Address, Calc, Date Book, and so on—and all you do is tap one to access that particular program.

> **NOTE**   *Say, didn't you just learn that you're supposed to press a button below the screen to load Date Book? In the Palm OS, there are often multiple ways to accomplish the same task. In this case, you can load certain programs either by tapping their onscreen icons or using their hardware-button equivalents.*

The Menus

As with most computers, you use drop-down menus to access program-specific options and settings. In most Palm OS programs, tapping the Menu icon (or the program's title bar at the top of the screen) makes a small menu bar appear at the top of the screen. You navigate this bar using the stylus as you would a mouse, tapping each menu item to make its list of options drop down (shown on the next page) and then tapping the option you want to access.

> **NOTE**   *These menus are not to be confused with those in the upper-right corner of the screen, which are usually used to select application categories, preferences, and so on.*

Entering Data into Your iQue

One of the first things you'll want to do with your new handheld is enter data—phone numbers, e-mail addresses, memos, to-dos, and so on—into your various applications. Hey, don't look so surprised. The core programs, such as Date Book, Address Book, Memo Pad, and To Do List, rely on you to fill them with interesting things you can later reference.

There are three primary ways to enter data into an iQue:

- Write it using Graffiti, the built-in handwriting-recognition software.

- "Tap type" using the onscreen keyboard.

- Enter data into Palm Desktop (or Outlook) on your PC and then HotSync the data to your handheld. This is the preferred method for people who are just starting out, because it's the path of least resistance. If you have an old-fashioned paper address book, for instance, and you want to copy all the names and addresses to your iQue, it's much easier to enter them into your PC than into the device itself. Similarly, if you have an electronic address book from another program or PDA, you can probably import the data into Palm Desktop or Outlook and then HotSync it all to your new PDA.

How to ... Find Out How Much Memory Your Handheld Has Left

As you start to add records and install new software on your iQue, you may wonder how to check the amount of memory that's available. From the Home screen, tap Menu | App | Info. The screen that appears shows the total amount of memory on your device and how much of it is free. Notice, too, some of the other options that appear when you tap Menu | App. There's Delete (used to delete third-party programs), Beam (used to beam third-party programs), and Copy (used to copy programs between internal memory and optional SD memory cards).

9

TIP   *You can also connect a full-sized keyboard to your iQue and type directly into the device—no PC required. The Palm Wireless Keyboard is a great option, as it folds up to pocket size but still provides a full-sized set of keys.*

If you're on the go, you definitely need to use either Graffiti or the onscreen keyboard to enter data. If you're at your desk, though, you might find entering data into the Palm Desktop and then HotSyncing easier because your desktop computer sports a full-sized keyboard.

Using Graffiti

Graffiti is a specialized handwriting-recognition system that enables you to enter text into a Palm handheld virtually error free. The iQue employs Graffiti 2, the second-generation version of the software, which allows you to write using fairly natural block characters. Want to know what those characters look like? Find the cheat-sheet that came with your iQue (and consider pasting it to the underside of the screen cover), or do this: with the Graffiti area showing, draw a line from inside it to the top of the screen. The iQue's built-in cheat sheet will appear.

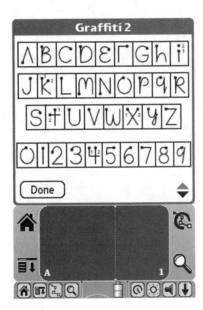

Here, in a nutshell, is how Graffiti works:

■ To actually enter data with Graffiti, your cursor has to be in a text field (for instance, in a memo or a to-do item).

■ You write characters one on top of the other within the Graffiti area. Most people find this weird at first, as they're accustomed to writing left to right.

■ You write letters and certain punctuation marks in the left side of the Graffiti area (which is slightly larger than the right). You write numbers and certain punctuation marks in the right side of the Graffiti area.

TIP *To get capital letters, write your letters across the dotted line separating the two sides of the Graffiti area.*

■ Your best bet for learning Graffiti is to experiment. Load the Memo Pad, tap New, and then just start writing. Remember to use the same block characters shown on the cheat sheet—*not* your usual handwriting. If you make a mistake, use the backspace stroke: a simple horizontal line drawn from right to left in either side of the Graffiti area.

NOTE *As you write in the Graffiti area, you'll notice a trail of "ink" beneath your stylus. When you lift your stylus, the trail disappears. This is the iQue's way of making data input a bit more like pen on paper. Unfortunately, it doesn't work very well, because the iQue doesn't draw the ink trail fast enough, so you wind up with what looks like a child's scribbles. If anything, this almost makes Graffiti input more confusing, because you don't get an accurate depiction of your characters as you make them. Hopefully, Garmin will issue a software patch that speeds up the ink-trail system.*

9

General Tips and Tricks for Graffiti

Despite Graffiti's simplicity, a few tips and tricks can make writing on your iQue a lot easier:

■ Draw your characters as large as possible, especially if you're having trouble with Graffiti misinterpreting what you're writing. Use almost the entire Graffiti area (top to bottom).

■ Don't cross the dotted line between the letter and number portion of the Graffiti area—unless you want a capital letter, that is. Make sure you write your characters on the correct side of the fence to get the characters you want.

■ Don't write at a slant. Some handwriting-recognition engines can account for characters being drawn at an angle to the baseline, but Graffiti can't. Vertical lines should be perpendicular to the Graffiti area baseline. In other words, make your characters straight up and down, as though you were in second grade and writing on ruled paper (and getting graded on it).

■ Don't write too fast. Graffiti doesn't care about your speed, but if you write too fast, you won't have sufficient control over the shape of your characters, and you can make mistakes.

Using the Onscreen Keyboard

Some people never get the knack of Graffiti, and others just plain don't like it. For both sides, there's the onscreen keyboard, which enables you to tap-type instead of write. You can use either method as you please, and even bounce back and forth between them as the need arises. For instance, even if you're adept with Graffiti, you may want to switch to the keyboard to, say, enter a password or record a phone number.

All it takes to use the onscreen keyboard is a tap. At the bottom of the Graffiti area, you see the letter *A* on the left and the number 1 on the right. Tap either spot to call up the appropriate keyboard (alpha or numeric).

NOTE *The keyboard appears only in situations where it's appropriate—specifically, when a cursor is in a data field. Just like with Graffiti. If no application is open in which you can insert text, you simply hear a beep when you tap a keyboard launcher.*

Once a keyboard is open, you can switch between letters and numbers by tapping the selector at the bottom of the screen. A set of international characters is available as well.

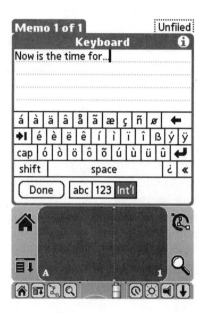

Remember the following tips about the onscreen keyboard:

- You can still use Graffiti even while the keyboard is active.

- Use the SHIFT key on the keyboard in the same way you use it on a real keyboard: tap it to create an uppercase letter.

- The CAP key is actually the CAPS LOCK key, which makes all subsequent letters uppercase until you tap it again.

- If you're typing with the CAPS LOCK on and you want to make a single character lowercase, tap the SHIFT key.

- The numeric keyboard provides access to special symbols and punctuation.

Introducing Palm Desktop

So far, we've talked mostly about the iQue itself: the hardware, the operating system, and so on. There's one area left to cover before you venture into real-world iQue use: Palm Desktop.

Wondrous as an iQue is in its own right, what makes it even more special is its ability to synchronize with your computer. This means all the data entered into your iQue can be copied to your PC, and vice versa. The software that fields all this data on the computer side is Palm Desktop. (If you use Microsoft Outlook or another contact manager, you needn't use Palm Desktop at all.)

Viewed in a vacuum, Palm Desktop resembles a traditional personal information manager (PIM) or contact-management program. It effectively replicates all the core functionality of the Palm OS, providing you with a phone list, appointment calendar, to-do list, and memo pad. If you've never used such software before, you'll no doubt find Palm Desktop an invaluable addition, because it helps keep you organized at home or in the office (whereas an iQue keeps you organized while traveling). Here's what Palm Desktop looks like alongside its iQue equivalent:

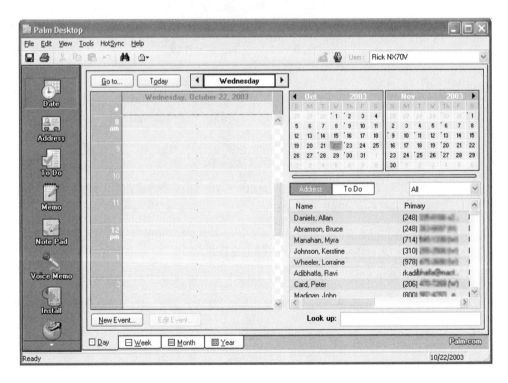

A Word About Synchronization

What happens when you synchronize your iQue with your PC? Essentially, three things:

- Any new entries made in your iQue are added to Palm Desktop.

- Any new entries made in Palm Desktop are added to your iQue.

- Any existing records modified in one place (the iQue, for example) are modified in the other (the desktop, same example), with the most recent changes taking precedence.

Therefore, synchronizing regularly ensures that your information is kept current, both in your iQue and in Palm Desktop.

NOTE   *One thing that can be a bit confusing about Palm Desktop is its Note Pad feature, as there's no corresponding application on the iQue. In tailoring Palm Desktop to work with the iQue, Garmin must have forgotten to remove the Note Pad module. There's not much you can do with it, so just ignore it.*

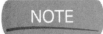

Already entrenched in Microsoft Office? The iQue comes with software—a special version of Puma Technologies' IntelliSync—that allows direct synchronization with Office (bypassing Palm Desktop). If you have a different contact manager (such as Lotus Organizer), you may need to upgrade to a different sync program, such as the full version of Puma's IntelliSync.

Map Selection in Palm Desktop

I find Palm Desktop to be a blissfully easy program to use, so much so that I'm not going to spend a lot of time explaining its features. However, I do want to talk about map selection: how it works, how to choose the right maps, and how to manage their storage on your iQue. Before we go any further, however, it's important that you install Palm Desktop and then perform the Install Detailed Maps option as detailed in the iQue Setup Guide.

How Map Selection Works

Garmin supplies street-level maps for all of the United States and parts of Canada. It would be nice if your iQue could hold a continent's worth of city streets, but that's just not possible (yet). It does, however, come with a basemap of North America, which shows the main highways, cities, waterways, points of interest (such as airports), and so on.

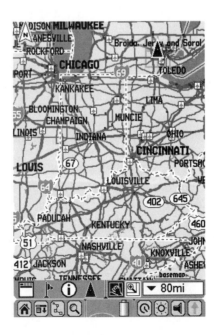

This is an important factor to consider as you plan your map selection. Suppose you're driving from New York to Los Angeles. Do you need street-level maps for the entire route? No, just for the start and end cities, because the iQue already has you covered for the highways that span the distance. In other words, you can pick and choose the maps you want to download to your iQue, and they don't necessarily have to be adjacent.

Let's walk through the map-selection process, which, surprisingly, isn't explained anywhere in Garmin's printed documentation.

1. Start Palm Desktop, then click the Map Install button on the left toolbar to load Garmin's Map Install wizard. Click Next when prompted to do so.

   Now you're presented with the Map Install window (see Figure 9-6), which is where you'll select the maps you want to download to your iQue. Notice

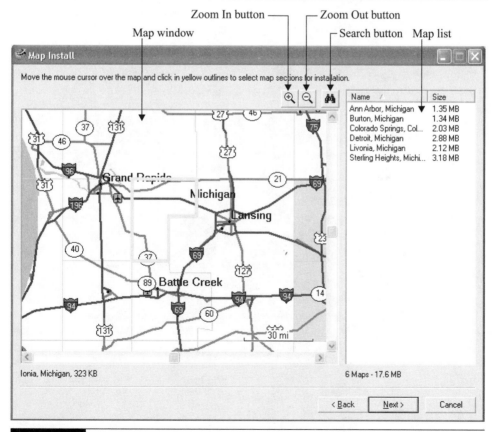

9

The Map Install window is where you choose maps to download to your iQue.

that as you move your cursor around the map, little yellow sections become highlighted. For any given section, you'll also see a city name and file size just below the map. This information is somewhat misleading, as the city that's listed isn't the only one contained in that map section. To get a more accurate idea of what's contained in any section, you need to zoom in.

TIP   *If you configured your iQue to synchronize with Outlook, you don't necessarily have to run Palm Desktop to install maps. Instead, you can choose Start | All Programs | MapSource | North American City Select v5 Map Installation Wizard.*

2. To zoom, use the up-down and left-right scroll bars to center the desired area in the map window, then click the magnifying glass with the plus sign a few times. The more you zoom in, the more detail you'll see. If you zoom in too far, you may lose the ability to see the boundaries of the map selection as designated by the yellow outline. If this happens, just zoom out again by clicking the magnifying glass with the minus sign.

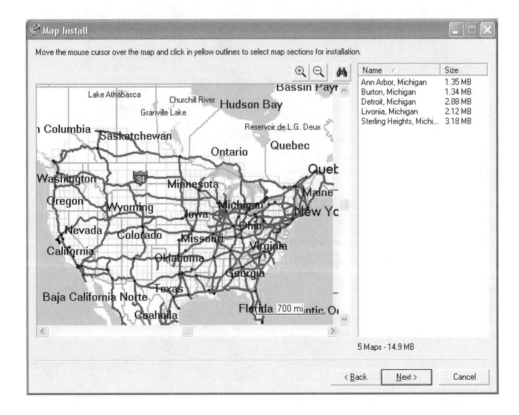

3. To select any given map area, point to it with your cursor and then click.

Maps for that area will immediately appear in the map list to the right of the map window. At the same time, the selected map area will become highlighted in pink. Now this map is ready for download to your iQue (after a few final steps, that is).

You may want to select more than one map. For example, I live in a suburb of Detroit. I could choose just the map that contains my hometown and the immediate surrounding areas, but what happens if I drive across town? I actually need five maps to get the coverage I need. Fortunately, selecting multiple maps is simple—just point and click. The only caveat is storage space: more maps require more memory, and the iQue has only so much internal space available. See "Managing Map Storage" later in this chapter for information on dealing with this issue.

4. Select any additional maps by clicking the areas for which you want maps.

Meanwhile, here's what the iQue map screen might look like if I had an unmapped area:

9

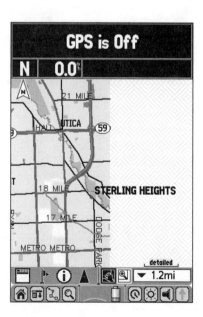

5. Once you've selected the maps you want to download, click Next. You're then presented with two fields: User and Destination. User should show the

HotSync name you chose when you first synchronized your iQue—if it doesn't, you probably have another PDA connected to your PC. Make sure to select your iQue HotSync name. Your choice for Destination is key: do you want the maps copied to the iQue's internal memory or to an SD expansion card? If you have an SD card, you should definitely use it (see "Managing Map Storage"). Choose your desired destination, then click Next.

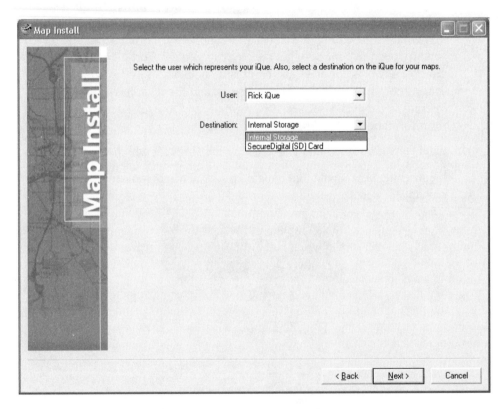

6. The software will go through the process of building map files (which it refers to as index files) for your iQue. This can take several minutes, depending on the number of maps selected and the speed of your computer. When the process is done, you'll see a message indicating that your maps are ready; now go ahead and HotSync.

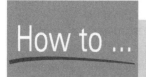

Delete Maps from Your iQue

Suppose you're back in New York after that long trip to L.A. You no longer need the L.A. maps on your iQue, so you decide to delete them to free up some storage space. Good thinking. Unfortunately, you can't do this on your iQue—although it enables you to delete all the detailed maps in one fell swoop, it doesn't let you delete individual ones. For that, you have to go back to the Map Install wizard, deselect the L.A. map (which you do just by clicking it), and then follow the rest of the steps. The software will rebuild all the map files and then require you to HotSync again. This is something of a hassle, to be sure, but it's also not something you're likely to have to do very often.

| NOTE | *The HotSync process itself will take longer than usual—possibly much longer, if you're installing a lot of map data. Indeed, if you've queued up, say, 50 megabytes' worth of maps and you're downloading them to a storage card (which is the only way you could copy that much data), the HotSync could take several minutes.* |

9

Managing Map Storage

As noted in the preceding example, I need to keep five metropolitan Detroit maps on my iQue so that I'm sure to have complete street-level coverage wherever I go in the area. These maps tally to about 13MB, which is a pretty big chunk of the roughly 23MB the iQue has available out of the box. (Technically speaking, the iQue has 32MB of RAM, but about 9MB are reserved for various behind-the-scenes functions, so they're inaccessible to us memory-starved users.) Factor in the 5MB North America basemap, and now I'm left with only about 5MB for games, e-books, and all the other goodies I'll tell you about later in the chapter.

Needless to say, I'm a prime candidate for a memory card. As mentioned in "The iQue's Key Features," you can buy a 128MB card for around $50. That's enough storage space for several states' worth of map data, with room left over for

MP3s and whatever else you want to carry. That's right: a memory card can be used for more than one kind of data.

Simply insert the card into the iQue's memory slot (you'll have to remove the plastic insert first), and then choose SD card when you reach the Destination step during map selection. HotSync Manager will automatically place the map files on the card instead of in the iQue's internal memory.

> **NOTE** *Maps don't have to be installed to one place or the other. The iQue can recognize map data in internal memory and on an expansion card.*

From Here to There: Routing with Your iQue

Routing on the iQue is a breeze, which is one reason I'm so fond of the device. By *routing,* I mean getting turn-by-turn driving directions from your current location to, well, anywhere. With just a few taps of the stylus, the iQue can route you to:

- **Any street address**   The maps you download to the iQue include a database of street addresses, meaning that you can route to pretty much anywhere within the map area just by entering a house (or business) number and street name.

- **Any contact in your address book**   This is one of the iQue's signature features. Your address book already contains the addresses of friends, clients, and everyone else in your life. The iQue can route you directly to any one of them.

- **Points of interest**   Garmin's street-level maps include huge listings of points of interest: restaurants, hotels, movie theaters, airports, gas stations—you name it. And you don't have to know the name of the place, either—you can find whatever's nearest to your current location. In a word: wow.

In the sections to come, I'm going to show you how to create these routes, modify the iQue's GPS settings, improve battery life, and make the most of your in-car usage. A lot of this information is covered quite clearly in Garmin's manual, so I'm not going to rehash it. My goal here is to help you understand a few concepts and procedures that aren't readily obvious.

Before You Hit the Road

Before you start using your iQue for in-car navigation, I highly recommend that you consider one particular accessory. It's the Garmin Auto Navigation Kit, and it provides a dashboard mount for the iQue, a cigarette-lighter adapter for constant power and charging, and a volume-adjustable speaker so you can hear driving directions more clearly.

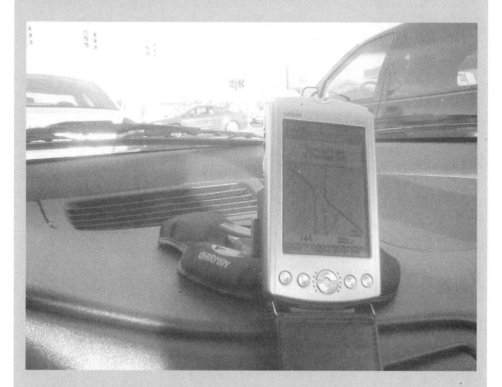

The kit is available from Garmin's online store for $79.99—not cheap, I know, but consider this: your iQue will be right up on the dashboard where you can view it safely (and it has an unobstructed view of the sky), and it'll be fully charged and ready for other duties when you reach your destination. Unless a passenger is doing all the navigating, I'd say don't leave home without this car kit.

Oh, and here's a little tip: at press time, **Amazon.com** was selling the kit for $59.99. Did I just save you the cost of this book or what!

Routing to a Street Address

Ready to hit the road? Once your maps are loaded and your battery is charged (or you have the aforementioned car kit), it's time to pick a destination. Let's start with a street address. Here's the procedure along with a few important notes:

1. Tap the Find icon (see Figure 9-3), either the one on the toolbar or in the Graffiti area.

2. You'll see the QueFind screen. Tap the Addresses icon if you want to navigate to a specific street address, or Intersections if that's what you'd prefer. (Suppose a friend wants to meet you at the new Starbucks store. She doesn't know the address, but she knows roughly where it is—"Corner of Tenth and Main." That's when you'd choose Intersections.)

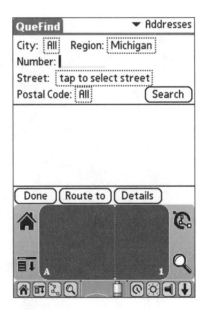

3. Now you're presented with a blank form containing several fields, with your cursor in the Number field. Using either Graffiti or the numeric keyboard, enter the address (house or building number only) of your destination.

4. Now tap the box next to the Street field: "tap to select street." A window will appear where you can enter the street name. With each letter (or number), notice how the list below the field is updated. The iQue is trying to find the

street without your having to enter the entire name. As soon as you see the street name in the list, tap it; then tap OK.

5. Back at the main form, you might think you need to select a city, region, and postal code as well. You probably don't. If you just tap Search, you should see the complete street address appear below the form. If, however, you're dealing with a fairly generic street name (Main Street comes to mind), you may wind up with lots of matches. At that point, you may want to enter a city name or postal code to narrow the search. Then tap Search again after you enter the additional info.

6. Tap the correct address from the list (you'll see it highlighted in yellow) and then tap Route To. Presto! In a few seconds (or perhaps even as long as minute, depending on the distance), the iQue will calculate the route, turn by turn, from your present location. To recap, all you did was tap Find, enter an address, tap Search, and then tap Route To. Pretty tough, huh?

NOTE   *The iQue couldn't find the address you were looking for? That's probably because the map data for that address wasn't installed. Remember, just because there's map data for your present location doesn't mean it's there for your desired destination. You may have to go back to the Map Install wizard and add more maps.*

Routing to a Contact's Address

Want to drive to a contact's home or office? The iQue gives you a couple ways to create such a route. This feature genuinely excites me, because it's exactly the way GPS should work. Instead of requiring you to enter data twice, it draws on data you already have.

Routing to a contact's address is fairly easy once you understand the process. This is what's going to happen:

1. You're going to find the desired contact in your iQue address book; then you're going to look up the address in the map database.

2. Once you've found the address, you're going to designate it as a Location for that contact.

3. When that's done, you'll be able to use the iQue's Route To function for that contact.

Got it? This can be a bit confusing, so I want to make sure you understand the steps before we go through them. Unless you tag a contact with a Location setting, you can't route to it. Okay, then; on to the step-by-step:

1. Press the Address Book button, then find and tap the entry for the contact you want to visit.

2. Tap the Location button.

The Set Location window opens. Now you're going to copy the contact's address information to the same QueFind form used to look up street addresses manually.

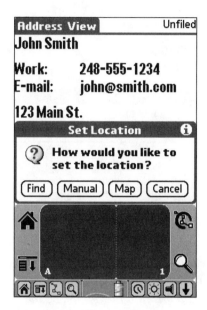

3. Tap the Find button to display the QueFind form.

4. The QueFind form appears with the key fields already filled in. Tap Search, tap the correct address from the list that appears (not necessary if only one address appears), and then tap OK.

5. You'll now see the address as represented on a map. Tap Done.

You'll see the main Address Book listing of contacts. Notice that the contact you just "located" now has a little flag next to his or her listing. That means that a Location setting has been established for that contact. You've just completed a one-time procedure for this person. The next time out, you can jump right to step 6.

6. Tap the contact's name to bring up his or her detailed listing and then tap the QueRoutes icon (see Figure 9-3). You'll see a big splashy option that says "Route to So-and-So" above a bunch of icons. Although it doesn't really look like a button, tap the area that says "Route to So-and-So."

Presto! Route generated.

NOTE   *Instead of tapping the QueRoutes icon, you can tap Menu | Que | Route To. That's three taps instead of two, so I'm not sure why you'd want to do that. Just thought I'd mention the option, as the Palm OS frequently gives you multiple ways to accomplish the same function.*

Routing to Points of Interest

Points of interest are the unsung heroes of GPS. Let's say you're out and about and suddenly realize your gas tank is nearly empty. You don't know the area—how are you going to find the nearest station so you don't wind up on the side of the road with a $75 tow truck bill? This is how:

1. Tap the Find icon (see Figure 9-3), either the one on the toolbar or in the Graffiti area.

2. On the QueFind screen that appears, tap the Services icon.

3. Two small arrows appear near the top of the screen. Tap the top one and then tap Near Current Location. Next, tap the bottom one and choose Auto Fuel.

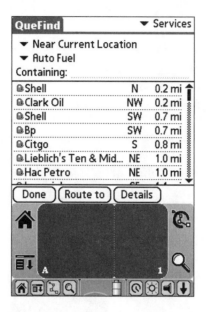

4. The list that appears shows the gas stations near your location, with the nearest one at the top. Tap it once to highlight it; then tap Route To.

Presto! Now you have a route to the closest station.

You can use more or less the same procedure to route to any point of interest, be it a natural landmark, a movie theater, a grocery store, or a police station or hospital. You needn't search by closest location, either—you can also enter the name of the destination if you know it. Just choose By Name from that first pop-up menu and then start writing the name in the Containing field.

A somewhat related example of this: We recently took our daughter to see the circus, which was being held at the Palace of Auburn Hills (home of the Detroit Pistons). I wasn't sure if the Palace would be categorized under Attractions or Entertainment, so I selected All Points of Interest. Then I wrote "palace of" in the Containing field, and there it was, right in the list. I tapped it, tapped Route To, and we were on our way. Took 20 seconds. Sometimes I really love technology.

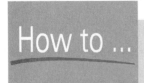 **Attach Locations to Appointments**

Just as Garmin tweaked the Address Book application so that you could add Location settings to contact listings, so did the company modify the Palm OS Date Book. You can attach a Location setting to any event in your calendar so that you can have quick access to a map of or route to your destination. When the time comes to head to your meeting, it'll take just two taps (on QueRoutes and then Route To) to start navigating.

It's easy enough to attach a Location setting to an appointment. Just set up your appointment like you normally would (with the time, description, alarms, and so on) and then tap Menu | Que | Attach Location. You'll see the QueFind menu, where you can select the destination in typical fashion. You can't, however, use Palm OS Find for this operation. If you're meeting with someone who's already in your address book, you'll still have to enter the person's address manually (by tapping Addresses).

When it's time for the appointment, simply tap it once; then tap the QueRoutes icon and then Route To.

How to ...

Route to Someplace You've Already Been

Once you've gone to all the trouble of setting up a route, you shouldn't have to go through the trouble of setting it up a second time. That's the beauty of Recent Finds, which you can access by tapping the Find icon and then the Recent Finds icon. The iQue keeps track of the addresses and destinations you've looked up or routed to, and it lists them starting with the most recent. To reroute to any of them, just tap it and then tap Route To.

QueFind	▼ Recent Finds		
▫ 123 S Main St	W	14.9 mi	
▫ 23800 Orchard Lak...	SW	160 ft	
▫ 30700 Glenmuer St	NW	3.9 mi	
⊘ Palace of Auburn Hills	N	16.9 mi	
▫ 672 Ridge Rd	NW	7.6 mi	
Ron Stefanski	NW	37.6 mi	
▫ 3399 Eastgate St	NW	37.6 mi	
▫ Playground	W	9.0 mi	
⊘ Palace of Auburn Hills	N	16.9 mi	
▫ 875 Drakeshire Dr	W	8.9 mi	
▧ Tuffy Auto Service ...	NW	8.0 mi	
▫ 300 W Merrill St	NE	8.9 mi	
▫ 6762 Red Cedar Ln	NW	10.1 mi	
▫ 18325 W 9 Mile Rd	E	6.8 mi	
▫ 30966 Club House Ln	N	4.2 mi	
1748 Albermarle Dr	E	423 mi	

(Done) (Route to) (Details)

9

Making Changes or Additions to a Route

Once you've plotted a route to wherever, you can make changes or additions to it as the need arises. To get to these options, tap the QueRoutes icon, which reveals the window shown on the next page.

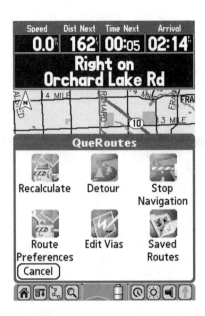

What's the scoop on these six icons? The scoop is this:

- **Recalculate** If you deviate from the designated route, you can tap this button to recalculate the route from your new position. However, this is necessary only if automatic route recalculation is turned off, which it shouldn't be.

- **Detour** Bump into heavy traffic? Construction? The iQue can come up with an alternate route to get you around the delay. Just tap the Detour icon and then choose the maximum distance you want the detour to take you away from the original route.

- **Stop Navigation** Even after you reach your destination, the iQue keeps on trying to route you there. Tap this button to turn off routing. If necessary, you can tap the QueRoutes icon again and then Resume Navigation to re-engage the route. Your route doesn't get erased just because you stop navigation.

- **Route Preferences** You can tweak dozens of iQue settings—everything from font size for points of interest to the options that appear when you cycle the Que button. I'd need another book to explain every preference in detail, so consult Garmin's electronic manual for further information. For the record, many of the options are self-explanatory, and if you get into trouble, you can always tap Defaults to return to the original settings.

■ **Edit Vias**   In all this talk about getting from point A to point B, I haven't said much about point C, which is a charming spot that's a bit out of the way but definitely worth visiting before you get to point B. In other words, if you want to make stops along the way, you can do so by adding a "via" to your route. Just tap Edit Vias, then select your desired stop by tapping Add via from Find (which brings up the standard QueFind menu) or Add via from Map (which lets you select a spot on the map just by tapping it). You can adjust the order in which you want to visit these stops by tapping one of them and then tapping the up or down arrow to change its order in the list. When you're done, tap Done, and the iQue will recalculate the route with the new stops added.

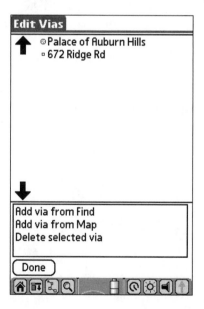

■ **Saved Routes**   Want to save a route for future use? You already know how to revisit previous destinations via the Recent Finds option, but that doesn't take vias into account, and eventually the older ones will be replaced by newer ones. You can save your current route by tapping Saved Routes and then Save Active. Then give your route a name you'll be able to recognize later.

Using the iQue in the Great Outdoors

In other chapters, you learned about using GPS for activities like hiking, Geocaching, and even marine navigation. Can you use the iQue for these sorts of things as well? After all, it has a perfectly good GPS receiver, right? It's just matter of finding the right software, right?

Right! But, also, wrong. While you can add other GPS navigation and mapping software to the iQue, there are a few caveats to consider. For starters, there's the matter of battery life. The iQue is good for only a couple hours between charges, and it's generally hard to find an AC outlet in the woods or on a boat (unless it's a really big boat). You can improve battery life by turning off the screen's backlight (hold down the power button for two seconds), which you don't need outdoors, but even that will get you only so far. You could use the iQue for a short Geocaching outing, but it might run out of juice for longer outdoor expeditions.

Then there's the bigger issue of durability. The iQue wasn't built for the rigors of the outdoors. One drop on a rock or in a puddle and you could wind up with a cracked or soggy paperweight. Garmin offers topographic maps for the iQue, but a company rep told me that the product really isn't recommended for serious outdoor use.

Ah, heck, you play by your own rules, right? You're going into the wild and the iQue is coming with you, dangit! If so, you might want to install ThatWay. This simplistic waypoint-navigation program is ideal for things like Geocaching, as it enables you to enter a set of coordinates and then navigate to them. Heck, even if you're going on a long hike and just need insurance that you can find your way back to your car or campsite, the combination of the iQue (which you can leave in your pocket most of the time) and ThatWay can't be beat. Plus, it's only 10 bucks.

Then there's Fugawi, a product I have to mention not only for its unique capabilities, but also because I love to say "Fugawi." This desktop mapping package enables you to import scanned maps or maps from any existing database and then convert them for use on your iQue. It includes detailed U.S. street maps—which are superfluous on the iQue, of course—as well as 80 nautical planning charts for the U.S., Bermuda, and the Bahamas. All told, it extends the mapping capabilities of your iQue considerably. For $99, it ought to.

Improving iQue Battery Life

The iQue's battery is its Achilles' heel, the one area in which improvement is definitely needed. Fortunately, there are three ways you can improve battery life while using your iQue, and two of them won't cost you a cent:

■ **Reduce screen brightness**   Tap the Brightness icon on the toolbar (it's the third one from the right) and then drag the slider to the left. Find a spot where the screen is still comfortably readable. The lower the brightness, the longer the battery will last. And if you're outdoors under bright daylight, turn off the screen's backlight altogether by holding down the power button for two seconds. Now you're really going to save some juice.

■ **Enable Battery Saver**   You can set the iQue to receive satellite data less frequently, which will conserve battery power quite a bit. To enable this option, tap the Prefs icon and then choose Que from the drop-down menu in the upper-right corner of the screen. Now choose GPS from the drop-down menu on the left side of the screen. Notice that WAAS Enabled is checked. When you check Battery Saver, you'll get a message about WAAS being disabled as a result. You're going to lose a bit of GPS accuracy by enabling Battery Saver, but for road navigation it's not a major issue.

■ **Buy Garmin's Auto Navigation Kit**   See "Before You Hit the Road" earlier in this chapter for information on this indispensable accessory, which will keep your iQue powered while you're driving and leave it fully charged when you get where you're going.

Charging on the Road

Although you use the HotSync cradle to charge the iQue when you're at your desk, you don't have to bring it along for charging on the road. Instead, you can disconnect the AC adapter from the cradle's USB cable and plug the connector directly into the bottom of the iQue (as shown in Figure 9-7).

Another option for charging on the road is a special cable that not only supplies power to the iQue, but enables you to HotSync it as well. I'm referring to so-called trickle charge cables like the BoxWave MiniSync, which features a USB connector on one end and a HotSync connector on the other. If you're traveling with a laptop or to someplace where you'll have access to a computer, a product like the MiniSync can be ideal. It uses a retractable cord system, meaning that when it's fully retracted,

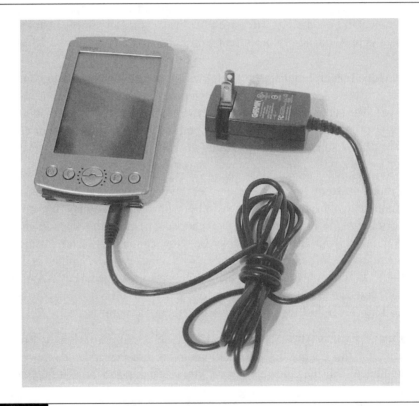

FIGURE 9-7   It's a little-known fact that you can plug the AC adapter directly into the iQue, meaning that you don't have to bring the HotSync along for charging on the road.

it fits easily into a pocket; plus it draws enough juice from the computer's USB port to power—and eventually recharge—the iQue.

At press time, the iQue-compatible version of the MiniSync was selling for just $15.50—quite a deal for such a valuable travel accessory.

Beaming Data and Programs

On *Star Trek,* transporters are used to beam people and equipment from one location to another. While we're a long way from being able to beam physical objects from place to place, the Palm OS makes it possible to beam almost any kind of data between PDA users.

As you learned earlier in the chapter, the iQue (like all Palm OS handhelds) has an infrared (IR) port. On the iQue, it's located on the top, just to the right of the memory card slot. Using this IR port, you can beam information in a surprising number of ways. You can:

- Use your iQue as a TV and stereo remote control
- Print data on an IR-equipped printer
- Beam data to other PDA users
- Give another PDA user your electronic business card
- Play two-player games head-to-head

These things are pretty cool, but mostly you'll probably use beaming to exchange mundane business data. All the core applications (Address Book, Memo Pad, and so on) support beaming, so you can beam:

- Contact listings
- Your own business card from the address book
- Appointments
- Memos
- Tasks

In addition, you can beam entire applications to other users. If you download a freeware program from the Internet and want to share it with friends or coworkers, go ahead: it's a snap to transmit the item wirelessly.

How to Beam

No matter what you're planning to beam—or receive—the process is essentially the same. Actually seeing the process demonstrated is faster than reading about it, but because I don't have time to stop by your office today, here's the process in a nutshell:

1. Orient the two PDAs so their IR ports face each other and are between three inches and three feet apart. If the PDAs are any closer than three inches, they may have a hard time locking onto each other; too far away, and the signal won't be strong enough to reach.

2. As the sender, you should choose the item you want to beam (for instance, open the memo or view the contact entry). Tap Menu, then choose the Beam command.

    A dialog box appears, indicating that the beam is in progress. First, you see a message indicating that your PDA is searching for the other PDA. That message then goes away and the data is transmitted. After the beam, your iQue goes back to business as usual—you won't get a message indicating that the beam was successful.

3. The receiver, on the other hand, sees a dialog box that asks permission to accept the beamed data. As the receiver, you need to decide what category to file the information in and then tap either Yes or No, depending on whether you want to keep the item. If you tap Yes, the data is integrated into your iQue in the category you specified. (There's no category decision to make if you're receiving an application or some other non-core-application data.)

Selecting Items for Beaming

So now that you know the rudiments of beaming, you're no doubt eager to start. I don't blame you—beaming is just really cool. I've seen it turn ordinary people into major geeks. And it's definitely better than writing notes by hand or trading easily scrunched business cards.

The most commonly beamed items are contacts from your address book. In fact, you can beam a single entry, an entire category, or your electronic business card. Let's take a look at the process of beaming a contact, which is pretty much the same as beaming an appointment, memo, or to-do item.

■   **Beam the current entry**   To send an address book entry to another user, find the name you want in the address list, tap it, and then tap Menu | Beam Address.

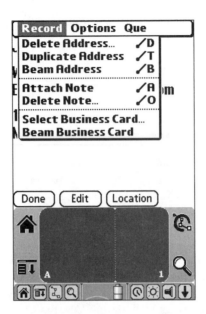

- **Beam a whole bunch of entries**   You can send any number of contacts—even every name in your iQue, in fact—using Beam Category. To do that, first choose the category you want to beam by picking the category from the list at the top-right corner of the screen. Then tap Menu and choose Beam Category. To beam all the entries in your entire address book, you should set the category to All—but if you do that, the recipient loses the categories, and everything ends up on the destination PDA as "Unfiled."

CAUTION   *Be careful before you beam or try to receive a whole category's worth of contacts—make sure it's something you really need to do. This operation could include hundreds of entries, which will take more time than either of you are willing to spend pointing your PDAs at each other.*

- **Beam your own entry**   What's more common than handing your business card to someone? You can configure your own address book entry as your personal business card and beam it to other handhelds. To do so, simply create a new contact with all the personal and business information that you want to share. When you're done, tap the new contact in the address list and then tap Menu | Select Business Card. You'll then see a little Rolodex-like icon at the top of your entry. To send it to someone, tap Menu | Beam Business Card.

TIP *There's a faster way to beam your business card to someone: hold down the Address Book button for two seconds. This automatically tells the iQue to beam your business card.*

Beaming Applications

Now for the best part. You can use the iQue's beaming prowess to transfer entire applications from one PDA to another. If you meet someone who shows you a cool new game or utility, for instance, you can ask that person to beam the program to your handheld.

NOTE *Not all applications are free, so don't use your iQue's beaming capability for piracy. Actually, many commercial programs are locked to prevent beaming, and shareware applications often require an unlock code to access all the features in the registered version. You can beam trial versions, but don't share registration codes—that's piracy.*

Not all programs can, in fact, be beamed. The core applications that come with your iQue are locked, making them nonbeamable. Many commercial programs are also locked, and some utilize supporting database files that can't be beamed. This means that you must go home and install the program the old-fashioned way, using your PC.

Now that you've read what you can't do, let's talk about what you can do. Beaming an application isn't much different than beaming data from one of the core programs. Do this:

1. Tap the Home button on your iQue to return to the applications screen.

2. Tap Menu and then tap Beam.

   A dialog box appears with a list of all the applications on your iQue, as in Figure 9-8. Some applications have little locks; these aren't beamable.

FIGURE 9-8   Choose a program from the list to beam it to another Palm. If it has a lock, however, it can't be beamed.

3. Select an application and tap the Beam button. If the desired program is stored on a memory card, tap the arrow next to Beam From and choose the card instead of Handheld.

You'll then see a list of the programs stored on the card. This designates only where programs are beamed from—programs you receive from others are always stored in main memory (though you can easily offload them to a memory card later).

If you want to beam more stuff, get a program called FileZ. This freeware file manager enables you to beam certain kinds of applications (like e-books and databases) that the Palm OS can't do on its own.

Working with Memory Cards

By now, you know the 21st-century spin on the old adage: you can never be too rich, too thin, or have too much memory. Sure, it's grammatically iffy—but it is accurate. What with RAM-devouring maps, e-books, games, AvantGo channels, productivity software, and even MP3 files, 32MB just don't go as far as they used to. Fortunately, the iQue offers simple, inexpensive, potentially limitless memory expansion in the form of MultiMediaCard (MMC) and Secure Digital media.

Should You Buy Software on a Card?

Companies like Mobile Digital Media and PalmOne sell a variety of memory cards that come preloaded with software. Because the software resides on the card, you can run it without sacrificing any of your iQue's internal memory. But if memory conservation is your only concern, you may not want to bother with software cards. Usually, your better bet is to buy a blank memory card and then load it up as you see fit. Same end result, but you can get a lot more storage capacity for the money.

However, there are some good deals to be had. Some of PalmOne's eBook and Game cards, for instance, pack multiple titles onto a single card—titles that would cost more if purchased separately. But the key point to remember is that virtually any software you can buy on a card, you can buy separately from sites such as **PalmGear.com**.

NOTE *What's the difference between MMC and SD cards? Physically, they're almost identical: about the size of a postage stamp. MMC media tends to cost a bit less; SD media offers faster data transfer rates and higher capacities. There's really no reason to opt for MMC these days, unless you find a great closeout deal (SD is rapidly becoming the dominant of the two media).*

What Price Memory?

Just what will it cost you to add a memory card to your iQue? That depends primarily on the size—the storage capacity—of the card. I spent some time shopping at **eCost.com**, where I found 128MB SD cards selling for about $50 and 256MB cards for about $67 (after a mail-in rebate). In general, you can find lower prices online than you can in retail stores, and many web-based vendors offer free shipping, thus saving you even more.

Memory 101

With the introduction of Palm OS 4.0, Palm also introduced the Virtual File System (VFS)—a way for the operating system to recognize removable memory cards and access the programs and data stored therein. Thus, you could relocate, say, Palm Reader and all your e-books to a card, freeing a fair chunk of your handheld's internal memory.

Getting Started with Memory Cards

You can move programs and data onto a memory card in two basic ways. First, if you have software that's already loaded in internal memory, you can use the Palm OS Copy tool to copy it to the card. (This procedure works both ways: you can copy items from a card back to internal memory as well.) To access this tool, tap the Home button to return to the main screen, then tap Menu | App | Copy. Select the program

9

you want to copy (you have to copy programs one at a time), making sure to select the desired Copy To and From locations. Tap Copy to begin the process.

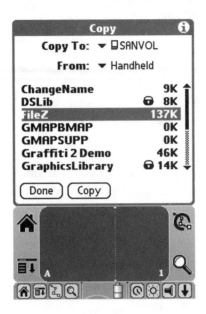

Alas, because there's no "move" option, the original file remains on your handheld. To claim the extra storage space you were after, you must then delete the software from internal memory. To do so, tap Menu | App | Delete; then tap the program you want to delete.

This is exactly as tedious as it sounds, which is why I strongly recommend a third-party file manager such as FilePoint (**www.bachmannsoftware.com**) or PocketFolder (**www.palmgear.com**). These programs make it much easier to move, copy, beam, and delete files. Just be sure you move the right files. If a program relies on more than one file for its operation (a good example is LandWare's Wine Enthusiast Guide 2003, which consists of the program file and several databases) and you move the wrong files or not enough of the files, you could wind up in trouble (as in the program no longer runs).

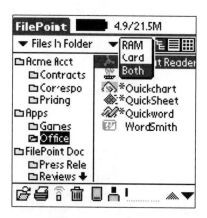

TIP *File managers can actually be a bit overcomplicated, especially for novice users who simply want to shuffle programs between internal and expansion memory. Instead, try an application launcher, which will not only organize all your programs, but also provide drag-and-drop simplicity for relocating them. Read on to learn more.*

A better way to place applications in external storage is by installing them there directly. The Palm OS Install Tool lets you specify the destination for new software at the time you install it, meaning that you can HotSync applications right onto a memory card. See Chapter 10 for instructions.

Ah, but what happens to the programs after that? Novice users often fall into the same trap: they install programs on their memory cards and then can't understand why they don't see the icons in the Home screen. The answer lies in a quirk of VFS: all applications stored on a memory card are automatically segregated into a category called Card. Thus, you must look in that category to find your newly installed stuff.

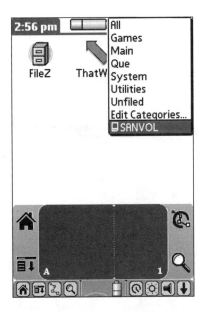

This can be inconvenient, to be sure, especially for users who like to keep their icons orderly. If you wind up with, say, 30 applications on a storage card, now you have an organization problem—you can't subcategorize the Card category. Fortunately, there's a solution in the form of third-party launchers, most of which now support external storage. One of my longtime favorites, Launcher X, lets you organize your icons however you see fit, regardless of where the actual applications are stored. MegaLauncher and Silver Screen, two more nice launchers, offer VFS support as well.

Beyond the Box: Doing More with Your iQue

By now, it's no secret that the iQue is capable of more than just street navigation—so much more, in fact, that the entire next chapter is devoted to its other functions. In Chapter 10, you'll learn about using your iQue for word processing, games, e-books, movies, and other fun and practical purposes. You'll also meet up with some handy accessories like keyboards and screen protectors and you'll learn how to troubleshoot your iQue in case of, well, trouble. See you there!

Where to Find It

Web Site	Address	What's There
BoxWave	**www.boxwave.com**	MiniSync
DataViz	**www.dataviz.com**	Documents To Go
Mark/Space	**www.markspace.com**	The Missing Sync for iQue 3600
PalmGear.com	**www.palmgear.com**	Almost every program mentioned in this chapter

9

Chapter 10

Doing More with Your iQue 3600

How to...

■ Install new software

■ Play games and music

■ Read books and watch movies

■ Turn the iQue into a mobile office

■ Add keyboards and other accessories

■ Troubleshoot the iQue

Your iQue is not just a mere organizer or navigation system—it's a full-fledged pocket computer, capable of running a huge variety of add-on software. In this chapter, I'm going to give you the scoop on popular applications like games, e-books, movies, and music and then talk about turning your iQue into a mobile office. The first step, however, is learning to install new programs.

How to Install Software

Installing software on your iQue involves little more than copying a few files, a process that's handled easy by Palm Desktop's Install Tool and the HotSync Manager. (If you sync with Outlook, don't fret—Install Tool works independent of your desktop contact manager. While you can run it directly from within Palm Desktop, you can also access it directly as a stand-alone program.)

There's a little mnemonic I like to share with novices: DUI: download, unzip, install. You're going to download programs from the Web, unzip them, and install them on your iQue.

The download part of the equation is pretty easy: you can find an endless variety of programs at sites like Handango and PalmGear.com. (See the end of this chapter for links to specific vendors.)

In most cases, the programs you download will be "zipped," meaning that they're a collection of files that have been compressed (using the Zip format) for faster, easier downloading. You have to "unzip" them before you can get to the file(s) you need to install on your iQue. Windows XP can do this automatically; if you have an earlier version of windows, download the shareware classic WinZip (**www.winzip.com**).

NOTE   *Some Palm OS programs are delivered as self-extracting files rather than Zip files. With these, you simply double-click the downloaded file and follow the instructions. The iQue files will automatically be queued in Install Tool for your next HotSync operation.*

After you've downloaded and unzipped the program, all that remains is to install it. This is accomplished using Install Tool, which is loaded on your PC when you first install Palm Desktop. Here's how to use it:

1. Run Install Tool by choosing Start | Programs | Palm Desktop | Install Tool.

2. Click the Add button.

3. The Open dialog box for selecting Palm OS applications (which have either a .pdb or .prc extension) appears.

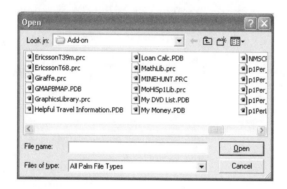

Locate the program you want to install (you'll have to navigate to the correct folder on your hard drive, the one where you unzipped the downloaded file). Suppose you're installing Bejeweled—look for bejeweled.prc and then click to select it. Click the Open button.

TIP   *You can select multiple applications at once by holding down the CTRL key as you click programs in the file list.*

4. With your application displayed in the Install Tool dialog box, click Done.

The next time you HotSync your iQue, the selected application is installed.

You can skip most of these steps by simply opening the Windows folder that contains the program you want to install and then double-clicking the program's icon. That will launch Install Tool and add the program to the queue. Click Done, HotSync, and you're finished!

Installing to a Memory Card

If your have a memory card, you can install applications directly to it. That's handy, especially if you want to install a huge application or data file that simply wouldn't fit if copied to the iQue's more limited internal memory.

After you've used Install Tool to select a program for installation, click the Change Destination button. You'll see the Change Destination dialog box. Then select the program that you want to install directly to the memory card and click the arrow to move it to the right side of the screen, which represents the iQue's memory card.

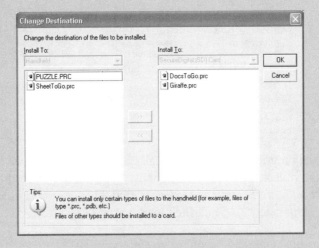

When you've configured your to-be-installed applications to your liking, click OK, close Install Tool (by clicking Done), and HotSync.

Playing Games

Maps, spreadsheets, and memos are all well and good. If that's all you ever plan to do with your iQue, that's fine—but don't blame me if people accuse you of being dull. Your iQue is a miniature general-purpose computer, and, as a result, it can do almost anything your desktop PC can do—including games. Sure, there are limitations. The display is pretty small, and the processor isn't nearly as fast as your desktop's, but the fact remains that your iQue is a great game machine for passing the time in an airport, on a train, at a meeting (where it looks like you're taking notes), or in any other place where you're bored with doing productive activities.

Indeed, games account for a pretty healthy chunk of all software sold for Palm OS handhelds, so it should come as no surprise that you can find hundreds upon hundreds of titles spanning every genre. Card games, action games, puzzle games— you name it, it's out there. Of course, I can't list all of them without doubling the size of the book. It's big enough already, don't you think?

As with other kinds of iQue software, games are easy to try before you buy. Most have a trial period, usually from two weeks to a month, after which the game becomes disabled unless you register it (that is, pay for a code to unlock it permanently). Games usually cost $10 to $20, though a few will set you back $30. There's also a treasure trove of great freebies like these (all of them available at **www.freewarepalm.com**):

■ **Cribbage 3.0**   Sure, you could pay 12 bucks or so for one of the commercial Cribbage games, but why? Well, the iQue tends to cheat a bit—but, otherwise, this is a freeware gem.

■ **Mulg II**   Use your stylus to guide a marble through a maze within a fixed amount of time. Devilishly addictive.

■ **Patience Revisited**   An amazing collection of solitaire games—21 in all, all in color, all free, free, free!

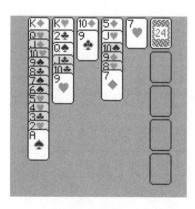

10

- **PilOth** A clone of the classic game of Othello.

- **Pocket Video Poker** Why take a trip to Vegas when you can gamble all you want for free? There's also Pocket Video Blackjack if that's more your speed.

- **Sea War** A nice implementation of the beloved game Battleship. There's even a high-resolution version.

- **Solitaire Poker** One of many variations on Solitaire, this one involving poker hands.

- **Vexed 2.1** One of the most addictive puzzle games ever, and a Palm OS freeware classic. The 2.1 version includes multiple puzzle packs with over 600 levels.

These freebies are a great place to start for anyone interested in a little fun on the run. In fact, there are enough freeware games to keep you entertained almost indefinitely. On the other hand, if you're willing to shell out a few bucks, you'll find some of the best mobile entertainment money can buy. Following are just some of my favorites, all of them available at **PalmGear.com**:

■ **Galax**   An excellent retread of the inimitable (but often imitated) Galaxian.

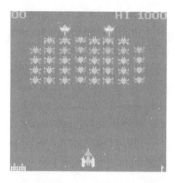

■ **Zap!2016**   A scrolling space-shooter with gorgeous graphics and terrific sound effects.

■ **AcidFreecell**   Freecell is one of my favorite Solitaire games, and this version includes sound effects, photographic backgrounds, and other nifty perks.

■ **Vegas Blackjack**   Without a doubt the best-looking blackjack game for the Palm OS, Vegas Blackjack plunks you down at a casino-style table for some serious hands of 21. Double down!

10

■ **Aggression**   Remember Risk? Aggression is a visually striking re-creation of the beloved board game. It even takes full advantage of the iQue's 320 by 480 pixel screen.

■ **Monopoly**   This needs no explanation, other than to say that one to four players can partake, human or computer, on the same handheld or on several of them (the game supports play via infrared).

■ **Rook's Revenge** Almost too fast-paced to qualify as a board game, Rook's Revenge is like chess with a jolt of caffeine. Move your pieces as fast as you can (they still have to be legal moves), without waiting for your opponent to move. A great change of pace from boring old chess.

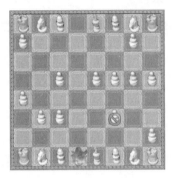

■ **Scrabble** Like Monopoly, no explanation needed here. But how cool to play this old favorite anytime, anywhere, without having to worry about tiles spilling all over the place.

■ **Bejeweled** Like TNT's "New Movie Classics," this game has been around for just a few years, but it's already achieved Tetris-like classic status. It requires zero time to learn to play—and all your free time once you do. If, by chance, you've never heard of it, trust us and give it a try. It might just be the perfect game for PDAs.

■ **NetWalk II** An oldie but goodie, NetWalk challenges you to make successful connections between your servers and your computers. Sounds like a tech-support nightmare, but it's a ton of fun.

■ **Crossword Puzzles for Palm OS** Whether you're a crossword-puzzle fanatic or you haven't looked at one in years, this excellent collection— derived from *Washington Post* puzzles—is an ideal way to pass the time. Sure beats carrying a big book of puzzles or getting newspaper ink on your fingers!

■ **Text Twist** The first game I reach for when I have five minutes to spare, Text Twist is a bit like Boggle. You're given six scrambled letters and a time limit; try to make as many words as you can from the letters and unscramble the six-letter word.

- **Billiards**   If you like pool, you'll love this dazzling interpretation.

- **Bump Attack Pinball**   Pinball is really hard to do right on a PDA, what with the small screen, lack of flippers, and so on. Bump Attack Pinball gets it right, and with several beautiful-looking tables to boot. It even has a few designed for big screens like the iQue's.

Listening to Music

The iQue is nothing if not versatile. Its entertainment capabilities don't end with books, games, and movies—it's also capable of playing music in the form of MP3 files. You know the sort: digital audio files "ripped" from CDs, downloaded from the Internet, or purchased from music sites like iTunes and MusicMatch.

NOTE   *Songs purchased from online music services may have restrictions, meaning that they might not be playable on your iQue. For example, at press time, Apple's iTunes Music Store sold only AAC-formatted music, which the iQue doesn't support. Other sites sell WMA files, also unsupported by the iQue. Ideally, you want plain-Jane MP3 files.*

The iQue comes with a program—QueAudio—designed expressly for playing MP3 files. (It can also play Windows-standard WAV files, which is the format often produced by voice recorders.) To use it, you simply need to copy some MP3 files from your PC to an SD memory card. There are two ways to accomplish this:

- Use Install Tool to HotSync your MP3 files directly to the SD card.

- Connect an SD card reader to your PC: then copy MP3 files to it using Windows Explorer.

NPR on Your iQue

I'm a huge fan of National Public Radio shows like *Car Talk*, *Fresh Air*, and *This American Life*. However, I'm never in the car at the right time, so I tend to miss the shows when they're broadcast. Thanks to an excellent program called Replay Radio (**www.replay-radio.com**), I can record NPR shows (and any other radio programs) on my PC in MP3 format and then copy them to my iQue for anytime, anywhere listening. You see, many radio stations stream their broadcasts over the Internet, and Replay Radio records that stream to your hard drive. You can set it to record a specific station at a specific time, TiVo-like, or start recording manually. (*This American Life*, for instance, maintains an archive of past shows that you can listen to on your PC at any time. Just start it playing, click Record in Replay Radio, and then press the computer's Mute button. In an hour, you'll have an MP3 that's ready to go.) FYI, a one-hour show recorded at FM quality takes about 28MB, so plan your memory-card space accordingly.

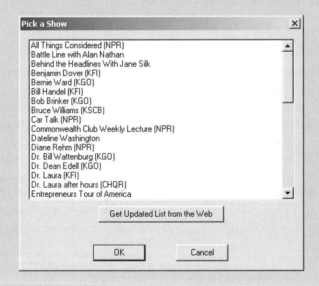

I highly recommend the latter option, because it can take forever—literally hours—to load MP3s on an SD card via HotSync. With a card reader, on the other hand, it should take no more than a few minutes. These readers plug into one of your computer's USB ports—when you insert a memory card, the card is assigned a drive letter and functions just like a disk. Now you can just drag and drop your MP3 files to the card and then pop the card back into your iQue when the files are done copying.

Lots of companies make these card readers (also known as media readers). I recommend buying a 6-in-1 reader, which accommodates not only SD cards, but also CompactFlash, Memory Stick, and other kinds of memory cards. You can buy a 6-in-1 reader for as little as $20 if you shop around—don't pay $50 to $60 for one.

As for QueAudio itself, it's a pretty rudimentary MP3 player. In other words, it gets the job done, but it doesn't have many features (like support for playlists). Therefore, you may want to consider a third-party alternative. I'm partial to Pocket Tunes, an attractive and feature-packed player that supports the use of skins— user-created wallpaper that customizes the look of the player.

The $19.95 Deluxe version includes a bookmark feature—ideal if you plan to listen to spoken-word MP3 files like audiobooks or radio shows (see "NPR on Your iQue").

Watching Movies

It wasn't all that long ago that watching an entire feature-length movie on a PDA would have been considered insanity. These days, though, there's no reason not to use your iQue to watch, say, *The Matrix* or an episode of *The Simpsons* on a long flight.

Of course, you'll need to have a lot of memory (see "The iQue's Key Features" in Chapter 9). A 128MB SD card is the bare minimum for watching a 30-minute TV show, and you'll need a 256MB or 512MB card for longer shows or movies.

Getting Video into Your iQue

Getting video into your iQue is a three-step process:

1. Download, record, or create video files on your PC.

2. Convert the files to an iQue-viewable format.

3. Copy the files to your iQue for viewing with one of several video-player applications.

The first step is without a doubt the most complicated. Although video can come from a variety of sources—TV, DVDs, your camcorder, the Internet, and so on—it can be a bit tricky to get it onto your PC in the proper digital format. For instance, suppose you have a DVD of *Chicken Run* (one of my all-time favorite movies, even though it's technically for kids) that you want to watch on your iQue. It's possible, believe it or not, but you have to jump through some fairly sizable hoops. Let's talk about the four main sources for video and how you work with them:

■ **TV** If you hate to miss Conan but just can't stay up that late, wouldn't it be great if you could record episodes and watch them later on your iQue? You have two options: either record the show on a standard VCR and then feed the video into your PC (bleh), or record the show right on your PC. I greatly prefer the latter option, which you can accomplish with a TV tuner card like the Hauppauge WinTV-PVR-250. In essence, it's like turning your PC into a low-grade TiVo (greatest invention ever, by the way). Just plug the cable-TV cable into the back of the card, set up the included software to record your show, and presto: you're on your way. (You'll still have to convert the recording for viewing on your iQue, which I'll discuss later.)

NOTE *You may be able to download some TV shows with one of the Internet file-sharing services like KaZaa or Morpheus. This gives you almost zero control over the quality of the recording, and shows can take a long time to download. On the other hand, you don't have to buy any new equipment. Personally, I'm a lot happier recording my own stuff.*

■ **Digital Video**   Got a digital video camcorder? You can pipe your home movies right into your PC (you need a FireWire or i.Link port to do so—consult your system manual if you need help) and then convert them for viewing on the iQue. Why show off a mere picture of the kids when you can show full-motion video?

■ **DVD**   Most of us watch movies on DVD these days, so it stands to reason that we'd want to be able to copy DVD to PDA. PDQ. Suppose you just rented *Terminator 3* but you're going out of town before you have a chance to watch it. The problem, of course, is getting the movie off the silver platter and onto your computer's hard drive. Because DVDs are copy protected, this might seem like a hopeless task. Fret not—there are several programs that make this possible. DVD-to-AVI (**www.dvd-to-avi.com**) and MovieJack (**www.moviejack.org**), for instance, can "rip" the content from DVD and store the movie as an AVI or MPEG file on your computer's hard drive. From there, it's a simple matter of converting the movie to an iQue-viewable format.

■ **The Internet**   Sites like **BMWfilms.com** are home to short films (good ones, in fact) that you can download to your PC and then convert for viewing on your iQue. These are nice because they don't eat up a ton of storage space, and you can view them in their entirety when you have just a few minutes to kill. Of course, you can also use a file-sharing service like KaZaa or Morpheus to download movies and TV shows. That's a violation of copyright laws, however, so let your conscience be your guide.

10

Converting Your Video

Let's say you've recorded (or downloaded) an episode of *The Simpsons* on your PC. Because of the vagaries and varieties of video formats, you can't just copy the file to your iQue and start watching (unlike with MP3 music files, which you can indeed copy and start listening to). Instead, you have to convert the file to a format that the iQue's video player can recognize.

Speaking of the video player, it's time to choose one, as the iQue doesn't come with one. I recommend either Kinoma Player or TealMovie. Both come with Windows-based utilities that you can use to convert your video files into the proper formats. I should also mention that both converters can be a little complicated, especially for novice users. Fortunately, you can download trial versions of both and see which one you like best before plunking down your money. TealMovie sells for $24.95; Kinoma Player is free, but the Kinoma Producer utility that converts videos will cost you $29.99.

NOTE   *I'm partial to the Kinoma product, not just because it's easier to use, but also because it supports the MPEG video format, which TealMovie does not. MPEG is the format you usually wind up with when recording TV shows or ripping DVD movies.*

Install Kinoma or TealMovie on your iQue like you would any other software; then follow the included instructions to use the converter. Pay special attention to resolution settings—the higher the resolution, the larger the resulting file will be, and the more space you'll need on your memory card. Set the resolution too low and you could wind up with video the size of a postage stamp—not exactly pleasant for viewing. My opinion: 320 by 240 is a good middle-ground resolution for viewing video on an iQue.

After you've converted a video, you'll end up with a file with a .pdb extension. If the file is reasonably small (under 10MB or so), you can load it on your iQue using Install Tool. Otherwise, I recommend copying it to your SD card using the same method described earlier in "Listening to Music."

One final note: video files come in lots of different formats, and it's not uncommon to discover that something you've downloaded (or even recorded) can't be converted using the Kinoma or TealMovie utilities. All is not lost—you simply need to perform a "pre-conversion," meaning that you need to use a different program to convert the file to a format recognized by one of the aforementioned converters. (Yes, this is a huge and obnoxious hassle. Someday, watching movies on your PDA will be much, much easier, but for now we have to go through all this silliness.) I recommend EO-Video, a $34.95 Windows utility that can convert just about any video format into any other video format.

10

Reading Books

You know the future has arrived when a device the size of a Pop-Tart can hold an entire Stephen King novel. Indeed, many users find electronic books (a.k.a. e-books) to be a major iQue perk. You can pay nothing at all and read hundreds of literary classics or pay discounted prices for mainstream titles.

Either way, you need a program that enables you to view e-book files on your iQue. I recommend Palm Reader, which supports not only commercial titles, but also public-domain freebies. It's a one-program-fits-all solution. Best of all, Palm Reader costs nothing—you can download it free from Palm Digital Media (which, incidentally, is also a prime spot for buying and downloading commercial e-books).

There are dozens of online sources for e-books, both free and commercial. The former are works considered public domain: either their copyrights have expired (as in the case of classic literature), or they're promotional freebies (Fictionwise, for example, often gives away short stories). Literally thousands of titles are available in the public domain, many of them already converted to the Doc format that Palm Reader requires.

NOTE   *This Doc format is not to be confused with Microsoft Word's .doc files. The latter is a file extension that has long been used by Microsoft's ubiquitous word processor. When electronic documents were first created for Palm OS handhelds, the guys who developed the software to read them chose the name Doc for the program. The program is long gone, but the file format remains, and the unfortunately coincidental Doc name along with it. Palm OS Doc files are not compatible with Microsoft Word, and vice versa. However, there are ways to convert files back and forth—see "Creating a Mobile Office" later in this chapter for details.*

Commercial e-books aren't unlike what you'd buy in a bookstore: they've simply been converted to an electronic format and authorized for sale online. The difference is, you don't have to get in the car and drive to a bookstore—or even wait three or four days while Amazon delivers your order. E-books are delivered instantly, which is definitely a nice perk. They're usually discounted off the cover price, too.

Finding Free Stuff

If one site is synonymous with public-domain e-books, it's MemoWare (**www .memoware.com**). Here you can find thousands of texts divided into categories such as business, history, travel, biography, sci-fi, and Shakespeare. Whether you're looking for a collection of Mexican recipes, a Zane Grey western, a sappy love poem, or a classic work by Dickens, this is the place to start.

MemoWare offers a convenient search engine, so you can type in a title or a keyword to quickly find what you're looking for. It also has links to other e-book sites, although none are as comprehensive.

Finding Commercial Stuff

The thing about public-domain e-books is that most of them are, well, old. Somerset Maugham and Jack London are all well and good for catching up on the classics, but sometimes you just want a little Stephen King. Or Anna Quindlen. Or Captain Kirk. Fortunately, you can have them all on your iQue, provided you're willing to pay for them.

The top place to go for contemporary, mainstream fiction and nonfiction is, without a doubt, Palm Digital Media (**www.palmdigitalmedia.com**). The site offers thousands of books from prominent authors like Stephen Ambrose, Elmore Leonard, and Kurt Vonnegut.

How to View Palm Digital Media Books

When you purchase a book from Palm Digital Media, you supply your name and credit card number and then receive a Zip file to download. (If you need a utility to expand Zip files—something Windows XP can do automatically, as mentioned earlier—I recommend downloading WinZip from **www.winzip.com**.) This file contains the e-book itself (in an encrypted .pdb format), along with the Palm Reader program. If you don't already have the Palm Reader installed on your PDA, be sure to install it.

When buying subsequent books, you need to install only the books themselves. You needn't install Palm Reader again.

You also receive, via e-mail, a code number that you'll use to unlock the e-book. You need to enter this number on your iQue the first time you open your e-book.

The code number is usually the credit card number you used to purchase the book. If you don't mind divulging it, you can, indeed, share the book with another handheld user. Just e-mail the file for them to install and then give them the number so they can unlock the book. This is pretty smart copyright protection, if you ask me, as it allows for sharing among family members and close friends, but essentially prevents you from giving books to strangers.

One more note about Palm Reader: you must use it to view books purchased from Palm Digital Media; no other e-book reader will let you read them. However, Palm Reader will let you view standard Doc files, such as those obtained at MemoWare and Fictionwise. Thus, it's a pretty good all-purpose program.

If you subscribe to Palm Digital Media's free weekly newsletter, which is distributed via e-mail, you'll receive a code that's good for 10 percent off every e-book you buy. Visit the site for details.

Other Sources for Contemporary E-Books

Palm Digital Media might be the largest source for commercial e-books, but a couple of other web sites are gaining notoriety.

- **Fictionwise** Here you'll find a growing collection of fiction and nonfiction stories and novels, all of them discounted. In fact, you can buy short stories for as little as a buck, sometimes even less. One nice thing about Fictionwise is that the books are provided in the standard Doc format, so you can use your favorite Doc viewing program. (The company also offers Palm Digital Media–format books, so you can read those with Palm Reader as well.) Furthermore, the site includes reader-supplied ratings for each book and story, so you can make more informed decisions on what to buy. Fictionwise also provides a decent collection of free short stories, so we highly recommend a visit.

- **Mobipocket** Mobipocket sells not only commercial fiction and nonfiction titles, but also loads of reference books. If you're looking for medical or

Reading in Bed Without Disturbing Your Spouse

Since the dawn of time, one seemingly insurmountable problem has plagued the human race: how to read in bed without disturbing one's spouse. Torches didn't work: they tended to set the bed on fire. Neither did battery-operated book lights: they never seemed to fit whatever kind of book you were reading. But, finally, there's an answer: the iQue. Just load up a novel and turn on the backlight. You'll have no trouble seeing the screen in the dark (in fact, you'll probably want to turn the brightness way down), and your spouse will barely know it's on. PDA or marriage-saver? You be the judge.

legal texts, encyclopedias, and so on, this is the place to start. However, you need the Mobipocket reader to view these titles.

> **NOTE**   *You can install multiple e-book readers on your iQue and switch back and forth between them as needed. There's nothing wrong with using, say, Palm Reader for fiction and Mobipocket for reference books.*

- **PerfectBound**   Individual book publishers are finally getting into the e-book act, as evidenced by this site offering titles from HarperCollins.

- **RandomHouse.com**   Another major-league book publisher offering e-books at discounted prices. At press time, Jon Krakauer's *Under the Banner of Heaven* was selling for $18—30 percent off the hardcover price.

Creating a Mobile Office

When I'm at the airport and I see business travelers schlepping nine-pound laptops inside overstuffed briefcases, I laugh derisively (but not out loud—that kind of thing can lead to a fat lip). My mobile office fits inside my pocket, thank you very much. For all its entertainment and GPS acumen, the iQue also does one heck of a job with word processing, spreadsheets, databases, and other business documents. You can use it to view Adobe Acrobat (also known as PDF) files, print important documents, and even send and receive e-mail.

NOTE *I interrupt this book to bring you an unpaid (but wholly self-serving) commercial announcement.* Mobility Magazine *is devoted solely to PDAs (and other mobile gear) and their business applications. It offers product reviews, business features, how-to advice, and plenty more. In short, if you're interested in exploring the business side of your iQue, it's a magazine you should get. At the same time, why not grab a copy of* Handheld Computing *(I'm the, ahem, editor), which leans more toward the fun and practical side of PDAs.*

The iQue comes with a very powerful piece of business software: Documents To Go 5. It enables you to view and edit Word and Excel files right on your iQue. An optional module, DataViz Mail, adds e-mail to the equation, sending and receiving messages when you HotSync with your PC. In short, this powerful suite turns your iQue into a pretty effective mobile office. You can compose new documents on the device or take desktop documents with you for on-the-road viewing and editing.

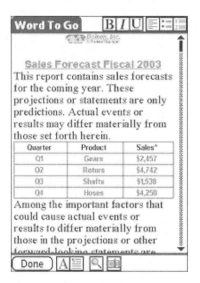

Unfortunately, the iQue comes with only a 30-day trial version of the package. You can buy the full version for $29.95 or upgrade to the Premium Edition for $49.95. The latter includes support for PowerPoint and PDF files, digital photos, and Excel-like charts. There are other office suites available for the Palm OS, as well as stand-alone word processors (in case that's all you really need), but I highly recommend Documents To Go—particularly because it offers native file support for Microsoft Office files. That means no conversion is necessary between PDA and PC.

There's one other ingredient you might want to consider for your mobile office: a keyboard. Yep, you can add a nearly full-size set of keys to your iQue, meaning that you can get some actual word processing done. See "iQue Accessories" later in this chapter for details.

Presentations in Your Pocket

Perhaps you read the last section and wondered, "Why in the world would I want to keep PowerPoint presentations in my iQue?" After all, it's not like you can connect the iQue to a projector and deliver your presentation with it, no laptop required, right?

Wrong!

As I keep telling you, there's almost nothing the iQue can't do. I mean, it can't drive a car or anything—although, now that I think about it, it does kind of steer the car by giving you driving directions, so I guess it can sort of "drive" a car. But it can't parallel park one!

It can, however, deliver PowerPoint presentations straight to a projector (or even a computer monitor), no laptop required. One of the products that makes this possible is Margi Presenter-to-Go (see Figure 10-1), which includes a special cable that links your iQue (via its SD slot) to a projector or monitor. It also comes with a wireless remote for controlling your presentations from a distance (no need to hold the iQue or stay tethered to the projector), and with software that shrinks your PowerPoint files down to a more iQue-friendly size. You can view notes on your iQue while delivering your presentation, change the slide order, remove specific slides from the presentation, and even integrate non-PowerPoint slides.

10

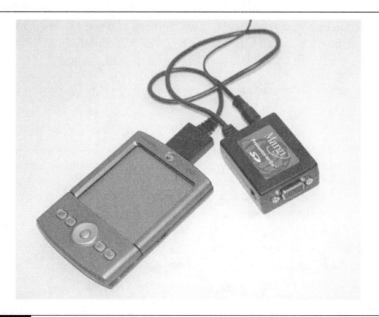

FIGURE 10-1   Margi's Presenter-to-Go, shown here with a Palm Tungsten T, enables you to connect your iQue to a projector and deliver PowerPoint presentations.

Presenter-to-Go doesn't enable you to edit slides on your iQue—but Documents To Go Premium Edition does (see the previous section). It also removes audio and fancy transitions from your presentations—something to keep in mind if you really need that stuff (though in my humble opinion, a good presenter needs neither). In short, it has a handful of limitations, but they're pretty minor in exchange for not having to lug a 9-pound laptop on your next business trip.

PDFs in Your Pocket

Adobe Acrobat files—also known as PDFs—are used for everything from software documentation to magazine distribution. That's because they maintain the exact look of a page—text, graphics, and all the rest—in a format that's viewable on nearly any platform: Windows, Macintosh, Linux, and, more recently, Palm OS handhelds like the iQue. Any PDF you can view on your desktop, you can now view on your handheld as well.

But do you really want to? Truth be told, PDFs and PDAs are not the best mix. A four-inch screen just doesn't do justice to a document meant for a full-size monitor. Because a PDF is essentially one big image, you have to zoom in quite a bit to read text, which translates to a ton of scrolling around the document. In other words, you can put PDFs on your PDA, but the viewing experience could best be described as annoying.

That said, there may be situations in which annoyance is a small price to pay to carry vital documents. Your company may have a PDF-formatted product catalog, one you'd like to be able to show customers. Perhaps you want to keep an instruction manual on hand for a particularly complex piece of software. Or maybe you've just received an e-mail with a PDF attached and need to peak inside.

The place to start is Adobe, makers of the free Acrobat Reader software (**www.adobe.com/products/acrobat/readerstep2.html**). Download the Palm OS version and install it on your iQue. Then use the Adobe Reader installation tool on your PC to add files.

I also recommend checking out RepliGo for Palm OS (**www.repligo.com**). This versatile viewer allows you to access not only Microsoft Office documents (replicated exactly as they appear in Windows), but also PDFs. The latter are "printed" from your PC using a special driver and then transferred to your PDA when you HotSync. Unlike Acrobat Reader, RepliGo sports a smart selection of zoom and navigation tools, making for a generally pleasant viewing experience. It can also "reflow" documents, removing graphics so all you see is the text—a huge help for getting to the meat of a PDF. Nice as RepliGo is, however, it's also pricey at $49.95.

Keeping the Kids Happy

Your toddler is bouncing around the restaurant booth. Your tween is sulking in the backseat because he forgot the Game Boy. Your six-year-old won't leave you alone for six seconds while you try to talk on the phone. At times like these, even the most patient of parents may feel the need to reach for the Prozac.

Reach for your iQue instead. Whether you have toddlers, teens, or a couple in between, you'll find software that's just right for keeping the kiddos occupied. I'm talking e-books, educational programs, paint programs, music, games, and more, all of it affordable, effective, and undeniably convenient.

Not wild about putting your precious PDA into the hands of a youngster? I hear you. The thought of sticky fingers mucking up the screen or a dunk into a glass of milk fills me with more dread than a *Barney* marathon. And make no mistake— there's a bit of risk in what I propose. At the very least, you may want to scope out a protective case—or at least a screen protector—before handing over the iQue (see "iQue Accessories" coming up).

I also recommend some advance instruction to let tykes know that this is not a Fisher Price toy. Say something like, "This little computer is very delicate, so it's important to hold it gently. If it gets dropped, it could break." The age of the child and the nature of the software will determine how much hands-on instruction is needed, but remember: kids love to do things for themselves, and excessive hovering might tarnish the experience for them.

Your iQue can be more than just a source of entertainment for the kids—it can also be an invaluable reference tool for you. For instance, web sites like **123Child.com** and **Parents.com** are home to dozens of feature articles covering everything from entertaining a toddler ("The Toddler Activity Pages," 123Child.com) to tantrum prevention ("40 Ways to Avoid Tantrums," Parents.com). Just copy and paste them into a memo, and you'll always have them at the ready.

Book Smarts

The diminutive iQue screen can't take the place of a large, colorful, tactile book page—but it can do in a pinch. For instance, check out Children's Illustrated eTales (**www.ddhsoftware.com**), a collection of four illustrated, toddler-oriented stories priced at $9.99.

You may also want to visit the Childrens section at PDA Bookstore (**www .pdabookstore.com**), home to three illustrated books—one each for different age groups (3 to 6, 7 to 10, and 8 to 12). They're priced at just $4.10, but unfortunately the Palm OS versions aren't illustrated.

Looking for freebies? You'll find them at MemoWare (**www.memoware.com**), which has a children's section containing several hundred classic titles (none of them illustrated, most intended for kids who can read) from authors like Hans Christian Anderson, Beatrix Potter, and the Brothers Grimm. Be aware, however, that most have been converted to the TomeRaider format, meaning that you'll need the $20 TomeRaider program, which is available from **www.tomeraider.com**.

Finally, don't forget the books you might want to read yourself. Palm Digital Media (see "Reading Books" earlier in this chapter) offers an extensive collection of titles on family and parenting—everything from *The World According to Mister Rogers* to *The Post-Pregnancy Handbook*. There's also a Young Adult section for your teens and tweens.

Photo Op

A digital camera can be the perfect toy for kids large and small, who can take funny pictures of themselves, snap "spy" photos of people around them, or just be creative. Because the shots show up on your iQue's screen, your little Ansel Adams gets instant gratification—and usually a lot of laughs. As with any digital camera, you can delete the pictures later to free up memory, or transfer them to your PC for viewing, printing, or whatever.

Obviously your iQue doesn't have a built-in camera (as some PDAs do), but you can add one: the Veo Photo Traveler. It features a swiveling, adjustable-focus lens, and it captures images at resolutions of up to 640 by 480 pixels—a far cry from today's multi-megapixel cameras, but more than adequate for fooling around. The Photo Traveler plugs into your iQue's SD expansion slot, so you'll have to remove your memory card if you have one inserted.

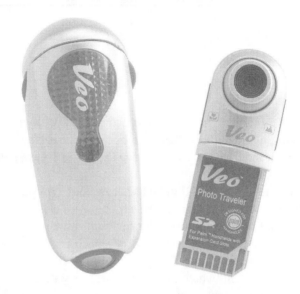

Paint and Scribble

Though lots of restaurants nowadays provide crayons and paper menus for kids to doodle, not many airlines, doctor's offices, or minivans do. Fortunately, you can turn your iQue into a small but versatile canvas for coloring, scribbling, even a little painting—and there's not a lick of cleanup required.

One of my favorites is Funny Faces (**adlsoftware.homestead.com/index.html**), which supplies the outlines of various faces, letting kids draw in the eyes, nose, mouth, and so on. Best of all, it's a freebie. For something a little more advanced, try TealPaint (**www.tealpoint.com**), which supplies a wealth of paint and sketch tools, and even allows drawings to be exported back to the PC for printing, e-mailing, or whatever.

Before you open the handheld art shop, I recommend you stop by
FreeScreenProtectors.com and order a box (of screen protectors, that is—they'll
help keep the screen safe from heavy-handed scribbling). At press time, they weren't
yet available for the iQue, but I'll wager they are by now—and if you enter **FREESP**
during the checkout process, you'll pay only the shipping charges. These transparent
sheets offer excellent screen protection without compromising readability or contrast.

Music Soothes the Savage Rugrat

You know those Barney, Wiggles, and Disney songs the kids insist on hearing every
time you pile into the van? You can load some of those tunes into your iQue for
easy listening just about anywhere. All you need to do is rip the songs from the
kids' favorite CDs, which you can do on virtually any computer with virtually any
CD-ROM drive, and convert them into MP3s. I recommend a program like Easy
CD Creator (**www.roxio.com**), though there are plenty of free and inexpensive CD
ripping utilities available online (try **www.download.com**).

For a great source of children's music that's already in MP3 format, visit
MP3.com. You'll find dozens of free sample songs to download, and low prices if
you decide to buy more. I'm partial to the music of Graham Clarke, who belts out
some of the most amusing kids' tunes I've ever heard. Just try not to smile during
"Old McDonald Goes Crazy."

10

That's Edutainment!

Most kids I know—young and old alike—love games like Bejeweled. But if you want something a bit more educational, fear not—you can find plenty of learning tools for the tykes. For instance, ABC Kiddie Cards and Learn ABC (**www .palmgear.com**) are flashcard-type programs designed to teach the alphabet. ABC Kiddie Cards uses color and cute pictures and costs $5; Learn ABC is free. After they've learned their letters, the little geniuses can move on to Count (**www.palmgear .com**), a cute and simple game that uses pictures to teach counting. As all kids software should, Count disables your handheld's buttons to prevent accidental application switching.

Hot Hangman 3.2 (**www.tblabs.com**) brings the classic game to your iQue, complete with color, high-score tables, and multiple databases containing hundreds of words. Next, check out Match Game 1.2 (**www.quizzlerpro.com**), a great freebie for the littlest of learners. A shape, color, number, or letter appears in the middle of the screen; the child taps the matching button from a selection at the bottom. The buttons are large enough to allow finger taps, and, as with Count, hardware buttons are disabled.

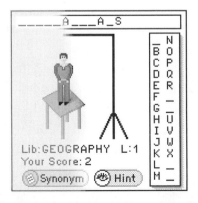

Finally, I'd be remiss if I didn't mention PDA Playground (**www.dataviz.com**), an entire collection of games designed expressly with little kids in mind.

Games to Go

What can an iQue offer that a Game Boy can't? An inexpensive, diverse, and mentally stimulating collection of games, all played on a screen that's bigger and infinitely easier on the eyes. Many adults have already experienced the joy that is Bejeweled, so why not give the kids a turn at the handheld arcade?

An absolute must-have for youngsters, Amusement Park Kids (**www.cakesoftware .com**) challenges your child's recognition, concentration, pattern matching, and reflex skills with ten different games. And don't stop with the Kids version—the developer has grown-up editions that are just as fun and accessible. Speaking of amusement parks, Bang Bang (**www.astraware.com**) evokes memories of the boardwalk shooting gallery, as you tap to knock down moving and stationary targets. Remember the old electronic game Simon? That's ATOM (**www.comcul.com**) in a nutshell: players must tap the molecules in sequence as they light up. Finally, no iQue-wielding parent should be without Kidz Pak 1.3c (**www.notionssoftware.com**), a collection of five familiar games, including connect the dots, word search, and matching pairs.

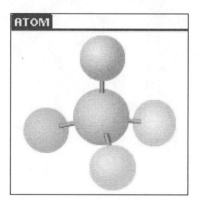

If you have tweens and teens, let them experience the classics of *your* youth. Galax and Froggy (**www.pilotfan.com**) are faithful recreations of Galaxian and Frogger, two of the all-time arcade greats. And don't forget Tetris (**www .pocketexpress.com**), which is just as addictive for kids as it was for you.

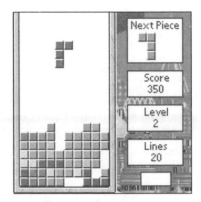

Finally, straight from the Game Boy itself (and most console systems) comes Rayman (**www.gameloft.com**), a faithful and gorgeous port of the popular side-scrolling action game. It features 31 levels, 8 different worlds, and an inexplicably armless/legless hero.

iQue Accessories

Like to accessorize? There are a handful of extras you may want to add to your iQue, starting with a pair of headphones. The unit's built-in speaker may be fine for voice directions, but it's pretty weak when it comes to music. Fortunately, the iQue has a standard-size headphone jack, so you can easily plug in your favorite pair. Or consider an FM transmitter like the Arkon SoundFeeder, which also plugs into the headphone jack and broadcasts your tunes (or audio programs) to any FM radio. This is an ideal solution for the car.

Next up: a keyboard. At press time, there were no keyboards designed specifically for the iQue, but it works just fine with the handful of wireless models now available. These keyboards rely on a PDA's IR port, meaning that they're universally compatible. Far and away the best option I've seen yet is Palm's own Wireless Keyboard (see Figure 10-2), which folds in half when not in use for easy storage and portability. It's $69.95.

Keyboards and FM transmitters are optional, but one accessory I strongly recommend is a screen protector. These are clear plastic sheets that install right over the screen, thereby protecting it from scratches and reducing glare. I've tried many such products over the years, and my favorite is still the BoxWave ClearTouch. It's $12.95, and it's so durable (you can even remove it and wash it if need be) that I'm still using the same one after about nine months.

Finally, consider a case for your iQue—especially if you plan to loan the unit to the kids once in a while (see "Keeping the Kids Happy" earlier in this chapter). At press time, the iQue was so new that few companies were offering cases for it. However, I did find one that looks pretty sweet: the Covertec Garmin iQue 3600 Case. It's available in black, brown, or red leather, and it includes slots for holding both credit cards and memory cards. It's designed so that you can flip up the iQue's antenna without having to remove the case (though obviously you can't close it while the antenna's up). The case is available exclusively from MobilePlanet (**www.mobileplanet.com**).

10

FIGURE 10-2 You can use the Palm Wireless Keyboard, shown here with the Tungsten T3, for comfortable typing while traveling.

Nine Great Tips and Tricks

These handy little secrets will help you on your way from novice user to iQue pro.

1. **Easy software installation** To save yourself the hassles of downloading, unzipping, and queuing Palm OS software (freeware and commercial applications alike) for installation, grab PalmGear's StreamLync utility. It's free, and it allows you to download and install software from PalmGear with just a few easy clicks.

2. **Hotwired HotSync** Can't HotSync all of a sudden? Try a soft reset of your handheld. More times than not, this solves the problem.

3. **HotSync with the Web** Did you know you can synchronize your handheld with Yahoo! Address Book and then access your calendar, contacts, and memos from any web-enabled computer? Just visit Yahoo! Mobile (**mobile.yahoo.com**), click the PDA Downloads link, and then look for Intellisync for Yahoo! It's free, as is the account you'll need to set up with Yahoo! Follow the instructions carefully, however, as you could accidentally wind up unable to HotSync with your PC.

4.   **Sync with your spouse**   It's one thing to sync two handhelds to the same PC. It's another to have access to each other's schedule. DualDate, a Palm freebie, puts your calendar side by side with a spouse, friend, coworker, or anyone else for at-a-glance comparison.

5.   **Happy holidays**   Want to add all the holidays to your date book? Just download 2004 USA Holidays 1.1 (**www.freewarepalm.com**). It contains 36 U.S. and religious holidays. While you're at it, get the 2005–2010 calendars as well. Just import the files into Palm Desktop and then HotSync.

6.   **Louder alarms**   If you've set the alarm volume to High in Preferences, but your alarms still aren't loud enough, try switching to a different alarm sound. In Date Book, tap Menu | Options | Preferences. Tap the arrow next to Alarm Sound and then choose a tune. You'll hear it played immediately. Find the one that's loudest and then tap OK.

7.   **Maximize your memos**   I find that most people tend to underutilize Memo Pad, which is an excellent tool for making lists. I use mine to keep lists of movies I want to rent, books I want to read, wines I've tried and liked, gifts my wife has hinted at, and so on.

8.   **A picture is worth a thousand words**   The iQue makes an excellent scratchpad. I'm talking about actual scribbles, not text notes you record in Memo Pad. With a program like DiddleBug, for instance, I can quickly jot down a phone number or draw the measurements of a room before heading to Home Depot to buy paint. DiddleBug is a freebie, but it doesn't let you use the entire iQue screen. For that, I recommend BugMe, which also allows you to attach alarms to your notes.

10

9.   **Graffiti at a glance**   Swipe the stylus from the bottom of the screen to the top, and a handy Graffiti reference chart appears.

Troubleshooting Your iQue

No computer is perfect. Windows is about as far from the mark as you can get, Macs have problems of their own, and even iQues suffer the occasional meltdown. Usually it's minor—some poorly written program causes a crash or something like that. But sometimes something downright scary happens, like a sudden and inexplicable lockup that wipes out the iQue's entire memory. In this section, I'll address some of the most common maladies and, hopefully, help you prevent the worst of them.

 *Many common problems are addressed on Garmin's web site (**www .garmin.com**). I'm not going to rehash them here, but I do suggest you check out the site if you have a problem I haven't addressed. Chances are good you'll find a solution.*

Cure Most Problems with a Reset

Just as rebooting a computer will often resolve a glitch or lockup, resetting your handheld is the solution to many a problem. And it's usually the first thing you need to do if your device crashes—or just acts a little strangely.

When a computer crashes, that generally means it has plowed into a brick wall and can no longer function. Fortunately, whereas a car in the same situation would need weeks of bump-and-paint work, a computer can usually return to normal by being rebooted. In the case of an iQue, a *reset* is the same as a *reboot*.

When an iQue crashes, one common error message is "Fatal Exception." Don't be alarmed; this isn't nearly as morbid as it sounds. It simply means that the iQue has encountered a glitch that proved troublesome to its operation. Very often, an onscreen Reset button will appear with this error, a tap of which performs a "soft reset" (as described in the next section). Sometimes, however, the crash is so severe that even this button doesn't work. (You know because you tap it and nothing happens.) In a case like that, you have to perform a manual reset.

Ways to Reset an iQue

On the back of your iQue is a little hole labeled RESET. Hidden inside this hole is a button that effectively reboots the unit. When the unit reboots, you see the Palm OS startup screen, followed a few seconds later by the Preferences screen. That's how a successful reset goes. About 98 percent of the time, everything will be as you left it: your data, your applications, everything.

TIP   *How can you press the Reset button inside that tiny hole? You can always bend open a paper clip and use one end of that. Or, better yet, unscrew the top end of the iQue's stylus. You'll find a reset pin conveniently located underneath it.*

10

Technically speaking, there are three kinds of resets: soft, warm, and hard. (Mind out of the gutter, please.) The details:

- **Soft**   Only in rare instances do you need to perform anything other than a soft reset, which is akin to pressing CTRL-ALT-DELETE to reboot your computer. You simply press the Reset button and then wait a few seconds while your iQue resets itself. No data is lost.

- **Warm**   A warm reset, performed by holding down the Scroll Up button while pressing the Reset button, goes an extra step by bypassing any system patches or special utilities you may have installed. Use this only if your iQue fails to respond to a soft reset—that is, if it's still locked up, crashing, or stuck in a boot loop (the Palm logo is flashing or the screen is displaying garbage). No data is lost, but you have to manually re-enable any system patches or utilities.

- **Hard**   With any luck, you'll never have to use a hard reset. A hard reset wipes out everything in your iQue's memory, essentially returning it to factory condition. In the exceedingly rare case that your iQue is seriously

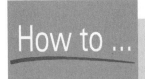 **Perform Warm and Hard Resets**

There's a bit of a trick to performing a warm or hard reset successfully. With your iQue on or off (it doesn't matter), hold down the Scroll Up button (for a warm reset) or the Power button (for a hard reset); then press and release the Reset button on the back of the unit. Now, here's the trick: *wait until the Palm logo appears on the screen* before releasing the Scroll Up or Power button. If you release both buttons simultaneously, before the logo appears, all you get is a soft reset.

hosed (it won't reset or even turn off), this should at least get you back to square one. If it doesn't, your handheld is toast and will need to be replaced. The good news is this: even after a hard reset, all it takes is a HotSync to restore all your applications and data. You may have to re-enter some registration codes for third-party applications, but otherwise you'll be good to go. Let's see a computer do that!

Beaming Problems

Having trouble beaming? Chances are good that the problem is caused by one of three factors. First, make sure the two handhelds aren't too close together. People often make the mistake of holding their PDAs right next to each other, which can cause trouble for the infrared transceivers. Keep the units at least a few inches apart (their maximum range is about five feet, by the way).

Second, make sure the Beam Receive option is checked on the Prefs | Power screen. While you may not have unchecked it yourself, sometimes it just seems to happen.

If neither of these suggestions solves the problem, try moving to a darker area. Beaming doesn't always work if you're in a brightly lit room or outdoors on a sunny day.

If all else fails, you might want to perform a soft reset on both handhelds; that should clear up whatever problem was keeping your devices from chatting with each other.

Other Sources for Help

While Garmin's web site is a good resource for troubleshooting assistance, several independent sites and newsgroups also offer tips, tricks, hints, and technical solutions. If you're looking for answers that aren't in this book or on the Garmin site, try some of these.

Site	Description
www.brighthand.com	There's a Garmin message board in the Palm Powered Devices section of Forums.
www.pdabuzz.com	Like Brighthand, this site has a message board area in which you can post questions and read answers to common questions. It also contains Palm OS–related product news and reviews.
alt.comp.sys.palmtops.pilot comp.sys.palmtops.pilot	These newsgroups are available to anyone with a newsreader like Outlook Express. They are threaded message boards that contain questions and answers about Palm OS issues. You can post your own questions, respond to what's already there, or just read the existing posts.

Where to Find It

Web Site	Address	What's There
Applian	www.replay-radio.com	Replay Radio
Arkon	www.arkon.com	SoundFeeder
BoxWave	www.boxwave.com	ClearTouch
DataViz	www.dataviz.com	Documents To Go
Electric Pocket	www.electricpocket.com	BugMe
Fictionwise	www.fictionwise.com	Commercial fiction and nonfiction e-books and short stories
Freewarepalm	www.freewarepalm.com	Free Palm OS games (and other programs)
Handango	www.handango.com	Thousands of Palm OS programs
Kinoma	www.kinoma.com	Kinoma Player and Producer
Margi Systems	www.margi.com	Presenter-to-Go
MemoWare	www.memoware.com	Public-domain e-books

Web Site	Address	What's There
MobilePlanet	**www.mobileplanet.com**	Covertec iQue case and other PDA accessories
Palm Digital Media	**www.palmdigitalmedia.com**	Commercial fiction and nonfiction e-books
PalmGear.com	**www.palmgear.com**	Almost every program mentioned in this chapter
PerfectBound	**www.perfectbound.com**	E-books from HarperCollins
NormSoft	**www.pockettunes.net**	Pocket Tunes
RandomHouse.com	**www.randomhouse.com**	E-books from Random House
TealPoint Software	**www.tealpoint.com**	TealMovie
Veo	**www.veo.com**	Veo Photo Traveler

Index

See the entry, Web addresses, for a comprehensive listing of the products and manufacturers referenced in this book.

Numbers

3D coordinate, explanation of, 22
6-in-1 readers, price range of, 253
9-pin serial cables, using with GPS receivers, 88–89
750NAV Plus, features of, 62

A

A and 1 buttons in Graffiti area of iQue 3600 PDAs, description of, 193
ABC Kiddie Cards, obtaining online, 270
AC adapters, plugging into iQue 3600 PDAs, 228
accounts, creating in Geocaching.com, 128
AcidFreecell, playing in iQue 3600 PDAs, 249
acquisition time, explanation of, 49–50
Acrobat Reader software, obtaining online, 265
addresses
    entering safely, 56–57, 65–66
    routing with iQue 3600 PDAs, 216–220
Aggression, playing in iQue 3600 PDAs, 249
A-GPS (Assisted GPS), explanation of, 22
Aircraft Owners and Pilots Association, Web address for, 167
AirMap 100 GPS receiver, features of, 156
alarms, adjusting volume of, 275
ALK Technologies, Web address for, 52, 79
Amusement Park Kids, obtaining online, 271
antennas for GPS receivers, types of, 49
Applian, Web address for, 279

applications
    beaming on iQue 3600 PDAs, 233–235
    installing to memory cards, 246
    placing in external storage, 239
AppointmentsEnd box, attaching locations to, 222
Arkon, Web address for, 279
ATOM, obtaining online, 271
Auto Navigation kit, features of, 215
autopiloting with marine GPS, 163
aviation
    choosing GPS receivers for, 29
    GPS receivers for, 158–160
    relationship to GPS, 5
    using GPS for, 9–10, 150–153
    using PDAs for, 158–160
aviation GPS simulator, example of, 157
avoid tolls routing option, explanation of, 68

B

Bang Bang, obtaining online, 271
battery life
    improving for iQue 3600 PDAs, 227–229
    significance of, 50
beaming
    applications, 233–235
    on iQue 3600 PDAs, 230–231
    selecting items for, 231–233
    troubleshooting, 278
Bejeweled, playing in iQue 3600 PDAs, 249
biking
    choosing GPS receivers for, 29
    using Garmin Forerunner 201 for, 46
    using GPS for, 102
billiards, playing in iQue 3600 PDAs, 251
Bluetooth, relationship to GPS, 38

boating, choosing GPS receivers for, 29
books, reading on iQue 3600 PDAs, 257–261.
   See also e-books; fiction e-books; nonfiction
   e-books
Book Smarts iQue application for children,
   features of, 266–267
BoxWave products
   MiniSync trickle charge cable with iQue
      3600 PDAs, 228–229
   Web address for, 241, 279
Brightness icon, accessing in iQue 3600 PDAs,
   194–195
BugMe, obtaining online, 279
Bump Attack Pinball, playing in iQue 3600
   PDAs, 251
business use of GPS, examples of, 13–14

C

caches
   choosing for Geocaching, 118–120
   creating and placing with Geocaching.com, 126
   finding on Geocaching.com, 122–124
   sample contents of, 111–112
   types of, 124–125
cameras, adding to iQue 3600 PDAs, 267–268
camping, using GPS for, 98–102
capital letters, writing in Graffiti, 203
card readers, features of, 253
car GPS receivers, features of, 18
car navigation, using GPS for, 7–8
carnivorous plants, using GPS for location of,
   105–107
carpool routing option, explanation of, 69
cars, obtaining GPS hardware for, 52.
   See also in-car navigation
cases, using with iQue 3600 PDAs, 273
cell phones
   using GPS with, 171–173
   using TeleNav with, 78–79
channels, significance of, 50–51
childrens entertainment and iQue 3600 PDAs.
   See also games
   ABC Kiddie Cards, 270
   Amusement Park Kids, 271
   ATOM, 271
   Bang Bang, 271
   Children's Illustrated eTales, 266
   Funny Faces doodling program, 268–269

Galax and Froggy, 271
Hot Hangman, 270
Kidz Pak 1.3c, 271
Learn ABC, 270
Match Game 1.2, 270
MemoWare e-books in public domain, 267
music, 269
PDA Bookstore and Childrens section, 267
PDA Playground, 271
Rayman, 272
TealPaint program, 269
Tetris, 271
Children's Illustrated eTales, Web address for, 267
child safety devices
   choosing GPS receivers for, 29
   features of, 46–47
ClearTouch, obtaining online, 279
clock, accessing on iQue 3600 PDAs, 194
cold start, explanation of, 49
Color Portable golf Unit
   features of, 140–141
   obtaining online, 140–141
contact addresses, routing with iQue 3600
      PDAs, 218–220
contact lists, choosing destinations from, 67
coordinates, entering in GPS receivers, 126–129
CoPilot Live GPS software
   features of, 41
   obtaining online, 40, 52, 79
   planning trips with, 64
   storage capabilities of and download options
      for, 62
course and heading, plotting with marine
   GPS, 163
Cribbage 3.0, playing on iQue 3600 PDAs, 247
CropTrak software, using for vineyard
   management, 181–182
cross-country skiing, choosing GPS receivers
   for, 29
Crossword Puzzles for Palm OS, playing in
   iQue 3600 PDAs, 249

D

D/2000 AutoDispatch Location Engine, features
   of, 174
DataViz products
   using with iQue 3600 PDAs, 262
   Web address for, 241, 279

date books, adding holidays to, 275
DeLorme products
    Topo USA, 104–105
    Web address for, 52, 107
destinations
    choosing from contact lists, 67
    entering from maps, 68
    entering in GPS receivers, 65–69
    entering safely, 56–57
Detour icon in QueRoutes window, purpose
    of, 224
detours, generating, 77
DGPS (Differential GPS), explanation of, 5, 23
digital video, using as video source for iQue
    3600 PDAs, 255
directions, entering safely, 56–57.
    See also mapping software
dispatching, using GPS for, 174–176
Doc format versus .doc files, 258
docks, marking when fishing, 96
Documents To Go
    obtaining online, 241, 279
    using with iQue 3600 PDAs, 262
DoD (Department of Defense), relationship
    to GPS, 4
drift, following when fishing, 96
DUI (download, unzip, install), significance
    of, 244
DVD, using as video source for iQue 3600
    PDAs, 255

E

E911 services, explanation of, 12, 171
Earthmate GPS for Handhelds, obtaining online,
    40, 52
Easy CD Creator, obtaining online, 269
EasyGPS freeware utility
    importing and exporting with, 90–91
    obtaining online, 92, 107, 135
    using with Geocaching, 130
e-books. *See also* books; fiction e-books;
    nonfiction e-books
    obtaining online, 280
    reading on iQue 3600 PDAs, 257–261
    reading with iQue backlight, 261
Edit Vias icon in QueRoutes window, purpose
    of, 225
Electric Pocket, Web address for, 279

Emtac products
    Web address for, 52
    Wireless Bluetooth GPS, 40
Enhanced 911 services, explanation of, 12, 171
EOTD (Enhanced Observed Time Difference),
    explanation of, 12
expansion slot on Garmin iQue 3600 PDA,
    features of, 188

F

"Fatal Exception" error message,
    troubleshooting, 277
favorites, entering in GPS receivers, 67
fiction e-books, obtaining online, 259, 279, 280.
    See also books; e-books; nonfiction e-books
Fictionwise, obtaining online contemporary
    e-books from, 260, 279
file managers, disadvantages of, 239
FileZ file manager, features of, 235
films, source of, 255
Find icon in Graffiti area of iQue 3600 PDAs,
    description of, 193
fish finding with marine GPS, 163
fishing
    choosing GPS receivers for, 29
    using GPS for, 91–97
Fishing Hot Spots, features of, 97
FleetBoss, Web address for, 182
fleet management, using GPS for, 172–173,
    176–177
Flight Simulator 2004, features of, 151–152
flying. *See* aviation
FM transmitters, using with iQue 3600 PDAs,
    273–274
fog mode routing option, explanation of, 69
Forerunner 201, features of, 44–45
Freewarepalm, Web address for, 279
FRS (Family Radio Service), explanation of, 83
Fugawi desktop mapping package, using with
    iQue 3600 PDAs, 227
Funny Faces doodling program, using with
    iQues, 268–269

G

Galax and Froggy
    obtaining online, 271
    playing in iQue 3600 PDAs, 249

games. *See also* childrens entertainment
and iQue 3600 PDAs
  AcidFreecell, 249
  Aggression, 249
  Bejeweled, 250
  Billiards, 251
  Bump Attack Pinball, 251
  Cribbage 3.0, 247
  Crossword Puzzles for Palm OS, 250
  Galax, 249
  Monopoly, 249
  Mulg II, 247
  NetWalk II, 250
  Patience Revisited, 247
  PilOth, 248
  playing, 247
  Pocket Video Poker, 248
  Rook's Revenge, 250
  Scrabble, 250
  Sea War, 248
  Solitaire Poker, 248
  Text Twist, 250
  Vegas Blackjack, 249
  Vexed 2.1, 248
  Zap!2016, 249
Garmin iQue accessories
  cases, 273
  FM transmitters, 272–273
  screen protectors, 273
  Wireless keyboards, 272–273
Garmin iQue 3600 PDA routing
  to contact addresses, 218–220
  to points of interest, 220–221
  to street addresses, 216–217
Garmin iQue 3600 PDAs
  adding Veo Photo Traveler cameras to, 268
  attaching Locations to AppointmentsEnd box
    in, 222
  beaming on, 230–235
  buttons on, 195–197
  creating mobile offices with, 261–265
  deleting maps from, 213
  determining amount of memory left on, 201
  entering data into, 200, 202–205
  features of, 32–33, 39, 67, 177–178
  getting video into, 254–257
  Graffiti area of, 190–193
  improving battery life of, 227–229

installing software on, 244–246
key features of, 188–189
listening to music on, 251–252
making presentations on, 263–264
obtaining help for, 279
obtaining online, 79
overview of, 185–186
versus PCs, 197–198
playing games on, 247–251
playing NPR (National Public Radio) on, 252
plugging AC adapters into, 228
preparing for in-car navigation with, 215
reading e-books on, 257–261
relationship to Palm OS, 187
reprogramming buttons on, 197
resetting, 276–278
routing to places visited already with, 223
as scratchpads, 275
shortcoming of, 194
storage capabilities of and download options
  for, 62
storing maps on, 213–214
and synchronization, 207–208
tapping versus writing on, 189–190
tips and tricks for use of, 274–276
toolbar in, 194–195
troubleshooting, 276–278
using for outdoor activities, 226–227
using Funny Faces doodling program with,
  268–269
using Graffiti with, 202–204
using memory cards with, 235, 237–240
using onscreen keyboard with, 204–205
using Recent Finds feature with, 223
viewing PDFs on, 264–265
watching movies on, 254
Garmin iQue 3600 PDAs and childrens
  entertainment
  ABC Kiddie Cards, 270
  Amusement Park Kids, 271
  ATOM, 271
  Bang Bang, 271
  Children's Illustrated eTales, 266, 267
  Funny Faces doodling program, 268–269
  Galax and Froggy, 271
  Hot Hangman, 270
  Kidz Pak 1.3c, 271
  Learn ABC, 270

Match Game 1.2, 270
MemoWare e-books in public domain, 267
music, 269
PDA Bookstore and Childrens section, 267
PDA Playground, 271
Rayman, 272
TealPaint program, 269
Tetris, 271
Garmin MapSource Fishing Hot Spots, features
   of, 97
Garmin products
   Auto Navigation kit, 215
   Forerunner 201, 44–45
   Geko 101, 85, 113–114, 127–128
   Geko 201, 135
   GPSMAP 76, 93, 94
   GPSMAP 196 receiver, 9–10, 156
   GPS V Deluxe, 32
   U.S. Topo, 104
   Web address for, 52, 79, 107, 135, 167, 182
Garmin Rino 110 and 120 GPS receivers
   features of, 43
   using for outdoor activities, 83
Garmin StreetPilot
   displaying street-level maps on, 31
   features of, 27
   obtaining online, 79
Garmin StreetPilot III
   features of, 32
   storage capabilities of and download options
     for, 62
Garmin TracBack feature, example of, 88
gas stations, locating with marine GPS, 164
Geko games, examples of, 134
Geko 101
   marking and managing waypoints with, 85
   using for Geocaching, 113–114, 127–128
Geko 201, obtaining online, 135
Geocaching
   choosing caches for, 118–120
   choosing GPS receivers for, 29, 113–115
   difficulties associated with, 123
   entering coordinates for, 126–129
   environmental impact of, 116–117
   example of, 130–134
   explanation of, 11
   future of, 117
   overview of, 110–112

   performing fairly and responsibly, 130
   performing responsibly, 117
   popularity of, 116
   preparing checklist for, 121–122
Geocaching.com
   creating accounts in, 128
   getting help with, 126
   interview with owner of, 116–117
   premium membership in, 126
   working with, 122–126
Geodashing game
   description of, 135
   Web address for, 135
GeoNiche software
   features of, 100–101
   obtaining online, 107
Geoteaming
   features of, 178
   Web address for, 182
GMRS (General Mobile Radio Service),
   explanation of, 83
golfing
   choosing GPS receivers for, 29
   dedicated receivers versus PDAs used for, 145
   using dedicated GPS receivers for, 140–142
   using GPS receivers for, 43–44, 139
   using GPS with, 10–11
   using PDAs for, 143–145
GolfLogix products
   Web address for, 147
   xCaddie, 140
Golf Position Solutions Pocket Caddie, features
   of, 144
GolfViaGPS, Web address for, 147
GPS add-ons for PDAs, table of, 40
GPS Bundles, obtaining online, 40
GPS business applications
   dispatching, 174–176
   examples of, 170
   fleet management and dispatching, 172–177
   vineyards, 181–182
GPS cell phones, features of, 19
GPS chartplotters, benefits of, 163–164
GPS Companion, obtaining online, 40
GPS constellation, completion of, 5
GPS-enabled phones, benefits of, 175
GPS features and tech specs, overview of, 47,
   49–51

GPS for Handhelds, obtaining online, 40
GPS games
    Geko games, 134
    Geodashing, 135
    MinuteWar, 135
GPS gear, obtaining online, 52
GPS (Global Positioning System)
    benefits to pilots, 153–155
    buying PDAs for, 37
    in cellular market, 171–173
    core benefits of, 170
    explanation of, 23
    features of, 2–4
    fees associated with use of, 5
    future of, 14–15
    having backup plan for, 60–65
    history of, 4–6
    navigating with, 177–178
GPS hardware
    GPS receivers, 15–19
    obtaining online, 52
GPS locator products, examples of, 19
GPSMAP 76, floatability of, 93, 94
GPSMAP 196 receivers, using for aviation,
        9–10, 156
GPS Master, using for aviation, 159
GPS Nav Kit
    features of, 39
    obtaining online, 40, 52, 79
    storage capabilities of and download options
        for, 62
GPS receivers
    accuracy of, 93, 123
    adjusting volume of, 58
    alarms available in, 93
    antennas used with, 49
    for aviation, 155–156, 158–162
    child safety devices, 46–47
    choosing for Geocaching, 113–115
    choosing prior to buying PDAs, 38
    compensating for inaccuracies of, 75–76
    connecting to PCs, 88
    construction considerations, 99
    dedicated receivers for golfing, 140–142
    entering coordinates into, 126–129
    entering destinations in, 65–69
    fishing with, 96–97
    floatability of, 93
    form factor of, 93–94

on golf courses, 139
    in-car GPS receivers, 18
    leveraging import-export capabilities of, 89–90
    loading maps into, 61–65
    mapping features of, 94–95
    marine applications of, 166–167
    mountable models of, 93–94
    navigating with, 70–79
    for notebooks, 17–18
    obtaining online, 135
    for PDAs, 17, 34–42
    raw data produced by, 15–16
    for runners, 44–46
    screen types of, 95
    setting zoom level for, 72–74
    sonar capability of, 95
    stand-alone GPS receivers, 16
    turn-by-turn directions on, 71–72
    two-way radio GPS receivers, 43
    types of, 29
    using for fishing, 91–97
GPS safety precautions, observing, 55–61
GPS SG2 Personal Digital Caddie, features of,
        141–142
GPS signals, impact of weather on, 9
GPS software
    CoPilot Live, 41
    functionality of, 22
    importance of, 19–21
    Mapopolis Navigator, 41
    MyNavigator, 42
    for outdoor activities, 100–101
    TomTom Navigator, 42
GPS systems
    mounting wisely, 58–60
    price range of, 31
GPS terminology
    3D coordinate, 22
    A-GPS (Assisted GPS), 22
    DGPS (Differential GPS), 23
    GPS (Global Positioning System), 23
    latitude, 23
    longitude, 23
    NMEA (National Marine Electronics
        Association), 23
    triangulation, 23
    WAAS (Wide Area Augmentation Service), 23
    waypoint, 23

GPS time, explanation of, 14
GPS TimeTrack, features of, 176
GPS usage
   by businesses, 13–14
   in car navigation, 7–8
   by consumers, 7
   Geocaching, 11
   with golf, 10–11
   in hiking, fishing, and other outdoor
       activities, 8–9
   personal and child safety, 12–13
   for private aviation, 9–10
GPS V Deluxe, features of, 32
GPS 3450, obtaining online, 40
Graffiti
   tips and tricks for use of, 203–204
   using to enter data on iQue 3600 PDAs,
       202–204
Graffiti area of iQue 3600 PDAs
   A and 1 buttons in, 193
   appearance of, 191
   Find icon in, 193
   hiding and showing, 191
   Home icon in, 192
   Menu icon in, 192
   QueRoutes icon in, 192
Graffiti reference chart, displaying
   on iQues, 276

H

Handango, Web address for, 279
handhelds, syncing, 275
hard resets, performing on iQues, 277–278
Hauppauge WinTV-PVR-250 TV tuner cards,
   using with iQue 3600 PDAs, 254
help, obtaining for iQue 3600 PDAs, 279
Hide & Seek a Cache option, explanation
   of, 122–123
hiking
   choosing GPS receivers for, 29
   using GPS for, 98–102
hitchhikers, relationship to Geocaching, 124–125
Home icon in Graffiti area of iQue 3600 PDAs,
   description of, 192
hospitals, locating, 76
Hot Hangman, obtaining online, 270
HotSync cradles, using with Garmin iQue 3600
   PDAs, 186

HotSync operations, troubleshooting on iQue
   3600 PDAs, 274
hunting, using GPS for, 98–102

I

iCN 630
   features of, 33
   mounting, 58–59
   obtaining online, 79
   storage capabilities of and download options
       for, 62
iGolfgps product, features of, 146–147
in-car navigation, choosing GPS receivers for,
   27, 29. *See also* cars
Install Tool, using with iQue 3600 PDAs, 245
IntelliGolf
   features of, 145–147
   Web address for, 147
Internet, using as video source for iQue 3600
   PDAs, 255
intersections, entering in GPS receivers, 66
iQue accessories
   cases, 273
   FM transmitters, 272–273
   screen protectors, 273
   Wireless keyboards, 273–274
iQue 3600 PDA routing
   to contact addresses, 218–220
   to points of interest, 220–221
   to street addresses, 216–217
iQue 3600 PDAs
   adding Veo Photo Traveler cameras to, 268
   attaching Locations to AppointmentsEnd
       box in, 222
   beaming on, 230–235
   buttons on, 195–197
   creating mobile offices with, 261–265
   deleting maps from, 213
   determining amount of memory left on, 201
   entering data into, 200, 202–205
   features of, 32–33, 177–178
   getting video into, 254–257
   Graffiti area of, 190–193
   improving battery life of, 227–229
   installing software on, 244–246
   key features of, 188–189
   listening to music on, 251–252
   making presentations on, 263–264

obtaining help for, 279
obtaining online, 79
overview of, 185–186
versus PCs, 197–198
playing games on, 247–251
playing NPR (National Public Radio) on, 252
plugging AC adapters into, 228
preparing for in-car navigation with, 215
reading e-books on, 257–261
relationship to Palm OS, 187
reprogramming buttons on, 197
resetting, 276–278
routing to places visited already with, 223
routing with, 214, 216–221, 223–227
as scratchpads, 275
shortcoming of, 194
storage capabilities of and download options
    for, 62
storing maps on, 213–214
and synchronization, 207–208
tapping versus writing on, 189–190
tips and tricks for use of, 274–276
toolbar in, 194–195
troubleshooting, 276–278
using for outdoor activities, 226–227
using Funny Faces doodling program with,
    268–269
using Graffiti with, 202–204
using memory cards with, 235, 237–240
using onscreen keyboard with, 204–205
using Recent Finds feature with, 223
viewing PDFs on, 264–265
watching movies on, 254
iQue 3600 PDAs and children's entertainment
    ABC Kiddie Cards, 270
    Amusement Park Kids, 271
    ATOM, 271
    Bang Bang, 271
    Children's Illustrated eTales, 266
    Funny Faces doodling program, 268–269
    Galax and Froggy, 271
    Hot Hangman, 270
    Kidz Pak 1.3c, 271
    Learn ABC, 270
    Match Game 1.2, 270
    MemoWare e-books in public domain, 267
    music, 269
    PDA Bookstore and Childrens section, 267
    PDA Playground, 271

Rayman, 272
    TealPaint program, 269
    Tetris, 271
IR port on iQue 3600 PDAs
    features of, 188
    location of, 229–230

J

jog dial on Garmin iQue 3600 PDA, features
    of, 188

K

Karrier Communications' IntelliGolf, features
    of, 145–147
keyboards, connecting to iQue 3600 PDAs, 201
Kidz Pak 1.3c, obtaining online, 271
Kinoma products
    Player and Producer, 256–257, 279
    Web address for, 279
Kivera's D/2000 AutoDispatch Location Engine,
    features of, 174

L

lakes, outlining when fishing, 96
latitude
    determining, 127–128
    explanation of, 23
Learn ABC, obtaining online, 270
location awareness feature of marine GPS,
    benefits of, 163
locations, attaching to AppointmentsEnd box, 222
longitude
    determining, 127–128
    explanation of, 23
Lowrance products
    AirMap 100 GPS receiver, 156
    Web address for, 167
LX200GPS telescope, features of, 14

M

Macintosh systems, using The Missing Sync
    for iQue 3600 with, 185
Magellan products
    750NAV Plus, 62
    GPS Companion, 40
    MapSend Topo, 104
    MapSentBlueNav Charts, 94

SporTrak Map, 27–28
SporTrak Marine, 94
SportTrak Topo, 104
Web address for, 52, 107, 135
major/local routing option, explanation of, 68
Map Install window in Palm Desktop,
    displaying, 209
Mapopolis products
    GPS Bundles, 40
    Navigator GPS software, 41–42
    Web address for, 52
mapping features, considering for GPS
    receivers, 94–95, 100
mapping software. *See also* directions
    considerations related to, 30–31
    examples of, 27–28
    features of, 19–20
    street-level mapping, 31–33
MapQuest, using as backup plan, 61
maps
    creation of, 179–181
    deleting from iQue 3600 PDAs, 213
    entering destinations from, 68
    loading into GPS receivers, 61–65
    obtaining online for mountain climbing, 92
    selecting in Palm Desktop, 208–214
    storing on iQue 3600 PDAs, 213–214
    topographic maps, 102–105
MapSend Topo, features of, 104
MapSentBlueNav Charts, features of, 94
MapSource Fishing Hot Spots, features of, 97
Margi Systems products
    Presenter-to-Go, 263–264
    Web address for, 279
marine GPS, overview of, 162–164, 166–167
MarkSpace, Web address for, 241
Match Game 1.2, obtaining online, 270
Meade's LX200GPS telescope, features of, 14
media readers, features of, 253
Memo Pad feature of iQues, using, 275
memory cards
    installing applications to, 246
    moving programs and data onto, 237–240
    price range of, 237
    using with iQue 3600 PDAs, 188, 213–214,
        235, 237–240
memos, maximizing on iQue 3600 PDAs, 275

MemoWare e-books in public domain, Web
    address for, 258, 267, 280
Menu icon in Graffiti area of iQue 3600 PDAs,
    description of, 192
Microsoft Flight Simulator 2004, features
    of, 151–152
MiniSync, obtaining online, 241
Minorplanet USA, Web address for, 182
MinuteWar game
    description of, 135
    Web address for, 135
The Missing Sync for iQue 3600
    obtaining online, 241
    using with Macintosh systems, 185
MMC (MultiMediaCards) versus SD cards, 237
mobile offices, creating with iQue 3600 PDAs,
    261–265
MobilePlanet, Web address for, 273, 280
Mobility Magazine, contents of, 262
Mobipocket contemporary e-books, features
    of, 260–261
Monopoly, playing in iQue 3600 PDAs, 249
mountain climbing, obtaining online map for, 92
MovieJack program, obtaining online, 255
movies, watching on iQue 3600 PDAs, 254
moving map, explanation of, 9
MP3 files, playing on iQue 3600 PDAs, 251–253
Mulg II, playing on iQue 3600 PDAs, 247
multi-caches, features of, 124
music, listening to on iQue 3600 PDAs, 251–253
Muskokatech, Web address for, 167
MyNavigator GPS software
    features of, 36, 42
    zooming with, 72–74

N

Navicache, Web address for, 135
navigation
    with GPS receivers, 70–79, 177–178
    relationship to GPS, 5
    by voice as safety precaution, 57–58
navigation screens, components of, 70
Navigator for Pocket PC, obtaining online, 107
Navigator GPS software, features of, 41–42, 42
Navigator USA
    features of, 39
    obtaining online, 40

Navman products
    GPS 3450, 40
    iCN 630, 33, 58–59, 79
    storage capabilities of and download options
      for, 62
    Web addresses, 52
    Web address for, 79, 167
NAVTECH (Navigation Technologies), digital
    maps created by, 179–181
Navy, relationship to GPS, 4
NetWalk II, playing in iQue 3600 PDAs, 249
NMEA compatibility, significance of, 50
NMEA (National Marine Electronics
    Association), explanation of, 23
nonfiction e-books, obtaining online, 259,
    279, 280.
    See also books; e-books; fiction e-books
NormSoft, Web address for, 280
notebooks, GPS receivers for, 17–18
NPR (National Public Radio), playing on iQue
    3600 PDAs, 252
numeric keypad, launching in Graffiti area
    of iQue 3600 PDAs, 193

O

offset caches, features of, 124
onscreen keyboard, using with iQue 3600 PDAs,
    204–205
Operation Desert Storm, relationship to GPS, 5
orchids, using GPS for location of, 105–107
OS (operating system), explanation of, 187
Otter Web address, 99
outdoor activities
    benefits of using GPS receivers for, 87
    choosing GPS receivers for, 29, 83–84
    GPS software for, 100–101
    using GPS for, 98–102
    using iQue 3600 PDAs for, 226–227

P

Palm Desktop
    map selection in, 208–214
    overview of, 206
    synchronizing iQue 3600 PDAs with, 207–208
Palm Digital Media
    viewing e-books with, 259–260
    Web address for, 259, 280

PalmGear, Web address for, 241, 280
Palm OS
    games and programs for, 279
    icons in, 198–199
    installing on iQue 3600 PDAs, 274
    menus in, 199–200
    relationship to Garmin iQue 3600 PDA, 187
    using for outdoor activities, 100–101
Palm Reader, features of, 257–261
Palms versus Pocket PCs, 35
parallel receiver, explanation of, 50
patch antenna, explanation of, 49
PathAway for Palm OS
    obtaining online, 167
    using for aviation, 158–159
Patience Revisited, playing on iQue 3600
    PDAs, 247
PCs (personal computers)
    connecting GPS receivers to, 88
    versus iQue 3600 PDAs, 197–198
PDA accessories, obtaining online, 280
PDA Bookstore, Childrens section of, 267
PDAs (Personal Digital Assistants)
    advisory about using for outdoor activities, 99
    benefits of, 31–32, 36–37, 67
    buying for GPS, 37
    disadvantages of, 37–38
    expense of, 38
    golfing with, 143–145
    GPS add-ons for, 40
    as GPS platforms, 28–29
    GPS receivers for, 17, 34–42
    mounting, 58–60
    obtaining hardware for, 52
    setting zoom levels on, 74
    using for airplane GPS, 158–160
    using for Geocaching, 114–115
    using for marine GPS, 166
    using travel chargers with, 37
    wiring of, 38
.pdb file extension, meaning of, 257
PDFs, viewing on iQue 3600 PDAs, 264–265
PerfectBound contemporary e-books
    features of, 261
    Web address for, 280
Persian Gulf War, relationship to GPS, 5
PilOth, playing on iQue 3600 PDAs, 248
pilots, use of GPS by, 153–155

PlayTime, Inc.'s Geoteaming, features
    of, 178, 181
Pocket Caddie
    features of, 144
    Web address for, 147
Pocket PC OS, disadvantages of, 37–38
Pocket PC PDAs, benefits of, 31–32
Pocket PC software, using for outdoor
    activities, 101
Pocket PCs versus Palms, 35
Pocket Tunes, obtaining online, 280
Pocket Video Poker, playing on iQue 3600
    PDAs, 248
points of interest
    entering in GPS receivers, 66–67
    routing option for, 69
    routing with iQue 3600 PDAs, 220–221
PowerPoint presentations, making on iQue 3600
    PDAs, 263–264
presentations, making on iQue 3600 PDAs,
    263–264
Presenter-to-Go
    obtaining online, 280
    using on iQue 3600 PDAs, 263–264
public-domain e-books, obtaining online, 280

Q

quad helix antenna, explanation of, 49
quadrifilar antenna, explanation of, 49
QueAudio program in iQue 3600 PDAs, features
    of, 251–253
QueGPS screen, accessing on iQue 3600
    PDAs, 194
QueRoutes window, displaying on iQue 3600
    PDAs, 192, 223–224
quickest/shortest routing option, explanation
    of, 68
QWERTY keyboard, launching in Graffiti area
    of iQue 3600 PDAs, 193

R

radio beacons, availability of, 153
RandomHouse.com contemporary e-books
    features of, 261
    Web address for, 280
RayDar LLC, Web address for, 107
Rayman, obtaining online, 272

Raymarine, Web address for, 167
real-time data, explanation of, 3–4
real-time routing, benefits of, 34, 65
Recalculate icon in QueRoutes window, purpose
    of, 224
Recent Finds feature, routing to places visited
    already with, 223
Replay Radio program
    obtaining online, 279
    using with iQue 3600 PDAs, 252
rerouting
    and detours, 77
    explanation of, 76–77
    and stopovers, 77
Rino 110 and 120 GPS receivers
    features of, 43
    obtaining online, 107
    using for outdoor activities, 83–84
RoboPhoto software
    obtaining online, 107
    using with GPS, 106–107
Rook's Revenge, playing in iQue 3600 PDAs, 249
Route Preferences icon in QueRoutes window,
    purpose of, 224–225
routes
    generating on the fly, 34
    making changes or additions to using iQue
        3600 PDAs, 223–225
    obtaining online, sharing and storing, 88–91
    significance of, 51
    studying in advance, 75
routing options, overview of, 68–69
running, GPS product for, 44–46

S

SA (selective availability), development and
    termination of, 5–6
satellites
    functionality of, 2
    spare satellites, 3
Saved Routes icon in QueRoutes window,
    purpose of, 225
ScanControl products
    CropTrak software, 181–182
    Web address for, 182
Scrabble, playing in iQue 3600 PDAs, 249
screen protectors, using with iQue 3600
    PDAs, 273

screens
    choosing for GPS receivers, 95, 100
    on Garmin iQue 3600 PDAs, 188
scroll buttons on iQue 3600 PDAs, using, 196
SD (Secure Digital) expansion slots
    versus MMC (MultiMediaCards), 237
    obtaining online, 188
Sea War, playing on iQue 3600 PDAs, 248
serial cables, using with GPS receivers, 88–89
shipwreck locations, finding with marine
    GPS, 164
SkyGolf GPS
    features of, 141–142
    Web address for, 147
SkyPlayer, obtaining online golf course data
    with, 142
Socket products
    GPS Nav Kit, 39, 40, 62, 79
    MyNavigator, 36
    Web address for, 52, 79
soft resets, performing on iQues, 277
software
    buying on memory cards, 236
    installing on iQue 3600 PDAs, 244–246
Solitaire Poker, playing on iQue 3600 PDAs, 248
sonar, availability in GPS receivers, 95
SoundFeeder, obtaining online, 279
speed alert routing option, explanation of, 69
speedometer in marine GPS, benefits of, 164
SporTrak products
    Map program, 27–28
    Marine program, 94
    obtaining online, 52
    Topo program, 104, 107
StarCaddy
    features of, 144–145
    Web address for, 147
Stop Navigation icon in QueRoutes window,
    purpose of, 224
stopovers, advisory about, 77
street addresses, routing with iQue 3600
    PDAs, 216–217
street-level mapping, considerations related
    to, 31–33
StreetPilot
    displaying street-level maps on, 31
    features of, 27
    obtaining online, 79

StreetPilot III
    features of, 32
    storage capabilities of and download options
        for, 62
surveying, relationship to GPS, 4
sychronizing iQue 3600 PDAs, 207–208

T

TealMovie video player
    obtaining online, 280
    using with iQue 3600 PDAs, 256–257
TealPaint program, obtaining online, 268
TealPoint software, Web address for, 280
team building, relationship to GPS, 178
TeleNav
    obtaining online, 79
    providing cell-phone navigation with, 78–79
TeleType for Pocket PC
    using for aviation, 159–160, 166
    Web address for, 167
Televigation, Web address for, 79, 182
Tetris, obtaining online, 271
Text Twist, playing in iQue 3600 PDAs, 249
Thales/Magellan, Web address for, 52
ThatWay waypoint-navigation program, using
    with iQue 3600 PDAs, 226
TomeRaider program, obtaining online, 267
TomTom Navigator USA, 42
    features of, 39
    obtaining online, 40
toolbar in iQue 3600 PDAs, features of, 194–195
TopoGrafix, Web address for, 107, 135
topographic maps, using with GPS, 102–105
Topo USA
    features of, 104–105
    obtaining online, 107
TracBack feature, example of, 88
tracking
    overview of, 87–88
    with Travel Bugs, 125
track point, explanation of, 51
Travel Bugs, relationship to Geocaching, 124–125
Travel by GPS, Web address for, 90
travel chargers, using with PDAs, 37
triangulation, explanation of, 23
trickle charge cables, using with iQue 3600
    PDAs, 228
Trimble, Web address for, 182

turn-by-turn directions, displaying on GPS receivers, 71–72
TV, using as video source for iQue 3600 PDAs, 254

U

USB ports, using with GPS receivers, 88–89
U.S. Topo, features of, 104
UTM (Universal Transverse Mercator), relationship to Geocaching, 121
U-turns, advisory about, 77

V

Vegas Blackjack, playing in iQue 3600 PDAs, 249
vehicle-installed GPS, benefits of, 175
Veo Photo Traveler cameras
    adding to iQues, 268
    obtaining online, 280
    Web address for, 280
Vexed 2.1, playing on iQue 3600 PDAs, 248
video
    converting, 256–257
    getting into iQue 3600 PDAs, 254
video players, choosing for iQue 3600 PDAs, 256–257
vineyard management, using GPS in, 181–182
virtual caches, features of, 124
visual map, explanation of, 9
VITO Technology, Web address for, 107, 135
voice navigation, using as safety precaution, 57–58

W

WAAS (Wide Area Augmentation Service)
    certification for aircraft use, 152–153
    explanation of, 23
    importance of, 51
warm resets, performing on iQues, 277–278
warm start, explanation of, 49
WASP system, explanation of, 15
waterproofing, significance of, 51, 99
waypoints
    explanation of, 23, 84
    finding when fishing, 96
    finding when hiking, hunting, and camping, 100
    marking automatically and manually, 84
    maximum number of, 84–85
    naming effectively, 85, 87
    obtaining online, sharing and storing, 88–91
    obtaining online when Geocaching, 128–129
    recognizing when Geocaching, 127–128
    storage capacities for, 95
Web addresses
    Acrobat Reader software, 265
    Aircraft Owners and Pilots Association, 167
    ALK Technologies, 52, 79
    Amusement Park Kids, 271
    Applian, 279
    Arkon, 279
    ATOM, 271
    aviation GPS receivers, 167
    Bang Bang, 271
    BoxWave, 241, 279
    BugMe, 279
    CD ripping utilities, 269
    Children's Illustrated eTales, 266
    ClearTouch, 279
    CoPilot Live Pocket PC 4, 40
    CropTrak software, 182
    DataViz, 241, 279
    DeLorme, 52, 107
    Documents To Go, 241, 279
    DVD-to-AVI program, 255
    Earthmate GPS for Handhelds, 40
    EasyGPS freeware utility, 92, 135
    e-books, 258, 279
    Electric Pocket, 279
    Emtac products, 40, 52
    fiction and nonfiction e-books, 259, 279
    Fictionwise e-books, 279
    FleetBoss, 182
    Freewarepalm, 279
    Galax and Froggy, 271
    games, 247
    Garmin products, 52, 79, 107, 135, 167, 182
    Geocaching sites, 135
    Geodashing, 135
    Geoteaming, 182
    GolfLogix, 147
    GolfViaGPS, 147
    GPS gear, 52
    GPS surveying products, 182

GPS terminology, 22
GPS TimeTrack, 182
Handango, 279
Hot Hangman, 270
iGolf Technologies, 147
IntelliGolf, 147
iQue 3600, 182
Kidz Pak 1.3c, 271
Kinoma, 279
Lowrance, 167
Magellan products, 40, 52, 107, 135
Mapopolis products, 40, 52
Margi Systems, 279
marine GPS receivers, 167
Mark/Space, 241
MemoWare e-books in public domain, 258,
    267, 280
MiniSync, 241
Minorplanet products, 182
MinuteWar, 135
The Missing Sync for iQue 3600 PDAs, 241
MobilePlanet products, 273, 280
MovieJack program, 255
Muskokatech, 167
Navicache, 135
Navman products, 40, 52, 79, 167
nonfiction e-books, 279
NormSoft, 280
Otter watertight cases, 99
Palm Digital Media, 259, 280
PalmGear products, 241, 280
Palm OS games and programs, 279
PathAway for Palm OS, 167
PDA Bookstore and Childrens section, 267
PerfectBound contemporary e-books, 280
Pocket Caddie, 147
RandomHouse.com contemporary e-books, 280
RayDar LLC, 107
Rayman, 272
Raymarine, 167
Replay Radio program, 279
RoboPhoto, 107
ScanControl, 182
SkyGolfGPS, 147

Socket products, 40, 52, 79
SoundFeeder, 279
StarCaddy, 147
TealPaint program, 268
TealPoint software, 280
TeleNavTrak, 182
TeleType, 167
Televigation, 79, 182
Tetris, 271
Thales/Magellan, 52
TomeRaider program, 267
TomTom Navigator USA, 40
TopoGrafix, 107, 135
Travel by GPS, 90
Trimble, 182
vehicle management systems, 182
Veo Photo Traveler cameras, 280
VitoNavigator, 135
VITO Technology, 107, 135
WinZip program, 244
Xora, 182
XY Golf, 147
Wherify GPS Locator, features of, 13, 46–48
WinTV-PVR-250 TV tuner cards, using with
    iQue 3600 PDAs, 254
WinZip program, obtaining online, 244
Wireless Bluetooth GPS, obtaining online, 40
Wireless keyboards, using with iQue 3600
    PDAs, 273–274

X

xCaddie
    features of, 140
    obtaining online, 147
Xora, Web address for, 182
Xora GPS TimeTrack, features of, 176
XY Golf products
    Color Portable Unit, 140–141
    Web address for, 147

Z

Zap!2016, playing in iQue 3600 PDAs, 249
zoom level, setting for GPS receivers, 72–74

INTERNATIONAL CONTACT INFORMATION

AUSTRALIA
McGraw-Hill Book Company
Australia Pty. Ltd.
TEL +61-2-9900-1800
FAX +61-2-9878-8881
http://www.mcgraw-hill.com.au
books-it_sydney@mcgraw-hill.com

CANADA
McGraw-Hill Ryerson Ltd.
TEL +905-430-5000
FAX +905-430-5020
http://www.mcgraw-hill.ca

**GREECE, MIDDLE EAST, & AFRICA
(Excluding South Africa)**
McGraw-Hill Hellas
TEL +30-210-6560-990
TEL +30-210-6560-993
TEL +30-210-6560-994
FAX +30-210-6545-525

MEXICO (Also serving Latin America)
McGraw-Hill Interamericana Editores
S.A. de C.V.
TEL +525-1500-5108
FAX +525-117-1589
http://www.mcgraw-hill.com.mx
carlos_ruiz@mcgraw-hill.com

SINGAPORE (Serving Asia)
McGraw-Hill Book Company
TEL +65-6863-1580
FAX +65-6862-3354
http://www.mcgraw-hill.com.sg
mghasia@mcgraw-hill.com

SOUTH AFRICA
McGraw-Hill South Africa
TEL +27-11-622-7512
FAX +27-11-622-9045
robyn_swanepoel@mcgraw-hill.com

SPAIN
McGraw-Hill/
Interamericana de España, S.A.U.
TEL +34-91-180-3000
FAX +34-91-372-8513
http://www.mcgraw-hill.es
professional@mcgraw-hill.es

**UNITED KINGDOM, NORTHERN,
EASTERN, & CENTRAL EUROPE**
McGraw-Hill Education Europe
TEL +44-1-628-502500
FAX +44-1-628-770224
http://www.mcgraw-hill.co.uk
emea_queries@mcgraw-hill.com

ALL OTHER INQUIRIES Contact:
McGraw-Hill/Osborne
TEL +1-510-420-7700
FAX +1-510-420-7703
http://www.osborne.com
omg_international@mcgraw-hill.com

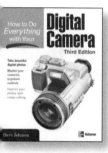 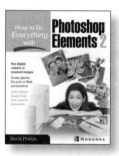 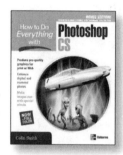 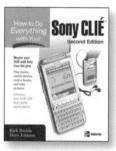 
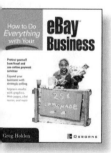    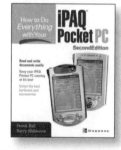

Subscribe Today!